INDICATIONS

OF THE

SECOND BOOK OF MOSES

CALLED

EXODUS.

BY

EDWARD B. LATCH,

AUTHOR OF "A REVIEW OF THE HOLY BIBLE," "INDICATIONS OF THE BOOK OF JOB,"
"INDICATIONS OF THE BOOK OF GENESIS"

WIPF & STOCK · Eugene, Oregon

Wipf and Stock Publishers
199 W 8th Ave, Suite 3
Eugene, OR 97401

Indications of the Second Book of Moses Called Exodus
By Latch, Edward B.
Softcover ISBN-13: 978-1-7252-9638-1
Hardcover ISBN-13: 978-1-7252-9640-4
eBook ISBN-13: 978-1-7252-9639-8
Publication date 5/12/2022
Previously published by J. B. Lippincott Company, 1892

This edition is a scanned facsimile of
the original edition published in 1892.

PREFACE.

IN the "Indications of Exodus" the same general interpretative system is taken up and continued as that set forth in the "Review of the Holy Bible," and as given in the "Indications of Genesis" and of "Job." The text used is the Bible as issued by the American Bible Society, New York, 1860 (Brevier, 12mo).

CONTENTS.

CHAPTER I.

(5) The seventy souls of Jacob's household. How are they made up? The Messiah as the Seed of Jacob. (6, 7) The death of Joseph. Remarkable prosperity, increase, and multiplication of the children of Israel. Who suffers the four hundred years' affliction? The Messiah as the Seed of Abraham 25

CHAPTER II.

(1–10) Moses born. Pertaining of Moses to time. The three past Ages of Man. (11, 12) Moses slays an Egyptian. The Euphratic age. (13, 14) "Who made thee a prince and a judge over us?" The Hiddekelic and Gihonic ages. (15–22) Moses flees to the land of Midian. The seven daughters of the priest of Midian. The seven daughters as allegory. Moses marries Zipporah. Zipporah as an Ethiopian woman. (23–25) The bondage of the children of Israel. The three great races that existed before the Deluge of Noah. God's covenant that brings a blessing to all families of the earth is the Second Covenant 27

CHAPTER III.

(1) Mount Horeb as pertaining to the Gihonic or Third age. (2–6) The Angel of the Lord appears unto Moses in a burning bush. God is God of the living. The dwellers of the dark valley not dead. Who are the dwellers of the dark valley? The people of the past ages of man as captives. Transmission of names, iniquity, blood, and char-

CONTENTS.

acteristics by the Law of Iniquity (7, 8) The deliverance of the Lord's people. The Lord's people are those of the Four Ages of Man. The land of Canaan as the earth in the Pisonic age. (10) Moses chosen as an instrumentality for bringing the children of Israel out of Egypt. The Egypt of the past (11, 12) Moses questions his own ability for the prescribed task. (13-15) Moses ignorant of the name of the God of those whom he is commanded to bring forth from Egypt. God's great name "I AM." Who were the fathers? (16-18) The three days' journey into the wilderness. The three ages of man under the veil. The Son in Egypt,—"Out of Egypt have I called my son." (19-22) The king of Egypt and the Egyptians shadow the Adversarial host. The Messiah shall possess the gate of his enemies 35

CHAPTER IV.

(10-17) Moses as shadowing the first three ages of man. Aaron as the mouth of Moses. (21-23) Israel as the Lord's first-born. The varied forms of creature life and existence. The first-born of every creature The Son as the first-born among many brethren. The exodus of the children of Israel shadows the deliverance of the captive from the land of darkness and shadow of death . . 44

CHAPTER V.

(1, 2) Pharaoh as shadowing Lucifer the angel Death. Lucifer's captives Lucifer as united to the Adversarial host. Lucifer's captives not absolutely dead . . . 50

CHAPTER VI.

(1-8) The bondage of the children of Israel to the Egyptians as simple history. The bondage of the children of Israel the father of nations. God Almighty as the Fulfilling Power of the Infinite Majesty, the Third Person of the Trinity. God as Jehovah, or as the unity of the Assenting and Fulfilling Powers of the Infinite Majesty, the Second and Third Persons of the Trinity. The unity of Moses and Aaron 51

CHAPTER VII.

(1-3) Moses clothed with more power than Pharaoh both in the allegorical and in the simple historical sense. Pharaoh as an instrumentality in the purpose of God (4, 5) Pharaoh as a sign to the great Adversarial host The judgments that came upon Pharaoh as signs to all beholders—earthly and heavenly—whereby to stamp the immutability of the most high God 52

CHAPTER IX.

(13-16) Pharaoh raised up as a positive instrumentality through whom the power of the Lord will be shown and declared throughout the earth. The hardening of Pharaoh's heart. The first four plagues. The seven remaining plagues. The power of the Adversary . . . 53

CHAPTER X.

(24-26) Pharaoh consents for the children of Israel to go and serve the Lord. The flocks and herds withheld. Moses' far-reaching reply, "not a hoof shall be left behind." Pharaoh as Lucifer. Lucifer as the destroying angel must disgorge the spoils of many generations . . 57

CHAPTER XII.

(1-6) The Four Ages of Man. Chief divisions of the Four Ages. The Messianic year The Messianic month. Advent of the Messiah as the son of man. The four hundred years' affliction. The lamb of the passover. The tenth day of the month. The Messiah as the branch of Jesse. The fourteenth day of the month. The fourteenth day of the month points to the day of the Messiah as Naboth the Jezreelite. The slaying of the lamb indicates the slaying of Naboth The fifteenth day of the month. The exodus of the children of Israel. The valley of the shadow of death. The fifteenth day of the month points to the return of the Messiah from the valley of the shadow of death The Messiah as Elisha the Prophet. The advent of the Messiah as the son of man. The ad-

vent of the Messiah as the Son of God. The lamb of
the passover identified with labors of the Messiah in
the Pisonic or Fourth age. (7–13) The blood of the
lamb of the passover. The upper door-post. The two
side posts. The priesthood of man The test by fire.
(14) The fourteenth day a day of memorial. (15–17) The
feast of unleavened bread. (40, 41) The sojourning of
the children of Israel. The hosts of the Lord that came
out of Egypt. General chronology of the first three ages
of man confirmed The Messiah as the son of man . . 58

CHAPTER XIII.

(1, 2) The sanctification of all the first-born seals them as
holy unto the Lord. (11–16) The land of Canaan as the
earth in the Pisonic or Fourth age. History of Pharaoh
as allegory. The result of sanctification is not oblivion . 81

CHAPTER XIV.

(1–18) Pharaoh as Lucifer The first three ages of man.
The escaping remnant of the Deluge. The six hundred
chosen chariots. The pursuit by Lucifer. Lucifer will
surely prevail against the people unless a redeemer arise
The Lord as the Redeemer. (19, 20) The House of Man
and the Adversarial army (21, 22) Dry ground in the
midst of the Red Sea. The Almighty as the Creator and
Governor. As an interpretative work simply the Bible
may be considered either as wholly truth, or as wholly
fiction. The veil thrown over the Scriptures becomes
proof of their inspiration and truth. The plagues of
Pharaoh a portion of the burden of the Pisonic age. The
children of Israel pass dry-shod into the midst of the sea.
This passage-way, with a wall of water on each hand,
indicates the valley of the shadow of death. (23–25)
Pharaoh pursues the children of Israel into the midst
of the sea. Lucifer and his host powerless in the valley
of the shadow of death The morning watch Allegorical apportionment thereof The Adversarial host
under bondage to the Edenic Law (26–28) Pharaoh's

host overwhelmed by the returning waters. Lucifer cannot return from the valley of the shadow of death. (29-31) Through the Messiah man can return from the dark valley, even as the Messiah, who was slain as Naboth the Jezreelite, came forth from thence manifest as Elisha the son of Shaphat 83

CHAPTER XV

(1) The song of Moses and the children of Israel The horse and his rider Lucifer the angel Death (see Rev. vi 7, 8). The pale horse. Death the last enemy. The Lord's glorious triumph over Lucifer the rider of the pale horse. (2) The habitation of the Lord The great battle of life. (3-8) The right hand of the Lord. The Messiah possessed of the gate of his enemies. Lucifer's captives. (9-10) Lucifer seeks a partial triumph through a division of the spoils (11-13) The holy habitation of the Lord, as the body that was created for the word of God in and as the very beginning of the creation of God The Living Bread. The communion of the Lord's body. The priesthood of Melchizedek (14-19) Pertainings of the dukes of Edom to the grand epoch from the beginning of the creation down to the end of time. The unblemishable creature body. The blemishable earthy body. The natural body. The spiritual body. The transmission of iniquity (20, 21) The song of Miriam reiterates the triumph of the Messiah over Lucifer. (22) The three days' journey into the wilderness The first three ages of man. (23-26) Marah. The Euphratic or First age of man The Tree of Life. The First Covenant or Law enters in. The bitter waters made sweet. Man proved by the Law. (27) Elim. The twelve wells of water, and the threescore and ten palmtrees. Elim as the Hiddekelic age 96

CHAPTER XVI.

(1-4) The wilderness of Sin lies between Elim and Sinai. Sinai as the Euphratic age, and Elim as the Hiddekelic age. The Law enters into the Hiddekelic race. The hidden manna and the visible manna. (8) Flesh chosen for food instead of manna The plague. Allegorical stand-point. (36) The tenth 116

CHAPTER XVII.

(1–7) Rephidim. The Hiddekelic famine. The Gihonic or Third race proved at Meribah. Their failure. (8–16) Amalek. The Adversarial host. The Subjugator. The escaping remnant 122

CHAPTER XVIII.

(1–12) The sojourning of the children of Israel. Jethro, Moses' father-in-law. The Red Sea as shadowing the Deluge of Noah. Moses as an instrumentality for bringing the children of Israel out of Egypt. The people whom Moses brought out from Egypt in the allegoric sense. Horeb shadows the Gihonic or Third age. The pertaining of Jethro. (13–27) Pertaining of Moses. The chief divisions of the grand epoch from the beginning of the creation of God down to the end of time. The rulers of thousands, the rulers of hundreds, the rulers of fifties, the rulers of tens. The Decade System of Chronology exemplified 128

CHAPTER XIX.

(1–6) The exodus of the children of Israel as allegory. The restoration of man of Adam's race but a small portion of the redemptive labors of the Messiah. Mount Sinai as an allegoric stand-point in the Euphratic age. "On eagles' wings." The regeneration of man. Man as a kingdom of priests. The Messiah as the Redeemer of and for the creature world, heavenly and earthly, animate and inanimate. The excellence of the creature reaches perfection through redemption and regeneration Direct regeneration. Indirect regeneration. The rich fruits that pertain to the six creative days. The priesthood of man openly confirmed at the Last Supper. (7, 8) The people express their acceptance of the covenant as given forth

CONTENTS. 11

PAGE

from Sinai. In the allegoric sense Sinai shadows the Euphratic or First age of man. (10–13) The sacredness of Mount Sinai. The sacredness of the Law or First Covenant. (21–25) The bounds of time. The Tree of Life Sin existed before the Law entered 139

CHAPTER XX.

(4, 5) The supremacy of God. The Law of Iniquity. Iniquity visited from the fathers upon the children unto the fourth generation. The Four Ages of Man. The iniquity of the whole rests upon the Fourth age The Ten Commandments embody the Law as given forth in the Euphratic age 151

CHAPTERS XXI, XXII., XXIII.

These chapters contain an analysis of the Ten Commandments, whereby the " Tree of the Knowledge of Good and Evil" is defined 151

CHAPTER XXIV.

(1–8) The acceptance of the First Covenant or Law by the people confirmed. The altar under the hill shadows the earth as an altar of sacrifice. The blood of sprinkling as a memorial and witness. Why should the people have been sprinkled with the blood of the sacrifice? The mission of man as a kingdom of priests. The consecration and sanctification of the creature. Christ as "the Head, from which all the body by joints and bands having nourishment ministered, and knit together, increaseth with the increase of God " The regeneration of the creature world. (16) The first seven semidivisions of the Four Ages memorialized 152

CHAPTER XXV.

(10–22) The ark of the covenant. Allegoric pertaining of the ark to the first three ages of man. The Son begotten. The Son as the first-born among many brethren. Man of Adam's race as a holy nation unto the Lord, and a kingdom of priests. To whom shall man as a kingdom of priests minister? The creatures that pertain to the six creative days. The ark of the covenant points to a perfect unit of labor from the beginning of the creation to the end of time. The mercy-seat. (23–30) Pertaining of the table for shrewbread to the Four Ages of Man. The two staves shadow the two Faithful Witnesses. The twelve cakes of shrewbread as pertaining to time. The unit of labor indicated by the table for shewbread. (31–37) The golden candlestick. The Four Ages of Man. The two Faithful Witnesses. The Trinity The seven lamps. The first seven semidivisions of the Four Ages . . 156

CHAPTER XXVI.

(1–6) The ten curtains of fine twined linen Pertaining of the ten linen curtains to time The unit of labor shadowed by the ten linen curtains (7–13) The eleven curtains of goats' hair Pertaining of the eleven curtains of goats' hair to the grand epoch from the beginning of the creation to the end of time. The unit of labor indicated by the curtains of goats' hair. The regeneration of the creature world. Melchizedek and Abraham What Abraham represents. Adam as perfect and upright The communion of the body that was created for the Word of God in and as the very beginning of the creation of God (15–30) The wooden tabernacle of the congregation. Pertaining thereof The burden of the creative days falls upon man of Adam's race The four short bars. The Four Ages of Man The middle bar The Messiah as the Redeemer. The Messiah "faithful unto death." The unit of labor indicated by the wooden tabernacle. The Living Bread The Holy One. The Priest of the Most High God (31–37) General construction of the tabernacle The veil of the tabernacle. The holy place. The most holy place. Chronology of the tabernacle. The Gihonic or Third age. The covering of rams' skins dyed red. The covering of badgers' skins. 171

CONTENTS. 13

CHAPTER XXVII.

PAGE

(1–8) The altar of burnt-offering. General construction.
Allegoric pertaining of the altar of burnt-offering to the
earth as a great altar of sacrifice. The four rivers of Eden.
The Messiah enters into these waters. Tribulations of
the Messiah The unit of labor indicated by the altar
of burnt-offering (9–19) The court of the tabernacle
Allegorical limits of the court of the tabernacle. The
great journey of life pertaining to all hosts finds culmination in the most holy place of the tabernacle The First
Covenant embodies life through righteousness by works.
The Messiah the only one that won the crown of life
through righteousness by works The subjugatory labors
of the Messiah as the son of man The general failure of
man of Adam's race The holy place or First Covenant
must be taken away or made old. The Second Covenant
or righteousness by the faith of Jesus Christ the Word of
God. (20) The continuity of the labors of the two Faithful Witnesses shadowed by the continual burning of the
lamps 198

CHAPTER XXVIII.

(4–7) The ephod. (8) The curious girdle of the ephod
(9–12) The two onyx stones. (13, 14) The ouches (15–
21) The breastplate of judgment. Apportionment of the
four rows of precious stones to the Four Ages The appertainings of the twelve tribes of Israel to the Four Ages
(22–30) The wreathen chains. The Urim and the Thummim. The breastplate of judgment as a perfect square
indicates a perfect unit of labor as established upon it as
a base (31, 32) The robe of the ephod. (36–88) The
mitre Holiness to the Lord. The Urim and the Thummim as an atoning element. The holy garments of
Aaron shadow the holy, the glorious, the beautiful.
Aaron's garments and the altar of burnt-offering as indicating parallel and embodiments 208

2

14 CONTENTS

CHAPTER XXIX.

PAGE

(1–9) Aaron and his sons chosen as priests. Aaron's holy garments shadow great magnitudes. Aaron revealed as priest whose ministrations reach throughout the Four Ages of Man. The priesthood of man bears upon the welfare of the creature world. (10–14) The four horns of the altar. The Four Ages of Man. The blood of the sin-offering. The promise carried with the sacrifice that the trespass shall be forgiven. Accumulation of these promises. The two onyx stones become a memorial to the children of Israel throughout the Four Ages, and, hence, take cognizance of the sacrificial promises. The Urim and the Thummim as an atoning element. The breastplate of judgment. With whom the care of the Thummim and the Urim rests. Melchizedek. The bread and wine. The Living Bread. The Law of Iniquity. The Messiah as the Seed of woman. The Messiah as the Son of man. The Messiah as the Redeemer. Atonement. The communion. The visible bread of the communion. The Urim as a power. Melchizedek as priest of the most high God. The Holy Trinity. Abraham as possessor of heaven and earth. The great temporal power of the Messiah as the son of man. Sisera. The raiment of needlework, "of divers colours of needlework on both sides, *meet* for the necks of *them that take* the spoil." The Messiah as the key of the house of David. The sin-offering as a sign. (15–18) The whole ram as a burnt-offering, and as a sweet savor. Tribulation. (19–21) The ram of consecration. The peculiar hallowing of Aaron and his sons and their garments. The consecration of the Four Ages of Man. The ear, the thumb, the great toe. The hallowing of man as a kingdom of priests, and a holy nation unto the Lord. Jesus washing his disciples' feet as allegory. The redemption of the creature world. (22–30) The ram of consecration, by equity, pertains to the grand epoch from the beginning of the creation of God to the end of time. The future welfare of inanimate creatures. The regeneration and restoration of the creature world—whether animal, plant, or mineral—entire probabilities. The new heaven

CONTENTS. 15

and new earth will be perfect in regard to material and
spiritual beauty   The earthy body left behind   The suit-
ability of the body created for the Word of God in and as
the very beginning of the creation of God as a habitation
for the creature irrespective of host. Plant life. The
ram of consecration denotes instrumentality on the part
of the animal kingdom. The death of the ram does not
make void this bearing. Plant life sanctified through the
consecrated eater. Sanctification is not regeneration.
Direct and indirect regeneration. The wave-offering.
(31-34) The body of the Redeemer must be eaten, in that
absolute atonement is made only through it, and by it.
Aaron's priesthood. Aaron and his sons, ministering in
the priests' office, "shall eat those things with which the
atonement was made, to consecrate *and* to sanctify them."
Consecration and sanctification seal the sacrifice unto redemption. The new earth will never cast away the laborer that helped to bear the burdens of the day. (35-
37) Sanctification of the earth as an altar of sacrifice.
The seven days' consecration of Aaron and his sons. Compensation cannot be made or brought about until after the
absolute death and resurrection of the Messiah. (38-46)
The continual burnt-offering. The sacrificial lambs.
Who will compensate the creature for its hapless lot?
The consecration and sanctification of the flesh of the
sacrifice after natural life has passed away point to restoration   218

CHAPTER XXX.

(1-10) The golden altar of incense. The horns of the altar.
The blood of the sacrifice. The promise of forgiveness.
Sacrifice and burnt-offering as signs and wonders. Christ's
manifestation in the flesh as the son of man   Pure substitution not probable. The yearly atonement. The seventh
month   Pertaining of the altar of incense to time. The
restoration of the creature after the natural life shall have
passed away   (11-16) The atonement money as a memorial. The Four Ages of Man   The bounds of time as set
according to the number of the children of Israel. The

CONTENTS.

PAGE

atonement money as an exponent of the bounds of time (17-21) The laver of brass Allegoric position of laver. The begetting of the Son The uttermost parts of the earth given to the Son for possession The six creative days What shall become of the clay, the earthy possessions of clay? Regeneration called for The general consecration of animal life and plant life. The descent of physical peculiarity from generation to generation The universal preying of animals upon each other may "work together for good to them that love God, to them who are called according to *his* purpose." Man of Adam's race not the only host that is called according to the purpose of God The possible regeneration of the creature world that existed before the creation of man of Adam's race Aaron the priest as shadowing the Four Ages of Man. Consecration and sanctification of the creature world to be considered in the Pisonic or Fourth age (22, 23) The four principal spices Their apportionment to the chief divisions of time. The holy anointing oil. (34-38) The sweet spices as a holy confection. The labors of the Messiah Regeneration of the creature world a portion of the wonderful mission of the Son of God 261

CHAPTER XXXI.

(12-18) The seven days of the week. The sabbath as a sign. The seventh day as the day in which the Most High rested "from all his work which he had made." The seven creative days. The general failure of man as a subjugator proved by the Deluge of Noah. The Messiah takes up the subjugatory labors in his person as the son of man The resting of the Most High indicates the immutability of his designs as set forth in his great purpose . . 291

CHAPTER XXXII.

(1-6) The molten calf. The crossing of the Red Sea as allegory The wilderness. The first three ages of man. Historic stand-point in the Euphratic or First age. The

CONTENTS. 17

Ten Commandments issued. The Pre-Euphratic Era. Fall of man in the Euphratic age. Lamentation for Israel, the House of Man (7-14) The threatened destruction of the people Who are the seed of Abraham, of Isaac, and of Israel? The Messiah as the first-born. (15-18) Moses and Joshua. Joshua the minister of Moses—not Oshea of the tribe of Ephraim—possibly the Messiah manifest as the son of man (19-24) The molten calf destroyed in the Gihonic or Third age. Transmission of iniquity. The Deluge of Noah The priesthood of man. (30-35) The abomination which maketh desolate Excessive idolatry of the people of the Gihonic age. Moses seeks to make atonement for the sin of the people. Such atonement is not possible. Atonement governed by equity 296

CHAPTER XXXIII.

(1-6) The Hiddekelic famine. The Gihonic age. The names of the people of the past ages raised up by the Messiah (8-10) The tabernacle of the congregation as the tabernacle of other hosts than the children of Israel simply. (11) The Lord speaks face to face with Moses as a man speaketh to his friend. The Lord who thus spoke with Moses doubtless is either the Lord as Melchizedek, or the Lord as the Messiah manifest in the flesh as the son of man. Joshua the minister of Moses fills the measures of the text. (12-16) Moses in ignorance of the people whom he is commanded to bring up. Who are they? They are the Lord's people of the past ages of man Egypt as the Hiddekelic and Gihonic ages. The Euphratic and Pisonic ages. The seventy years' desolation of Jerusalem as allegory. Daniel's comprehension of the allegory. Confirmations by the prophets Isaiah and Ezekiel. (17-23) The Lord reveals to Moses the history of the world 312

CHAPTER XXXIV.

(1-4) The two sets of tables of stone. (5-9) Proclamation of the name of the Lord The Law of Iniquity. Trans-

b   2*

mission of iniquity from father to son. Forgiveness cannot clear the guilty by blotting out sin. Forgiveness transfers the debt. Forgiveness does not prevent accumulation of the debt. The Edenic Law absolutely irrevocable. The Redeemer. The irrevocability of the Edenic Law brings absolute condemnation upon all transgressors irrespective of host. (10, 11) The ruling of the Ten Commandments in the Pisonic or Fourth age. The trials and tribulations of the Messiah as the Seed of Abraham forms a portion of the burden of the Pisonic age. The four hundred years of affliction. The Messiah as the Subjugator and Replenisher. (27, 28) The fast of Moses for forty days and forty nights. Elijah's fast. The fast of Jesus (29–35) The skin of Moses' face shone on Mount Sinai. Elijah on Mount Horeb. The transfiguration of Jesus 327

CHAPTER XXXVIII.

(1–31) The gold, silver, and brass, used in the construction of the tabernacle of the congregation, as chronology. The bounds of the people, or of time, as set according to the number of the children of Israel. The ransom money as an exponent of the bounds of the people, or of time. The bounds of the people of the Euphratic age as set by the talents of gold. The bounds of the people of the Hiddekelic and Gihonic ages combined as set by the talents of brass. The age of gold is the one in which the Word of God was begotten as the Son of God that he might do the will of God 341

DIAGRAMS.

DIAGRAM	PAGE
1. The birth and pertaining of Moses (ii. 1–10)	29
2. Moses slays an Egyptian (ii 11–25)	32
3. Moses at the burning bush (iii)	38
4. Aaron as Moses' spokesman (iv. 10–14)	46
5. Israel as the Lord's first-born (iv. 21–23)	47
6 The lamb of the passover (xii 1–6)	58
7. The blood of the passover lamb (xii. 7–13)	64
8. The sojourning of the children of Israel (xii. 40, 41)	74
9 The Messiah as the son of man (xii 40, 41)	77
10. Pharaoh pursues the Israelites (xiv.)	86
11. The morning watch (xiv)	93
12 The song of Moses and the children of Israel (xv. 1–21)	100
13. The children of Israel at the waters of Marah (xv. 23–26)	111
14. The twelve wells of water, and the seventy palm-trees (xv. 27)	114
15. The journey from the Red Sea to the wilderness of Sin (xvi. 1–4)	118
16. The journey from the wilderness of Sin to Rephidim (xvii)	125
17. Jethro's meeting with Moses after the exodus (xviii. 1–12)	128
18. The Decade System of Chronology (xviii. 13–27)	136
19 The journey from Rephidim to Sinai (xix. 1–13)	138
20. The blood of sprinkling (xxiv. 1–8)	152
21. The ark of the covenant (xxv. 10–22)	159
22. The table for shewbread (xxv 23–30)	164
23. The golden candlestick (xxv 31–37)	169
24. The ten linen curtains for the tabernacle (xxvi. 1–6)	172

DIAGRAM		PAGE
25	The curtains of goats' hair (xxvi. 7–13)	176
26.	The wooden tabernacle of the congregation (west side) (xxvi. 15–30)	182
27.	The wooden tabernacle of the congregation (north side) (xxvi 15–30)	184
28	The altar of burnt-offering (xxvii 1–8)	199
29.	The court of the tabernacle (east side) (xxvii. 9–19)	205
30	The court of the tabernacle (north side) (xxvii. 9–19)	206
31	The breastplate of judgment (xxviii. 15–30)	214
32.	The bullock of the sin-offering (xxix. 10–14)	223
33.	The whole ram as a burnt-offering, and as a sweet savor (xxix. 15–18)	239
34.	The consecration of the Four Ages of Man (xxix. 19–21)	241
35.	The ram of consecration (xxix. 22–30)	246
36.	Sanctification of the earth as the altar of burnt-offering (xxix 35–37)	256
37.	The continual burnt-offering (xxix. 38–46)	259
38.	The altar of incense (xxx. 1–10)	267
39.	The atonement money as a memorial (xxx 11–16)	273
40.	The laver of brass (xxx 17–21)	277
41.	The holy anointing oil (xxx. 22–33)	285
42	The perfume as a holy confection (xxx. 34–38)	289
43.	The seven days of the week (xxxi. 12–18)	293
44.	The molten calf (xxxii)	297
45	The molten calf (xxxii)	307
46.	The people Moses brought out of Egypt (xxxiii.)	322
47.	The Law of Iniquity (xxxiv. 5–10)	333
48.	The gold, silver, and brass, as chronology (tabernacle) (xxxviii 24–31)	345

BASES.

(Extract from the "Review.")

First Basis: *The Holy Trinity.*—The triune character of the Creator is self-evident,—that is, three separate Persons in One.

These are, first, the Power which conceives; second, the Power which signifies assent as the Word or Command; third, the Power which carries out or performs the thought signified or expressed. Each are equal, the one with the other; for the Power which conceives would not be a Power if each conception was carried out or accomplished without assent. The Word would be no Power without Thought and Action. The Power which acts would be no Power without the Thought and Command; therefore it follows that these three are equal, the one with the other, and that they combine into the One Infinite Majesty, perfect and supreme in all his attributes, and above all other powers; yet each is separate and distinct, the one from the other. They possess the attribute of manifesting themselves separately and distinctly as Persons; and it follows that the Power which creates matter can invest itself in it, endow it with life, and become visibly clothed with it.

It also follows that no inharmonious relation can exist between the Three; that they all work together; and that without the Three was nothing made that was made. It further follows that the fulness of the Three dwells in each one as a Person.

Second Basis: The Overthrow of Evil and the Redemption of the Fallen.—This embodies the ends and aims of the labors involved in the Scriptural Records according to the great work Mount Zion, which was laid down in the beginning.

Third Basis: The Antiquity of Man.—This basis brings to light four separate, independent, consecutive creations of man; of which the present race is the fourth and last. It embraces a period of time of about thirty-three thousand seven hundred and fifty-two years' duration. The Revelation of St. John the Divine unlocks the history of the human races, and sheds, also, much light on the Overthrow of Evil.

Fourth Basis: The Great Law of Iniquity.—By which the iniquity of the fathers is visited upon the children, and upon the children's children, unto the third and to the fourth generation. Divine in its origin, laid down from the beginning, and upon which hinges the plan of the redemption of man as recorded in the Scriptures.

Fifth Basis.—The Mystery of our Lord and Saviour Jesus Christ, who entered upon his mission as the Redeemer of man from the day Melchizedek met Abram returning from the slaughter of the kings. This is the revelation of the Apostle Paul.

Sixth Basis.—The Veil, under which are hidden the mysteries of the Scriptures.

LANDMARKS.

SPACES a, a, of the Landmarks No. 2, indicate the four rivers of Eden in their pertainings to the Four Ages of Man; b, b indicate the Four Ages; c, c indicate the Four Ages by the first four seals of the vision of St. John the Divine (see Rev. vi. 1-8); d, d indicate the four races of men of Adam's race,—Adam being the generic name (see Gen. v. 1, 2) of each race; e, e indicate twenty chief divisions of the grand epoch from the beginning of the creation down to the end of time; f, f indicate approximate years of chief divisions of time; g, g indicate time; h, h indicate the seven creative days; i, i indicate approximate chronology pertaining to time.

Probably indeterminate	Determinate Time				Indeterminate
Creative days	1st Age of man	2nd Age	3rd Age	4th Age	Infinity
	Determinate Minimum length of sixth day 25892 yrs			Pisonic Era	
Probably indeterminate	The Son begotten was in heaven Satan cast out into the earth · a time ·	times	· a half time ·	a half time	Infinity

Creation of a body for the Word of God in and as the very beginning of the creation of God (see Col 1 18-18, Rev iii 14)

First day — Creation of light   Creation of the earthy

Second day — Creation of the firmament

Third day — Creation of vegetation

Fourth day — Creation of sun, moon, and stars

Fifth day — Creation of fishes and fowl

Sixth day — Creation of cattle, creeping thing, and beast of the earth

The Word of God is begotten as the Son of God by investing with life the body that was created in and as the very beginning of the creation of God (see Rev xii, Lev xxvii)   Beginning of Time

The Pre-Euphratic Era forms a portion of the First age or time

Creation of the Euphratic or White race (Adam's)

The earth in the Euphratic age

Creation of the Hiddekelic or Red race

Destruction of the Euphratic race by fire and earthquake.

The earth in the Hiddekelic age

Creation of the Gihonic or Black race

Destruction of the Hiddekelic race by famine

The earth in the Gihonic age

The abomination that maketh desolate set up (Daniel)   Creation of the Pisonic or Pale race

Destruction of the Gihonic race by the Deluge of Noah

Advent of the Messiah the Prince in the flesh of man as the Redeemer of man

The Messiah born of the Virgin

The earth in the Pisonic age   Crucifixion of the Messiah   The dividing of a time or age

Transgression come to the full (Zechariah) } Judgmental Era

Transgression come to the full (Daniel)

Advent of the Messiah as King of the thousand years } Thousand Years' Era

The thousand years fulfilled

The approximate end of Time.

Realms of eternity.

Creative days						Pre-Euphratic Era	Euphratic Era	Hiddekelic Era	Gihonic Era	Pisonic Era					Eternity
1st day	2nd day	3rd day	4th day	5th day	6th day										
3963						27789	23017	21414	13465	12098	7355	5897	2241	1827	
														AD 1	
														34	
														1998	
														2133	
														2803	
														3803	
														3963	Indeterminate
Probably indeterminate						2074 yrs	Bounds of time as set according to the number of the children of Israel 35752 yrs								indeterminate

INDICATIONS

OF THE

BOOK OF EXODUS.

I. 1–4. "Now these *are* the names of the children of Israel, which came into Egypt; every man and his household came with Jacob.

2. "Reuben, Simeon, Levi, and Judah,

3. "Issachar, Zebulun, and Benjamin,

4. "Dan, and Naphtali, Gad, and Asher."

These verses specify, by households, the children of Israel which came into Egypt with Jacob.

I. 5. "And all the souls that came out of the loins of Jacob were seventy souls: for Joseph was in Egypt *already*."

How is this number of souls made up? By Genesis xlvi. 26, it is stated that "All the souls that came with Jacob into Egypt, which came out of his loins, besides Jacob's sons' wives, all the souls *were* threescore and six;" therefore if Joseph and his two sons be added, the sum would be threescore and nine. Whence, then, the statement of the text that seventy souls came out of the loins of Jacob? The statement, doubtless, is made and recorded in order that the actual physical presence of the Seed of Abraham—who was called in Isaac (see Gen. xxi. 12), and who was with Jacob (see

Gen. xxviii. 4)—may become manifest as the flesh of Jacob in the day of Jacob; hence the Messiah as the son of Jacob is the one that raises the number threescore and nine to the seventy called for by the text of Exodus, and also as called for in Gen. xlvi. 27; all of whom are the souls of his sons and daughters.

I. 6, 7. " And Joseph died, and all his brethren, and all that generation.

7. " And the children of Israel were fruitful, and increased abundantly, and multiplied, and waxed exceeding mighty; and the land was filled with them."

From the above verses it is seen that prosperity follows the descendants of Abraham unto, and even after, the death of Joseph. How can this possibly be so, since Abraham was assured to a certainty that his seed (see Gen. xv. 13) should be afflicted four hundred years? As already indicated (verse 5), the Messiah as the Seed of Abraham is present as the Seed of Jacob, and, therefore, it is possible that the prophecy given Abraham is fulfilling to the very letter, and that the Messiah as the Seed of Abraham is suffering, in the flesh of man, as the son of man, more than falls to the lot of any one of Adam's race.

Isaac was sixty years old when Jacob was born, and Jacob was about ninety-one when Joseph was born, and Joseph lived one hundred and ten years: here, then, over two hundred and sixty years out of the four hundred have expired, and the blessing of God, involving peace and plenty, surrounds them on every side.

Is the prophecy a mistake, a defective translation, a general approximation, or is the Messiah as the Seed of Abraham actually fulfilling the prophecy? By the

INDICATIONS OF THE BOOK OF EXODUS.

lifting of the veil it becomes clearly evident that he is fulfilling it, and that he has been fulfilling it from the day of Abraham. If the man hidden by the text of Genesis is not the Messiah, who is it? Nobody? for this prophecy expires with the exodus (see Acts vii. 17, 18). The indications of the presence of the Messiah in his mission as the son of man multiply at every step, and they will continue to multiply until he, in the flesh of man, overthrows and subjugates the Adversary and his evil host. By the context, however, the children of Israel really did suffer affliction from the hands of the Egyptians, but it was after the death of Joseph, and his brethren, and all that generation; but this limited experience cannot fill the measure of the Lord's assurance in Abraham.

II. 1–10. "And there went a man of the house of Levi, and took *to wife* a daughter of Levi.

2. "And the woman conceived, and bare a son: and when she saw him that he *was* a goodly *child*, she hid him three months.

3. "And when she could not longer hide him, she took for him an ark of bulrushes, and daubed it with slime and with pitch, and put the child therein; and she laid *it* in the flags by the river's brink.

4. "And his sister stood afar off, to wit what would be done to him.

5. "And the daughter of Pharaoh came down to wash *herself* at the river; and her maidens walked along by the river's side: and when she saw the ark among the flags, she sent her maid to fetch it.

6. "And when she had opened *it*, she saw the child:

and, behold, the babe wept. And she had compassion on him, and said, This *is one* of the Hebrews' children.

7. "Then said his sister to Pharaoh's daughter, Shall I go and call to thee a nurse of the Hebrew women, that she may nurse the child for thee?

8. "And Pharaoh's daughter said to her, Go. And the maid went and called the child's mother.

9. "And Pharaoh's daughter said unto her, Take this child away, and nurse it for me, and I will give *thee* thy wages. And the woman took the child, and nursed it.

10. "And the child grew, and she brought him unto Pharaoh's daughter, and he became her son. And she called his name Moses: and she said, Because I drew him out of the water."

In Diagram 1, spaces a, a indicate the Four Ages of Man; b, b indicate the Four Ages by the land Abraham passed through (see Gen. xii. 1–7); of which Canaan represents the earth in the Fourth age as the promised land; c, c indicate the first Three Ages, as hidden under the veil, by the three months Moses was hidden; d, d indicate the allegorical pertaining of Moses to the first Three Ages of Man; e, e indicate the time during which Moses was hidden; f, f indicate the Four Ages by the four rivers of Eden (see Gen. ii. 10–14).

The land of Canaan (see Diagram 1, spaces b, b) shadows the earth in the Fourth age. The three months during which Moses was hidden, as allegory, point to time from the beginning thereof down to the advent of the Fourth age. Inasmuch, however, as by the simple history Moses was not permitted to cross over into the land of Canaan (see Deut. xxxii. 52;

INDICATIONS OF THE BOOK OF EXODUS. 29

Ex. i. 1–10, considered as allegory.

DIAGRAM 1.

THE BIRTH AND PERTAINING OF MOSES.

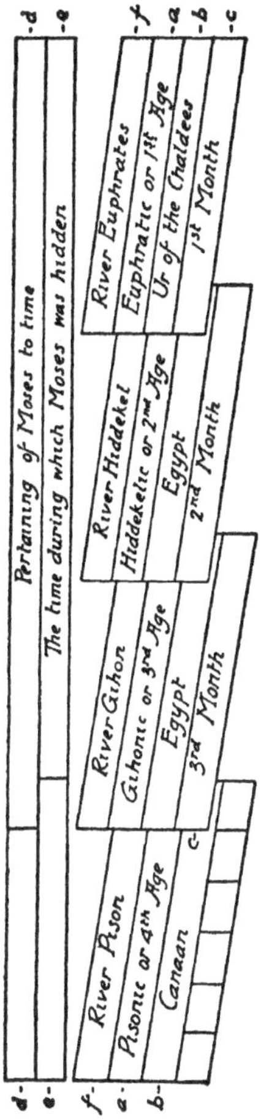

Beginning of Time.
Pre-Euphratic Era.
Creation of the Euphratic or First race (Adam's).

The earth in the Euphratic age.

Creation of the Hiddekelic or Second race.
Destruction of the Euphratic or First race

The earth in the Hiddekelic age.

Creation of the Gihonic or Third race ;
Destruction of the Hiddekelic or Second race.

The earth in the Gihonic age

Creation of the Pisonic or Fourth race   Brink of the river (see verse 3, also Landmarks No 1)
Antediluvian Epoch
Deluge of Noah   Destruction of the Gihonic or Third race
Epoch of replenishment (see Gen ix 1)
Advent of the Messiah as the son of man in the day of Abraham
The earth in the Pisonic age
Advent of the Messiah as the seed of woman
Absolute death of the Messiah for the sins of the creature world at the dividing of the Pisonic age
Judgmental Era
Thousand Years' Era
Era of Destruction
End of Time.

Side labels (left to right):
- Pertaining of Moses to time
- The time during which Moses was hidden
- River Euphrates / Euphratic or 1st Age / Ur of the Chaldees / 1st Month
- River Hiddekel / Hiddekelic or 2nd Age / Egypt / 2nd Month
- River Gihon / Gihonic or 3rd Age / Egypt / 3rd Month
- River Pison / Pisonic or 4th Age / Canaan

3*

xxxiv. 4), so his pertaining to time, as allegory, extends from the beginning of the First age down to the end of the Third age, or down to the Deluge of Noah.

The end of the third month (see Diagram 1) finds place in Egypt; hence an allegorical stand-point is established in the latter part of the Third age. From this stand-point the indication becomes manifest that Moses, as representative of the three great ages under the veil, can be hidden no longer; for (see Diagram 1) the river's brink is reached, the Fourth age is ushered in, and, shortly, the Messiah will come forth in his labors for the subjugation of the earth (see Gen. i. 28) and for the release (see Isa. xlii. 5–8) of the captives that have slumbered for ages in the dark valley. If these captives shall thus be released, then the indication is clear that, like unto Moses, the time is approaching when they can be hidden no longer.

When, however, Moses went with Pharaoh's daughter, and became her son, he leaves the allegorical stand-point just established, and takes up other bearings of the past to which he pertains.

II. 11, 12. "And it came to pass in those days, when Moses was grown, that he went out unto his brethren, and looked on their burdens; and he spied an Egyptian smiting a Hebrew, one of his brethren.

12. "And he looked this way and that way, and when he saw that *there was* no man, he slew the Egyptian, and hid him in the sand."

The stand-point of these verses is, evidently, towards the end of the Euphratic or First age, or during the overlap of the First and Second races, at which time the Adversary sadly oppressed the human family;

INDICATIONS OF THE BOOK OF EXODUS. 31

wherefore, as there was no man that was able to fulfil the Divine commands to subdue the earth, and have dominion over every living thing that moved upon it, the people of the Euphratic age, as shadowed through the simple history of Moses and the Egyptian, were swept away, and hidden in the sand by earthquake and volcanic eruption (see Diagram 2), even as further indicated in Num. xvi. 28–34; Jer. iv. 22–29.

In Diagram 2, spaces *a, a* indicate the Four Ages of Man; *b, b* indicate the Four Ages by the land passed through by Abraham (see Gen. xii. 1–7); *c, c* indicate the First and Second ages by the first and second days Moses went out unto his brethren; *d, d* indicate the pertainings of the seven daughters of Reuel, priest of Midian; *e, e* indicate pertaining of Reuel, priest of Midian; *f, f* indicate pertaining of Moses to the first Three Ages.

II. 13, 14. "And when he went out the second day, behold, two men of the Hebrews strove together: and he said to him that did the wrong, Wherefore smitest thou thy fellow?

14. "And he said, Who made thee a prince and a judge over us? intendest thou to kill me, as thou killedst the Egyptian? And Moses feared, and said, Surely this thing is known."

In these verses the stand-point is placed in the midst of Egypt,—that is, during the overlap of the Hiddekelic or Second and the Gihonic or Third Ages of Man. As before, the oppressor is at work (see Isa. xix. 19, 20), but, in addition, man's own transgression becomes manifest; for Hebrew fights against Hebrew (see Diagram 2), or Egypt against Egypt. Thus, by the alle-

32 INDICATIONS OF THE BOOK OF EXODUS.

Ex. ii. 11-25, considered as allegory.

DIAGRAM 2.

MOSES SLAYS AN EGYPTIAN.

Beginning of Time.
Pre-Euphratic Era.
Creation of the Euphratic or First race (Adam's).

Dividing in the midst of the Euphratic or First age (see Gen. xv 7-10).

Creation of the Hiddekelic or Second race.

Destruction of the Euphratic or First race by volcanic eruption and earthquake (see Num xvi 28-34, Jer iv 22-29, Rev viii 7). This destruction is shadowed by the Egyptian whom Moses slew and hid in the sand

Dividing in the midst of the Hiddekelic or Second age.

Creation of the Gihonic or Third race
Two Hebrews strive together. Overlap of the Hiddekelic and Gihonic races
Destruction of the Hiddekelic or Second race

Dividing in the midst of the Gihonic or Third age.

Creation of the Pisonic or Fourth race.
Well dug by Isaac (see Gen xxvi 22) shadows the Fourth race, and doubtless is shadowed by the well to which Moses came
Deluge of Noah   Destruction of the Gihonic race
Epoch of replenishment (see Gen. ix 1)
Advent of the Messiah as the Redeemer of man
Messianic Epoch,
Dividing in the midst of the Pisonic or Fourth age   Crucifixion, absolute death, and resurrection of Jesus Christ the Messiah
Judgmental Era.
Thousand Years' Era
Era of Destruction.
End of Time

INDICATIONS OF THE BOOK OF EXODUS. 33

gory the three ages under the veil are disclosed, together with indications of their moral condition and standing.

II. 15–22. "Now when Pharaoh heard this thing, he sought to slay Moses. But Moses fled from the face of Pharaoh, and dwelt in the land of Midian: and he sat down by a well.

16. "Now the priest of Midian had seven daughters: and they came and drew *water*, and filled the troughs to water their father's flock.

17. "And the shepherds came and drove them away: but Moses stood up and helped them, and watered their flock.

18. "And when they came to Reuel their father, he said, How *is it that* ye are come so soon to-day?

19. "And they said, An Egyptian delivered us out of the hand of the shepherds, and also drew *water* enough for us, and watered the flock.

20. "And he said unto his daughters, And where *is* he? why *is* it *that* ye have left the man? call him, that he may eat bread.

21. "And Moses was content to dwell with the man: and he gave Moses Zipporah his daughter.

22. "And she bare *him* a son, and he called his name Gershom: for he said, I have been a stranger in a strange land."

The allegorical stand-point is now taken up in the overlap of the Third and Fourth ages; hence when Moses, as shadow, fled from the Hiddekelic age he came into the Gihonic. The Gihonic age (see Gen. ii. 10–14) is shadowed by the river Gihon that compasseth the whole land of Ethiopia; wherefore, when Moses took Zipporah, the daughter of the priest of Midian, to

c

wife, after he had fled from the face of Pharaoh, the indication becomes manifest that Moses (see Num. xii. 1) married an Ethiopian woman.

From these positions indications follow (see Diagram 3) that the seven daughters of the priest of Midian are emblematic of, or memorialize, the first seven semidivisions of the Four Ages; that they represent or memorialize the same magnitudes as seven of the daughters of Zion, and hence, as such, that they care for the people, the sheep, of these semidivisions of time. The shepherds which came and drove them away are emblematic of the host of the Adversary (see Jer. xxv. 34–36), and as, by the text, Moses stood up and watered the flock of the seven daughters of Midian, so will the Messiah water the sheep of the Four Ages when the seven semidivisions of time shall have expired.

II. 23–25. "And it came to pass in process of time, that the king of Egypt died: and the children of Israel sighed by reason of the bondage, and they cried, and their cry came up unto God by reason of the bondage.

24. "And God heard their groaning, and God remembered his covenant with Abraham, with Isaac, and with Jacob.

25. "And God looked upon the children of Israel, and God had respect unto *them.*"

As already indicated, the bondage of the children of Israel is emblematic of the bondage of those dwelling in the dark valley; it is emblematic of the bondage of the three great races which existed before the flood; and, therefore, God remembered his covenant with Abraham, with Isaac, and with Jacob. Why should he remember this covenant? Because through it all families of the earth shall be blessed. God does not remember his covenant simply that the children of Israel may return to the land of Canaan again; for Paul says (Heb. xi. 15), " If they had been mindful of that *country* from whence they came out, they might have had opportunity to have returned." No, the covenant embraces a magnitude far beyond the mere worldly possession of the land of Canaan by the progeny of Abraham; for by it, the Second Covenant, even the heathen, through faith (see Gal. iii. 7–9), shall be counted the children of Abraham.

The exodus of the children of Israel is but one link in the great chain of events evolving from it; while the bondage and afflictions set forth by the simple history of the text are not merely those of Abraham's progeny, but they comprehend those of the Seed, the Messiah the Prince, who shall come forth out of Egypt with a treasure far more precious than jewels of silver and jewels of gold; hence God had respect unto them when he heard their cry, and when he saw their bondage.

The death of the king of Egypt (see Diagram 2) points to the end of the Gihonic age and to the near approach of the One who shall deliver the captive from the oppressor.

III. 1. " Now Moses kept the flock of Jethro his father in law, the priest of Midian: and he led the flock to the back side of the desert, and came to the mountain of God, *even* to Horeb."

This verse indicates that the stand-point is in the overlap of the Third and Fourth ages, wherefore (see

36 INDICATIONS OF THE BOOK OF EXODUS.

Diagrams 2, 3) the desert or the first barren ages of man having been passed through, the land as the earth in the Pisonic age (see ii. 11-14; Gen. xxvi. 22) will now be fruitful. (See, also, the blessings of Joseph, Deut. xxxiii. 13-16.) In this light the allegoric standpoint of Mount Horeb becomes established at or about the end of the Gihonic or Third age.

III. 2, 6. "And the Angel of the Lord appeared unto him in a flame of fire out of the midst of a bush: and he looked, and, behold, the bush burned with fire, and the bush *was* not consumed . . .

6. "Moreover he said, I *am* the God of thy father, the God of Abraham, the God of Isaac, and the God of Jacob. And Moses hid his face; for he was afraid to look upon God."

By verse 6, God is the God of Abraham, the God of Isaac, and the God of Jacob, and by St. Mark xii. 27, God is not God of the dead, but the God of the living; therefore it becomes evident that the dwellers of the dark valley are not dead, but that they sleep, and shall, at some time, rise again among their brethren.

Who are the dwellers of the dark valley? They are in part the people of the first Three Ages of Man; they are the people whom Moses, in the allegoric sense, is now commanded to bring forth out from the Egypt of the past (see Diagram 3) into the Fourth age, that their names and their iniquity may fall upon the Messiah as the Redeemer of man. This bringing forth, however, is invisible, it is under the veil, but through the perfected labors of the Messiah they will eventually become visibly manifest as presences. When, therefore, they shall rise again into existence as manifest presences, will the penalty of death still be over their heads? It does not seem possible; for by the labors of the Messiah—which culminated in the Messiah's absolute death—man is freed from his debt. If man is freed from his debt, who will replace it upon him that his bondage should be re-established? or if the iniquity of man falls upon the Saviour, and he pays the penalty thereof, what power exists that can make his death of no avail? There is none, or the life-giving Power would become secondary. Abraham was not dead; Isaac was not dead; Jacob was not dead; but their names, blood, and iniquity were borne by the Seed that, eventually, he might pay their debts, and redeem them from captivity in the dark valley and from the absolute death that hovered over them; hence, as with Abraham, Isaac, and Jacob, so with all those which shall be counted the seed of Abraham as a father of nations, that shall be counted the seed of Isaac as a father of nations, and that shall be counted the seed of Jacob as a father of nations.

In Diagram 3, spaces a, a indicate the Four Ages; b, b indicate the Four Ages by the land passed through by Abraham (see Gen. xii. 1–7); c, c indicate the first Three Ages as the wilderness; d, d indicate the first Three Ages by the three days' journey into the wilderness; e, e indicate the pertaining of Abraham as a father of nations; f, f indicate the pertaining of Isaac as a father of nations; g, g indicate the pertaining of Jacob as a father of nations; h, h indicate the pertaining of Jethro to time; i, i indicate the pertaining of Moses to time.

III. 7, 8. "And the Lord said, I have surely seen

38 INDICATIONS OF THE BOOK OF EXODUS.

Ex. iii., considered as allegory.

DIAGRAM 3.

MOSES AT THE BURNING BUSH.

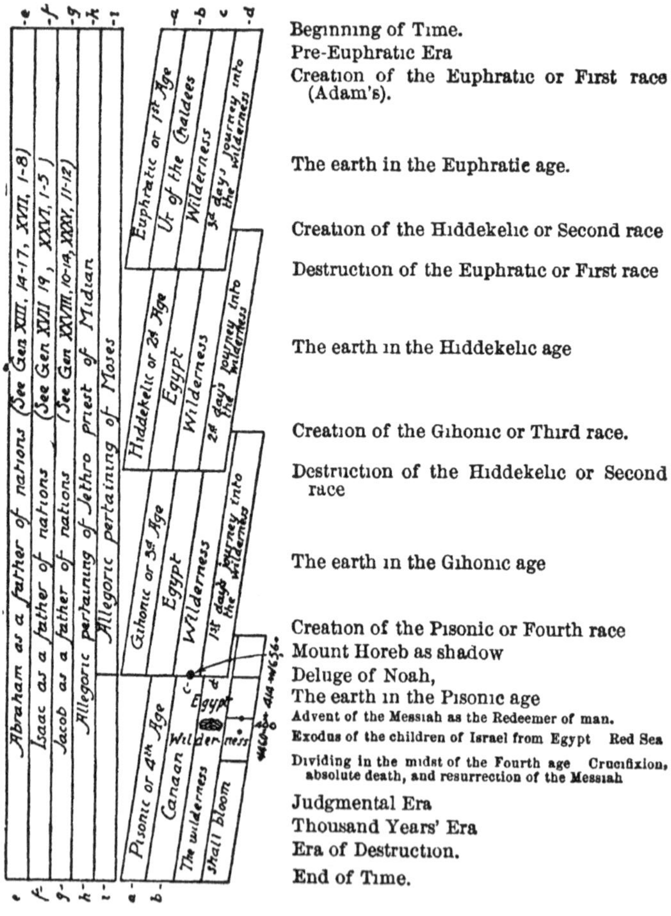

Beginning of Time.
Pre-Euphratic Era
Creation of the Euphratic or First race (Adam's).

The earth in the Euphratic age.

Creation of the Hiddekelic or Second race

Destruction of the Euphratic or First race

The earth in the Hiddekelic age

Creation of the Gihonic or Third race.

Destruction of the Hiddekelic or Second race

The earth in the Gihonic age

Creation of the Pisonic or Fourth race
Mount Horeb as shadow
Deluge of Noah,
The earth in the Pisonic age
Advent of the Messiah as the Redeemer of man.
Exodus of the children of Israel from Egypt   Red Sea
Dividing in the midst of the Fourth age   Crucifixion, absolute death, and resurrection of the Messiah

Judgmental Era
Thousand Years' Era
Era of Destruction.
End of Time.

Diagram labels:
- Abraham as a father of nations (See Gen XIII, 14-17, XVII, 1-8)
- Isaac as a father of nations (See Gen XVII, 19, XXVI, 1-5)
- Jacob as a father of nations (See Gen XXVIII, 10-14, XXXV, 11-12)
- Allegoric pertaining of Jethro priest of Midian
- Allegoric pertaining of Moses
- Euphratic or 1st Age — Ur of the Chaldees — Wilderness — 3d day's journey into the wilderness
- Hiddekelic or 2d Age — Egypt — Wilderness — 2d day's journey into the wilderness
- Gihonic or 3d Age — Egypt — Wilderness — 1st day's journey into the wilderness
- Pisonic or 4th Age — Canaan — The wilderness shall bloom — Egypt — Wilderness — Which did not so

the affliction of my people which *are* in Egypt, and have heard their cry by reason of their taskmasters; for I know their sorrows;

8. "And I am come down to deliver them out of the hand of the Egyptians, and to bring them up out of that land unto a good land and a large, unto a land flowing with milk and honey; unto the place of the Canaanites, and the Hittites, and the Amorites, and the Perizzites, and the Hivites, and the Jebusites."

In these verses the Lord expresses his determination of delivering his people from the hand of the Egyptians, and of establishing them in the land of the Canaanites, the Hittites, and others; from which, as simple history, it becomes manifest that the Canaanites shall be driven out according to the promise given to Abraham, to Isaac, and to Jacob. In the allegoric sense, however, the Lord's people are those of the Four Ages, and unto them the land of Canaan shall be given forever,—which land, symbolically (see Diagram 3), is the earth in the Fourth age,—and from which the Adversary and his adherents, the oppressor and his army, shall be driven out never more to return.

III. 10. "Come now therefore, and I will send thee unto Pharaoh, that thou mayest bring forth my people the children of Israel out of Egypt."

By this verse Moses is chosen as an instrumentality for bringing the children of Israel out of Egypt; hence, as allegory, although the people of the Second age refused him as a ruler and as a deliverer (see ii. 11–14), yet their names will be brought out with the hosts of the Lord when and where the exodus from the Egypt of the past shall find place.

III. 11, 12. "And Moses said unto God, Who *am* I, that I should go unto Pharaoh, and that I should bring forth the children of Israel out of Egypt?

12. "And he said, Certainly I will be with thee; and this *shall be* a token unto thee, that I have sent thee: When thou hast brought forth the people out of Egypt, ye shall serve God upon this mountain."

These verses indicate that Moses comprehends to a limited extent the magnitude of the hosts which shall be brought forth out of Egypt, and, consequently, he feels his unworthiness for the fulfilment of so great a purpose. When, as simple history, Moses smote the Egyptian he thought (see Acts vii. 25) that his brethren would have understood how that God by his hand would deliver them; but they understood not. This deliverance, in all probability, related simply to the souls of the house of Jacob,—that is, to the progeny of Abraham; but afterwards, when the Lord appeared unto Moses, the magnitudes to be delivered then, through the simple history as allegory (see Diagram 3), were much increased, by which Moses felt his unfitness for the task, although (see Acts vii. 22) he was learned in all the wisdom of the Egyptians, and was mighty in words and deeds. The greatness of the task is further indicated where the Lord said, "Certainly I will be with thee;" for the presence of the Fulfilling Power of the Infinite Majesty will be unmistakable. The token given by the Lord to Moses, after Moses shall have brought the children of Israel out from the land of Egypt,—viz., Moses's service upon Mount Horeb,—doubtless is set forth in the book of Deuteronomy.

III. 13–15. "And Moses said unto God, Behold, *when* I come unto the children of Israel, and shall say unto them, The God of your fathers hath sent me unto you; and they shall say to me, What *is* his name? what shall I say unto them?

14. "And God said unto Moses, *I am that I am:* and he said, Thus shalt thou say unto the children of Israel, *I am* hath sent me unto you.

15. "And God said moreover unto Moses, Thus shalt thou say unto the children of Israel, The Lord God of your fathers, the God of Abraham, the God of Isaac, and the God of Jacob, hath sent me unto you: this *is* my name for ever, and this *is* my memorial unto all generations."

These verses indicate that Moses is ignorant of the name of the God of the fathers of the children of Israel. Why should this be so, since God had already declared unto him, "I *am* the God of thy father, the God of Abraham, the God of Isaac, and the God of Jacob"? Moses knew that the Hebrews were his brethren, and if so, why should he be ignorant of the name of the God of their fathers? It undoubtedly is because the term "their fathers" relates to the ages which existed prior to the Deluge, the history of which had passed out of remembrance; therefore, in this emergency, God gave unto Moses his great name "*I am,*" by which he is, was, and shall be known to all generations; hence, the God of the fathers was known in the preceding ages by the name "*I am.*"

III. 16–18. "Go, and gather the elders of Israel together, and say unto them, The Lord God of your fathers, the God of Abraham, of Isaac, and of Jacob, appeared unto me, saying, I have surely visited you, and *seen* that which is done to you in Egypt:

17. "And I have said, I will bring you up out of the affliction of Egypt unto the land of the Canaanites, and the Hittites, and the Amorites, and the Perizzites, and the Hivites, and the Jebusites, unto a land flowing with milk and honey.

18. "And they shall hearken to thy voice: and thou shalt come, thou and the elders of Israel, unto the king of Egypt, and ye shall say unto him, The Lord God of the Hebrews hath met with us: and now let us go, we beseech thee, three days' journey into the wilderness, that we may sacrifice to the Lord our God."

As simple history pertaining to the Fourth age these verses embody the great decree, "Out of Egypt have I called my son." Who is the son? He is the Seed of Abraham, the Seed of Isaac, the Seed of Jacob, the Desire, the Replenisher, the Deliverer, the Messiah the Prince, whose presence and works as the Redeemer of man in the flesh of man, as the son of man, are traceable from the day Melchizedek met Abraham returning from the slaughter of the kings unto the end of the Sacred Records. His labors, however, as a Faithful Witness are brought to light through the simple history of the Fourth age, which history is taken up as allegory and as parable of illustration. Wherefore in the text the term "wilderness" (see Diagram 3) becomes emblematic of time before the Deluge, and hence the three days' journey into the wilderness indicate the Three Ages into which that time was divided, during which the Faithful Witnesses labored for the overthrow of Evil. One of these Witnesses (see Rev. i. 4–6) is Jesus Christ, the Son of God.

III. 19–22. "And I am sure that the king of Egypt will not let you go, no, not by a mighty hand.

20. "And I will stretch out my hand, and smite Egypt with all my wonders which I will do in the midst thereof: and after that he will let you go.

21. "And I will give this people favour in the sight of the Egyptians: and it shall come to pass, that, when ye go, ye shall not go empty:

22. "But every woman shall borrow of her neighbour, and of her that sojourneth in her house, jewels of silver, and jewels of gold, and raiment: and ye shall put *them* upon your sons, and upon your daughters; and ye shall spoil the Egyptians."

In this history, as allegory, the king of Egypt, and the Egyptians, become emblematic of the Adversary and his host; and, by the allegory, they will be spoiled of every good thing which they possess or appear to possess, because they heeded not the wonders done in their midst by the Lord of hosts. The certainty of their spoliation is expressed in St. Matt. xiii. 12 as follows: "For whosoever hath, to him shall be given, and he shall have more abundance: but whosoever hath not, from him shall be taken away even that he hath." From this history, therefore, indications follow that the Messiah, who is among the hosts of Israel, shall possess the gate of his enemies, and that not only Israel shall be his, but that the Gentiles also, the great host which fell before man was brought forth as an instrumentality and a field, shall be wrenched out of the hand of the Adversary, while the adversarial host will be stripped of all but their evil garments.

IV. 10–17. "And Moses said unto the Lord, O my Lord, I *am* not eloquent, neither heretofore, nor since thou hast spoken unto thy servant; but I *am* slow of speech, and of a slow tongue.

11. "And the Lord said unto him, Who hath made man's mouth? or who maketh the dumb, or deaf, or the seeing, or the blind? have not I the Lord?

12. "Now therefore go, and I will be with thy mouth, and teach thee what thou shalt say.

13. "And he said, O my Lord, send, I pray thee, by the hand *of him whom* thou wilt send.

14. "And the anger of the Lord was kindled against Moses, and he said, *Is* not Aaron the Levite thy brother? I know that he can speak well. And also, behold, he cometh forth to meet thee: and when he seeth thee, he will be glad in his heart.

15. "And thou shalt speak unto him, and put words in his mouth: and I will be with thy mouth, and with his mouth, and will teach you what ye shall do.

16. "And he shall be thy spokesman unto the people: and he shall be, *even* he shall be to thee instead of a mouth, and thou shalt be to him instead of God.

17. "And thou shalt take this rod in thine hand, wherewith thou shalt do signs."

In the light that Moses shadows the first Three Ages of Man, then that he may become manifest as an intelligence, a mouth is given him in Aaron his brother; hence much of that which pertains to Moses as representative of the Three Ages under the veil will, as allegory, be made manifest through Aaron (see Diagram 4).

The slow speech of Moses also becomes indicative of the allegories with which his words are veiled, and, hence, to the spokesman of Moses, whomsoever he may be, the words of Moses will be as the words of God through their inspiration.

In Diagram 4, spaces a, a indicate the Four Ages of Man; b, b indicate the Four Ages by the land Abraham passed through in his journey from Ur of the Chaldees to Canaan; c, c indicate the first Three Ages as the wilderness; d, d indicate epochs of the Fourth age; e, e indicate the bounds of time; f, f indicate pertaining of Moses to time; g, g indicate pertaining of Aaron as Moses's spokesman.

IV. 21–23. "And the Lord said unto Moses, When thou goest to return into Egypt, see that thou do all those wonders before Pharaoh, which I have put in thine hand: but I will harden his heart, that he shall not let the people go.

22. "And thou shalt say unto Pharaoh, Thus saith the Lord, Israel *is* my son, *even* my firstborn:

23. "And I say unto thee, Let my son go, that he may serve me: and if thou refuse to let him go, behold, I will slay thy son, *even* thy firstborn."

In Diagram 5, spaces a, a indicate the Four Ages of Man; b, b indicate the Four Ages by the land through which Abraham journeyed (see Gen. xii. 1–7); c, c indicate the first Three Ages as the wilderness; d, d indicate epochs in the Fourth age; e, e indicate the grand epoch from the beginning of the creation unto the end

46 INDICATIONS OF THE BOOK OF EXODUS.

Ex. iv. 10–17, considered as allegory.

DIAGRAM 4.

AARON AS MOSES'S SPOKESMAN.

Beginning of Time
Pre-Euphratic Era
Creation of the Euphratic or First race (Adam's).

The earth in the Euphratic age

Creation of the Hiddekelic or Second race
Destruction of the Euphratic or First race.

The earth in the Hiddekelic age.

Creation of the Gihonic or Third race
Destruction of the Hiddekelic or Second race.

The earth in the Gihonic age.

Creation of the Pisonic or Fourth race.
Mount Horeb as shadow
Deluge of Noah   Destruction of the Gihonic or Third race
The earth in the Pisonic age
Advent of the Messiah as the Redeemer of man.
Exodus of the children of Israel from Egypt
Dividing in the midst of the Fourth age   Crucifixion, absolute death, and resurrection of the Messiah as Jesus Christ.
Judgmental Era
Thousand Years' Era.
Era of Destruction
End of Time

INDICATIONS OF THE BOOK OF EXODUS. 47

Ex. iv. 21-23, considered as allegory.

DIAGRAM 5.

ISRAEL AS THE LORD'S FIRSTBORN.

The firstborn of every creature is established in the creation of a body for the Word of God. This body (see Col i 13-19) obtains pre-eminence in all things, and hence is and must be (see Rev iii 14) the very beginning of the creation of God

Creative days. Creation of light, of the earthy, of the firmament, of vegetation, of the sun, moon, and stars, of fishes and fowl, of cattle, of creeping thing, and beast of the earth.

The Son begotten as the firstborn among many brethren (see Rom viii 29, Rev xii 1-5, Deut xxxii 9-14) Beginning of Time
Creation of the Euphratic or First race (Adam's).

The earth in the Euphratic age

Creation of the Hiddekelic or Second race
Destruction of the Euphratic or First race

The earth in the Hiddekelic age

Creation of the Gihonic or Third race
Destruction of the Hiddekelic or Second race

The earth in the Gihonic age.

Creation of the Pisonic or Fourth race.
Mt Horeb as shadow Allegoric stand-point of the text
Deluge of Noah Destruction of the Gihonic or Third race
The earth in the Pisonic age.
Advent of the Messiah as Jacob the Seed of Jacob The name of the Seed of Jacob changed to Israel (see Gen xxxii 24-30) Exodus of the children of Israel from Egypt as simple history of the Fourth age The simple history of the Exodus shadows the bringing forth from the land of darkness and shadow of death (see Diagram 5) of those dwelling in the wilderness or the Three Ages of Man under the veil
Judgmental Era
Thousand Years' Era
Era of Destruction
End of Time

of time; *f, f,* through the regeneration of the creature world, indicate the pertaining of Israel, the Lord's firstborn, to the grand epoch from the beginning of the creation unto the end of time.

The stand-point of the text, as allegory, is in the overlap of the Third and Fourth ages; hence, when Moses shall return into Egypt (see Diagram 5), the pertaining will be to the Egypt of the past, to the ages of man under the veil.

When Moses shall have returned unto Pharaoh he is commanded to say (see verse 22), "Thus saith the Lord, Israel *is* my son, *even* my firstborn." Such being the command, how is it possible that Israel be the son of God, and, also, that Israel be his firstborn?

The harmonious solution of these questions is clearly indicated by the Scriptures; for (see Num. xxiii. 20–23) the perfection of Jacob—in that no iniquity is beheld in Jacob—points to him as being the Messiah, while Jacob's name (see Gen. xxxii. 24–30) was changed to Israel. Of Israel it is said (see Num. xxiii. 21), "Neither hath he seen perverseness in Israel: the Lord his God is with him;" hence the perfection of Jacob as Israel, and the perfection of Israel as Jacob, indicate that this perfect one (see Deut. xxxii. 3, 4) is the Messiah under the name of Jacob, the Seed of Jacob (see Gen. xiv. 18–20; xxvii. 4, 10–14, 33), in whom all families of the earth shall be blessed.

In the light that Israel is the Messiah, then (see Col. i. 15; Rev. iii. 14) Israel the Messiah, through the body created for him, in and *as* the very beginning of the creation of God, truly is the firstborn of every creature (see Diagram 5). The first-born of every creat-

INDICATIONS OF THE BOOK OF EXODUS. 49

ure, however, is not, of necessity, endowed with life (see Gen. i. 1-2); hence this first-born, like unto the earth in the first stage of its creation, may also have been without form and void. Further, this first-born may be just as suitable for the habitation of the varied forms of creature life as the earth itself is suitable for the varied forms of creature life which pertain to it.

When, therefore, the Word of God invested this body it, the body, became endowed with the life of the Word of God, and thus was begotten to God as the Son of God. By this begetting the Son (see Rom. viii. 29) became the first-born among many brethren,—the text of Romans does not say the first-born among all brethren, but among many brethren; hence creature life (see, also, Rev. xii. 1-5) existed before the Word was begotten as the Son of God. Indications follow from Rev. xii. that the brethren called for by the text of Romans are found in man of Adam's race, and, hence, that the Son was begotten (see Lev. xxvii.) shortly before the creation of man of Adam's race (see, also, Diagram 5).

Thus Israel the Messiah, through the body created for him that he might do the will of God, as the first-born, is the beginning of the creation of God, and Israel the Messiah, as the begotten Son of God, is also the first-born among many brethren.

If Israel the Messiah was begotten as the Son of God before the creation of man of Adam's race, then his presence in the Egypt of the past as the Son of God (see Rev. xi. 3-8) becomes manifest (see, also, Diagram 5); wherefore the words of the Lord unto Pharaoh (see verse 23), "Let my son go, that he may serve me,"—from the allegorical stand-point of the text,

—are susceptible of actual fulfilment; hence, when the Son of God shall thus come out of Egypt that he may serve the Lord, he will (see Diagram 5) very shortly thereafter, or very shortly after the creative days shall have come to an end, take up in his own Person the great subjugatory labors called for in Gen. i. 28.

The context indicates that the circumcision of the past races of men will be fulfilled in the circumcision that pertains to the Fourth age; hence by the allegory (see verses 24–26, also 11, 21, 22) the stand-point may be placed in the Fourth age at or about the time of the exodus. From this stand-point the work pertaining to the exodus, both as simple history and as allegory, can be more clearly manifested.

V. 1, 2. "And afterward Moses and Aaron went in, and told Pharaoh, Thus saith the Lord God of Israel, Let my people go, that they may hold a feast unto me in the wilderness.

2. "And Pharaoh said, Who *is* the Lord, that I should obey his voice to let Israel go? I know not the Lord, neither will I let Israel go."

Pharaoh evidently shadows Lucifer, the angel Death (see xv. 20, 21; Rev. vi. 7, 8). This powerful being is united to the adversarial host, and he holds captive the people of the past ages of man in the dark valley of death. These people (see Diagram 5) dwell in the wilderness, and the command of the Lord is for them to hold a feast unto the Lord in the wilderness, whereby they will be released from their captivity and rise into renewed life.

As, by the simple history of the text, Pharaoh acknowledged not the Lord, and refused to let the people go, so Lucifer, the destroying Angel, acknowledges not the supremacy of the Lord (see Isa. xiv. 12–14), and will not let his captives go that they may serve the Lord. It must be kept in mind that the stand-point is now placed at or about the time of the exodus of the children of Israel from Egypt.

VI. 1–8. "Then the Lord said unto Moses, Now shalt thou see what I will do to Pharaoh: for with a strong hand shall he let them go, and with a strong hand shall he drive them out of his land.

2. "And God spake unto Moses, and said unto him, I *am* the Lord:

3. "And I appeared unto Abraham, unto Isaac, and unto Jacob, by *the name of* God Almighty; but by my name JEHOVAH was I not known to them.

4. "And I have also established my covenant with them, to give them the land of Canaan, the land of their pilgrimage, wherein they were strangers.

5. "And I have also heard the groaning of the children of Israel, whom the Egyptians keep in bondage; and I have remembered my covenant.

6. "Wherefore say unto the children of Israel, I *am* the Lord, and I will bring you out from under the burdens of the Egyptians, and I will rid you out of their bondage, and I will redeem you with a stretched out arm, and with great judgments:

7. "And I will take you to me for a people, and I will be to you a God: and ye shall know that I *am* the Lord your God, which bringeth you out from under the burdens of the Egyptians.

8. "And I will bring you in unto the land, concerning the which I did swear to give it to Abraham, to Isaac, and to Jacob; and I will give it you for a heritage: I *am* the Lord."

Through the bondage of the children of Israel to the Egyptians, as simple history, the bondage of the children of Israel as the father of nations is brought to notice (see Diagram 3). Wherefore as by the simple history the children of Israel shall be delivered from their Egyptian bondage, so shall the children of Israel the father of nations be delivered from the adverse power that holds them in bondage.

The God that appeared unto Abraham, Isaac, and Jacob was known by the name of God Almighty; wherefore indications arise (see Gen. xiv. 18–20; xvii. 1, 2) that the Fulfilling Power of the Infinite Majesty, the Third Person of the Trinity, was known to Abraham, to Isaac, and to Jacob, by the name of God Almighty.

Now, however, in that the captives lying in the valley of the shadow of death are to be brought forth from that valley, the Second and Third Persons of the Trinity unite in the work, whereby God becomes manifest and known by the name JEHOVAH. This unity doubtless is shadowed by the unity of Moses and Aaron (see iv. 13–16).

VII. 1–3. "And the Lord said unto Moses, See, I have made thee a god to Pharaoh; and Aaron thy brother shall be thy prophet.

2. "Thou shalt speak all that I command thee; and Aaron thy brother shall speak unto Pharaoh, that he send the children of Israel out of his land.

3. "And I will harden Pharaoh's heart, and multiply my signs and my wonders in the land of Egypt."

Thus, by the Lord's endowment—"I have made thee a god to Pharaoh"—Moses, from the simple historical stand-point, is clothed with more power than Pharaoh, both in the allegorical and in the simple history sense; hence a Power greater than Lucifer will loose the bands of Lucifer's captives. Pharaoh, clearly (see verse 3), is an instrumentality raised up through whom the power and supremacy of the Lord will be made manifest.

VII. 4, 5. "But Pharaoh shall not hearken unto you, that I may lay my hand upon Egypt, and bring forth mine armies, *and* my people the children of Israel, out of the land of Egypt by great judgments.

5. "And the Egyptians shall know that I *am* the Lord, when I stretch forth mine hand upon Egypt, and bring out the children of Israel from among them."

In these verses indications are further given that the great adversarial hosts pertaining to the ages of man under the veil shall know that the Lord is God, and that the Lord's people pertaining to these ages shall be delivered from their hands, even though they are apparently overwhelmed by death.

As simple history pertaining to the Fourth age, the judgments that came upon Pharaoh and the Egyptians become signs and wonders (see verse 3) in the eyes of all beholders,—whether such beholders be earthly or heavenly,—to stamp the immutability of the most high God.

IX. 13-16. "And the Lord said unto Moses, Rise up early in the morning, and stand before Pharaoh,

54 INDICATIONS OF THE BOOK OF EXODUS.

and say unto him, Thus saith the Lord God of the Hebrews, Let my people go, that they may serve me.

14. "For I will at this time send all my plagues upon thine heart, and upon thy servants, and upon thy people; that thou mayest know that *there is* none like me in all the earth.

15. "For now I will stretch out my hand, that I may smite thee and thy people with pestilence; and thou shalt be cut off from the earth.

16. "And in very deed for this *cause* have I raised thee up, for to shew *in* thee my power; and that my name may be declared throughout all the earth."

From these verses indications become evident that Pharaoh was raised up that through him the power of the Lord might be shown, and that the name of the Lord be declared throughout the earth. Why should Pharaoh have been raised up as an instrumentality for showing the power of the Lord? Why should his heart have been hardened that he would not let the children of Israel go? It was that the power and majesty of the Lord should be made manifest to the great host of evil which roamed throughout the earth, and which sought to overthrow every good thing. The command was given man in the beginning to subdue the earth and to have dominion over it; but the evidences of his failure became visible on every side; yet through man in his fallen condition the power of God is made manifest that none be deceived by the Power of Evil in his apparent triumph. For four hundred years the Messiah, as the Seed of Abraham, to whom all things were promised and to whom all things were given, has been suffering affliction even to its greatest depths; afflictions which were poured upon him with an unsparing hand by the Adversary and his host of adherents, who, in their seeming triumph, thought to prevail.

The plagues, therefore, that came upon Pharaoh, with scarcely a doubt, were for the purpose of showing to this host that, although the Seed had suffered more than fell to the lot of any man, the promise made to him was steadfast and sure; and that the sufferings which he had experienced were no evidence of weakness, or indication of failure on the part of him who gave the promise. It seems fitting before the Seed the Son came out of the land of Egypt that a great manifestation of power be made, that great rejoicing prevail, and also that, by the judgments which came upon Pharaoh and the Egyptians, the evil host could comprehend the certainty of their overthrow when, in the last day, judgment shall have been rendered against them. Indications also follow from the calling of Pharaoh, that Lucifer, the angel Death, was raised up as an instrumentality for the final destruction of evil.

It is stated, Deut. xxix. 2–4, " Ye have seen all that the Lord did before your eyes, in the land of Egypt unto Pharaoh, and unto all his servants, and unto all his land;

" The great temptations which thine eyes have seen, the signs, and those great miracles :

" Yet the Lord hath not given you a heart to perceive, and eyes to see, and ears to hear, unto this day." And by Psalm cvi. 7, "Our fathers understood not thy wonders in Egypt." If, therefore, Pharaoh was raised up that the power of God be made manifest

56 INDICATIONS OF THE BOOK OF EXODUS.

and his name declared throughout the earth, and if the children of Israel understood not the wonders which were done in their midst and in their presence, of what avail were these wonders? The indications point very clearly to the conclusion that they were manifest to Satan and his army, the great host which was cast out of heaven into the earth (see Rev. xii. 9), and also to the great host (see Heb. ii. 14) which is under bondage to Satan through fear of death.

In the great exhibitions of power given by the Lord before Pharaoh, three of them were duplicated by the magicians through enchantment, or probably by legerdemain, whereby the power of the Adversary is shadowed. It will be noticed in regard to these three plagues that they pertain directly to the earth into which Satan was cast,—that is, the serpents, the rivers which became blood, and the frogs which came out from the waters, pertain directly to the earth. So, also, the lice may be directly connected with the earth, but the flies, the dust in the air, the locusts, the murrain, the darkness, and the hail pertain more to the heavens from which Satan was cast, and to which he cannot return, and which he cannot command except it be given him for a purpose as expressed in Rev. xiii. 5. The indications are probable that the first four signs given Pharaoh shadow (see Ezek. xiv. 21, 22) the four sore judgments that shall come upon Jerusalem as the Four Ages of Man, three of which—viz., the destruction of the First race by volcanic eruption and earthquake (see Num. xvi. 1–40), the destruction of the Second race by drought and famine (see Rev. viii. 8, 9), and the destruction of the Third race by the Deluge of

INDICATIONS OF THE BOOK OF EXODUS. 57

Noah (see Gen. vii. 17-20)—are all matters of the past, while the fourth may now be in the course of fulfilment. From this position the seven plagues that remain shadow the seven last plagues (see Rev. xv. 1-7; vi. 7, 8) pertaining to the final epochs of the Fourth age.

The power of the Adversary in the earth is made manifest in I. Kings xix. 11, 12 as follows: "And a great and strong wind rent the mountains, and brake in pieces the rocks before the Lord; *but* the Lord *was* not in the wind: and after the wind an earthquake; *but* the Lord *was* not in the earthquake:

"And after the earthquake a fire; *but* the Lord *was* not in the fire: and after the fire a still small voice."

If the Lord was not in the wind, and not in the earthquake, and not in the fire, it becomes evident that the Adversary must have produced them. This is the mount—evidently the earthy creature body—which can be touched (see Heb. xii. 18-21) by the power of the Adversary, and of his power who can doubt? since (Rev. xiii. 13, 14) "He doeth great wonders, so that he maketh fire come down from heaven on the earth in the sight of men,

"And deceiveth them that dwell on the earth by *the means of* those miracles which he had power to do in the sight of the beast."

X. 24-26. "And Pharaoh called unto Moses, and said, Go ye, serve the Lord; only let your flocks and your herds be stayed: let your little ones also go with you.

25. "And Moses said, Thou must give us also sac-

rifices and burnt offerings, that we may sacrifice unto the Lord our God.

26. "Our cattle also shall go with us; there shall not a hoof be left behind; for thereof must we take to serve the Lord our God; and we know not with what we must serve the Lord, until we come thither."

By verses 9–11 Pharaoh consented for the men of Israel to go and serve the Lord; but the young, the sons and daughters, together with the flocks and herds, he withheld. Now, however, he consents for the little ones to go with Moses, but that the flocks and herds, shall remain. To this Moses will not listen, and he declares that not a hoof shall be left behind.

If Pharaoh shadows Lucifer, then the simple history recorded above indicates that the destroying angel shall disgorge the spoils of many generations, young and old, sons and daughters, men and little ones; and, more, that not a single hoof shall be left behind to mark a triumph for the spoiling Power. Truly, therefore, the seed of Abraham shall be as the dust of the earth, as the sand that is by the sea-shore, and as the stars of heaven for multitude.

XII. 1–6. "And the Lord spake unto Moses and Aaron in the land of Egypt, saying,

2. "This month *shall be* unto you the beginning of months: it *shall be* the first month of the year to you.

3. "Speak ye unto all the congregation of Israel, saying, In the tenth *day* of this month they shall take to them every man a lamb, according to the house of *their* fathers, a lamb for a house:

4. "And if the household be too little for the lamb,

DIAGRAM 6.

THE LAMB OF THE PASSOVER.

The Son begotten. Beginning of Time or of Months
Pre-Euphratic Era
Creation of the Euphratic or First race (Adam's)

The earth in the Euphratic age

Creation of the Hiddekelic or Second race
Destruction of the Euphratic or First race

The earth in the Hiddekelic age

Creation of the Gihonic or Third race
Destruction of the Hiddekelic or Second race

The earth in the Gihonic age

Creation of the Pisonic or Fourth race
Antediluvian Epoch
Deluge of Noah   Destruction of the Gihonic or Third race
Epoch of replenishment (see Gen ix 1)
Advent of the Messiah the Prince (see Dan ix 25)
Tenth day of the month Jesse the Seed of Jesse as the Messiah (see Isa xi 1-5).
Fourteenth day of the month The Messiah as Naboth slain (see I Kings xxi 1-22)
Fifteenth day of the month The Messiah manifest as Elisha, in whom (see II Kings xlii 20-21) the dead revive.

End of Time

Euphratic or 1st Age	Hiddekelic or 2d Age	Gihonic or 3d Age	Pisonic or 4th Age
Ur of the Chaldees	Egypt	Egypt	Canaan
1st Month	2nd Month	3d Month	4th Month	5th Month	6th Month	7m mo	8m mo	9m mo	10m mo	11m mo	12m mo

≈1860 ≈≈ 4/4 1656/7

The Messianic Year

INDICATIONS OF THE BOOK OF EXODUS. 59

let him and his neighbour next unto his house take *it* according to the number of the souls; every man according to his eating shall make your count for the lamb.

5. "Your lamb shall be without blemish, a male of the first year: ye shall take *it* out from the sheep, or from the goats:

6. "And ye shall keep it up until the fourteenth day of the same month: and the whole assembly of the congregation of Israel shall kill it in the evening."

In Diagram 6, spaces *a, a* indicate the Four Ages of Man; *b, b* indicate the Four Ages by the land through which Abraham journeyed; *c, c* indicate chief divisions of the Four Ages as months; *d, d* indicate the Four Ages or Time as the Messianic year. The figures at *f, f* indicate the years of the first three divisions or epochs of the Fourth age.

The Fourth age is divided into six epochs, of which the third is the Messianic Epoch or month. In the beginning of this epoch the Messiah made his advent (see Gen. iii. 15, 16; xiv. 18–20; Dan. ix. 25) as the Son of man. Four hundred years after this advent (see Gen. xv. 13, 14; Acts vii. 15–36) the exodus of the children of Israel was on the eve of fulfilment as simple history pertaining to the Fourth age. This simple history, however, as allegory, shadows very great magnitudes, which, by the lifting of the veil, become traceable on every side.

The stand-point of the text is in the Messianic Epoch; wherefore, by considering twelve of the chief epochs, into which time is divided, as twelve months, the ninth month coincides with the Messianic Epoch. As already indicated, the Messiah made his advent as the Son of man in the beginning of this epoch or month, or upon the first day of this month. Upon the tenth day of the month, as simple history, a lamb of the first year, a male without blemish, shall be taken from the sheep, or from the goats, and shall be kept up four days.

This lamb, that is without blemish, doubtless shadows (see St. John i. 29; Rev. v. 5–13) " the Lamb of God which taketh away the sins of the world." Wherefore as upon the tenth day of the month the lamb of the passover was made manifest, so, as shadow, the tenth day of the Messianic month points to the manifest presence of the Messiah (see Isa. xi. 1–5) as Jesse the branch of Jesse, and (see Rev. v. 5) as the Root of David, whose perfection marks him as being the Messiah; hence, by the shadow (see Diagram 6), the tenth day of the Messianic month points to the year 2690 of the Fourth age, at or about which time the Messiah as the Seed of Jesse was manifest as a presence (see, also, Isa. ix. 6, 7).

By the simple history of the text (see verse 6) the lamb of the passover shall be killed in the evening of the fourteenth day of this month; hence as this lamb shadows the Messiah, so, by the slaying thereof on the fourteenth day of the month, the slaying of the Messiah on the fourteenth day of the Messianic month is indicated. The fourteenth day of the Messianic month points to the year 2938 of the Fourth age, at or about which time (see I. Kings xxi. 1–22) the Messiah as Naboth the Jezreelite was slain, although not one fault or blemish was found in him by his bitterest enemies.

The exodus of the children of Israel (see Num.

INDICATIONS OF THE BOOK OF EXODUS. 61

xxxiii. 3-5) took place on the fifteenth day of the month; hence as the exodus of the children of Israel out of the land of Egypt shadows the exodus of the people of the past ages out from their land (see Diagram 6), so, inasmuch as they must be raised out of the valley of the shadow of death, the Messiah, who was slain as Naboth the Jezreelite, must come forth again from the dark valley.

Therefore, as the exodus of the children of Israel, by the simple history, was upon the fifteenth day of the month, so the return of the Messiah from the dark valley, to which he was sent as Naboth the Jezreelite, is made manifest upon the fifteenth day of the Messianic month; for the fifteenth day of the Messianic month points to the year 3000 of the Fourth age, at or about which time the Messiah was physically manifest as Elisha the Prophet, whose works (see II. Kings v. 1-14) were only paralleled (see I. Kings xvii. 1) by those of Elijah, and (see St. Luke v. 12, 13) by those of Jesus Christ the Messiah.

If, therefore (see St. Luke vi. 44), "every tree is known by his own fruit," who can distinguish between these trees? for in the healing of the leper (see II. Kings v. 11) even Naaman was wroth because Elisha did not come out, and stand, and call on the name of the Lord his God.

Through the wonders pertaining to the Messianic month, the lamb of the passover, as shadow, becomes identified with the Messiah; hence, inasmuch as, by the simple history of the text (see verse 2), the month in which the exodus took place shall be the beginning of months, and as it shall be the first month of the year to the children of Israel, so, through it as shadow, the Messianic month indicates the beginning of months or the beginning of time as the Messianic year; hence the Messianic month, as shadow, points to the first month of the allegoric year (see Diagram 6, spaces *d, d*), during which the Messiah fulfilled the commands of the Lord (see Gen. i. 28) for the subjugation of the earth, and of every living thing that moved upon it. Wherefore, in perfect harmony with what has gone before, as the Messiah made his advent as the Son of man in the beginning of the Messianic month, so, also, the Messiah made his advent in the beginning of time, or in the beginning of the Messianic year, as the Son of God, in the body (see Heb. x. 5–7; Ps. xl. 5–10) that was prepared for him, that he might do the will of God.

Thus the lamb of the passover, as shadow, now becomes identified with the labors of the Messiah in the Fourth age, but the labors of the Messiah as the Son of God (see Diagram 6) commence with the beginning of time.

XII. 7–13. "And they shall take of the blood, and strike *it* on the two side posts and on the upper door post of the houses, wherein they shall eat it.

8. "And they shall eat the flesh in that night, roast with fire, and unleavened bread; *and* with bitter *herbs* they shall eat it.

9. "Eat not of it raw, nor sodden at all with water, but roast *with* fire; his head with his legs, and with the purtenance thereof.

10. "And ye shall let nothing of it remain until the morning; and that which remaineth of it until the morning ye shall burn with fire.

11. " And thus shall ye eat it; *with* your loins girded, your shoes on your feet, and your staff in your hand; and ye shall eat it in haste: it *is* the Lord's passover.

12. " For I will pass through the land of Egypt this night, and will smite all the firstborn in the land of Egypt, both man and beast; and against all the gods of Egypt I will execute judgment: I *am* the Lord.

13. " And the blood shall be to you for a token upon the houses where ye *are:* and when I see the blood, I will pass over you, and the plague shall not be upon you to destroy *you,* when I smite the land of Egypt."

In Diagram 7, spaces *a, a* indicate the Four Ages of Man; *b, b* indicate the Four Ages by the countries through which Abraham passed in his journey from Ur of the Chaldees to Canaan (see Gen. xii. 1–7), of which Canaan represents the earth in the Fourth age; *c, c* indicate the first Three Ages by the upper door-post and the two side-posts, and also the Fourth age with its six divisions; *e, e* indicate the years of the six divisions of the Fourth age.

The upper door-post shadows the First age, the two side-posts shadow Egypt as the Second and Third ages; wherefore when, by the simple history of the text, the blood of the passover lamb shall be struck on the posts which pertain to the houses wherein the lamb was eaten, so the shadow and memorial is given that the blood of the Messiah will seal the Lord's host that pertains to the Egypt of the past, that they be not harmed when the Lord shall execute judgment (see Dan. vii. 1–12) against the gods of the Egypt of the past.

In this light indications follow that the houses in which the lamb was eaten shadow the children (see

64 INDICATIONS OF THE BOOK OF EXODUS.

Ex. xii. 7-13, considered as allegory.

DIAGRAM 7.

THE BLOOD OF THE PASSOVER LAMB.

The Son begotten   Beginning of Time or of months.
Pre Euphratic Era.
Creation of the Euphratic or First race (Adam's).

The earth in the Euphratic age

Creation of the Hiddekelic or Second race. (Second Adam.)
Destruction of the Euphratic or First race.

The earth in the Hiddekelic age

Creation of the Gihonic or Third race. (Third Adam.)
Destruction of the Hiddekelic or Second race.

The earth in the Gihonic age

Creation of the Pisonic or Fourth race. (Fourth Adam.)
Antediluvian Epoch
Deluge of Noah   Destruction of the Gihonic or Third race
Epoch of replenishment (see Gen ix 1).
Advent of the Messiah as the Son of man.
The Messianic Epoch or month   The earth in the Pisonic age.
Crucifixion and absolute death of the Messiah as Jesus Christ.
Judgmental Era.

Thousand Years' Era.

Era of Destruction
End of Time.

INDICATIONS OF THE BOOK OF EXODUS 65

xxxiv. 6, 7) upon whom the blood and iniquity of the past ages of man had been visited; hence (see Diagram 7) when the children—those of the Fourth age—shall partake of the Living Bread, which bread is the body of the Messiah, the Lamb of God, then the fathers also, the people of the past ages (see Job xiv. 19–22), through the children as temples and as priests, will become sealed with the blood of the Lamb who was slain (see Rev. v. 9, 10), that God's people, God's inheritance, might be redeemed by his blood out of every kindred, tongue, people, and nation.

Thus, by the allegory the possibility of a general priesthood of man is brought to notice, and that through man of Adam's race, as a holy nation and a kingdom of priests (see xix. 5, 6), man will be a peculiar treasure to the Lord above all people pertaining to the earth; hence the indication further follows (see xxix. 32, 33) that, through man as a priesthood and as a nation of priests, the sealing of God's inheritance even to the uttermost possession (see Ps. ii. 6–8; Isa. xi. 6–9) may be accomplished to the exclusion of everything that is hurtful; hence again, from these positions the text also indicates that the overthrow and destruction of Evil will be fulfilled in due time, and that the lamb of the passover shadows the Redeemer or the one who shed his blood that the penalty resting over man might be paid.

By verse 9 the flesh of the passover lamb shall be roast with fire, thus indicating (see Rev. xx. 9) the baptism of fire which, finally, shall envelop all, but not destroy all, even as indicated in verse 13, "The plague shall not be upon you to destroy *you*, when I smite the land of Egypt," and, also (see Gen. xv. 17), by the smoking furnace and burning lamp that passed between the pieces that represented the Lord's inheritance (see, also, Zech. xiv. 12–21).

The test by fire also seems imperatively called for in verse 9, "Eat not of it raw, nor sodden at all with water, but roast *with* fire," and again (verse 10), "Let nothing of it remain until the morning; and that which remaineth of it until the morning ye shall burn with fire," which still further indicates that when the body of the Saviour shall have fulfilled its high calling it shall be eaten no more. Therefore it follows that, in the final era of time, the last hope of the Evil Kingdom will be blotted out forever, and that no resurrection can ever restore the dead of that last dread day; hence the subjugation of the Adversary will be complete, and the Tree of Life will never fall within his grasp that he should re-establish his kingdom through its regenerating, life-giving power.

XII. 14. "And this day shall be unto you for a memorial; and ye shall keep it a feast to the Lord throughout your generations: ye shall keep it a feast by an ordinance for ever."

This memorial-day is the fourteenth day of the month, and (Lev. xxiii. 5) " In the fourteenth *day* of the first month at even *is* the Lord's passover;" also (see Num. xxviii. 16), "And in the fourteenth day of the first month *is* the passover of the Lord;" therefore the passover was killed and eaten and preparation made for the exodus on the fourteenth day of the month.

XII. 15–17. "Seven days shall ye eat unleavened

bread; even the first day ye shall put away leaven out of your houses: for whosoever eateth leavened bread from the first day until the seventh day, that soul shall be cut off from Israel.

16. "And in the first day *there shall be* a holy convocation, and in the seventh day there shall be a holy convocation to you; no manner of work shall be done in them, save *that* which every man must eat, that only may be done of you.

17. "And ye shall observe *the feast of* unleavened bread; for in this selfsame day have I brought your armies out of the land of Egypt: therefore shall ye observe this day in your generations by an ordinance for ever."

By the text of Exodus the actual date of the commencement of the feast of unleavened bread seems under the veil, but where it is specially proclaimed as an ordinance,—which proclamation the text of Exodus calls for,—as given in Lev. xxiii. 6, 7, the feast of unleavened bread is on the fifteenth day of the month, and it continues for seven days, the fifteenth day being a holy day. Also by Num. xxviii. 17, the limits of this feast are clearly defined as seven days from and including the fifteenth day of the month. The same books and chapters also establish the memorial day in which the passover was killed and eaten as the fourteenth day of the month; therefore it follows that while the fourteenth day is a day of preparation and a feast day, the fifteenth also is a feast day, and in it shall be a holy convocation in which no work shall be done "save *that* which every man must eat, that only may be done of you."

The indication further follows from the text that the exodus of the children of Israel commenced with the fifteenth day of the month; by which the return of those dwelling in the dark valley is shadowed forth; for the Saviour did not pay the penalty of man's transgression until the close of the fourteenth day, that they should return from their bondage before the fifteenth. Moreover it is clearly stated (Num. xxxiii. 3), "And they departed from Rameses in the first month, on the fifteenth day of the first month; on the morrow after the passover the children of Israel went out with a high hand in the sight of all the Egyptians," from which it becomes clear that the passover was killed and eaten on the fourteenth day of the first month, while the feast of unleavened bread, which was for seven days, commenced on the fifteenth.

XII. 29–39. "And it came to pass, that at midnight the Lord smote all the firstborn in the land of Egypt, from the firstborn of Pharaoh that sat on his throne unto the firstborn of the captive that *was* in the dungeon; and all the firstborn of cattle.

30. "And Pharaoh rose up in the night, he, and all his servants, and all the Egyptians; and there was a great cry in Egypt: for *there was* not a house where *there was* not one dead.

31. "And he called for Moses and Aaron by night, and said, Rise up, *and* get you forth from among my people, both ye and the children of Israel; and go, serve the Lord, as ye have said.

32. "Also take your flocks and your herds, as ye have said, and be gone; and bless me also.

33. "And the Egyptians were urgent upon the peo-

INDICATIONS OF THE BOOK OF EXODUS. 69

ple, that they might send them out of the land in haste; for they said, We *be* all dead *men*.

34. "And the people took their dough before it was leavened, their kneadingtroughs being bound up in their clothes upon their shoulders.

35. "And the children of Israel did according to the word of Moses; and they borrowed of the Egyptians jewels of silver, and jewels of gold, and raiment:

36. "And the Lord gave the people favour in the sight of the Egyptians, so that they lent unto them *such things as they required:* and they spoiled the Egyptians.

37. "And the children of Israel journeyed from Rameses to Succoth, about six hundred thousand on foot *that were* men, beside children.

38. "And a mixed multitude went up also with them; and flocks, and herds, *even* very much cattle.

39. "And they baked unleavened cakes of the dough which they brought forth out of Egypt, for it was not leavened; because they were thrust out of Egypt, and could not tarry, neither had they prepared for themselves any victuals."

By verses 29, 30 all the first-born in the land of Egypt were smitten with death, both of man and of cattle, but (see Num. iii. 11–13) the Lord's claim to all the first-born is positively set forth in the words, "All the firstborn *are* mine; *for* on the day that I smote all the firstborn in the land of Egypt I hallowed unto me all the firstborn in Israel, both man and beast: mine they shall be: I *am* the Lord." If such be the case according to the Scriptures, then who can gainsay it according to the Scriptures? more especially since Israel (see Gen. xxviii. 10–14; xxxv. 9–12) is the father of many nations, and in whom all families of the earth shall be blessed.

By verses 31, 32 the children of Israel are almost driven out from the land of Egypt, the Egyptians being urgent upon them, and saying unto them, "Also take your flocks and your herds, as ye have said, and be gone;" by which, as allegory, not only the children of Israel who dwelt in the Egypt of the past will come forth from their captivity in the dark valley, but that their flocks and herds will come forth also; the Lord having said, "Mine they shall be: I *am* the Lord." If, however, the first-born of man and of beast, in their pertainings to the past ages, shall not reappear, then the Lord's claim would simply be the graceless grace that marks the head-stones of victorious graves. This position will not stand; for (see Zech. iv. 6, 7; I. Cor. xv. 54, 55) Zerubbabel shall bring forth the head-stone with shoutings, crying, "Grace, grace unto it;" while the Lord's claim will empty every hold wherein the Lord's inheritance lies bound. Truly, grave, "Where *is* thy victory?"

By verses 37, 38 about six hundred thousand men of the children of Israel journeyed from Rameses to Succoth, beside the children, and the mixed multitude, and the flocks, and the herds. Through the simple history thus given, when taken as an allegory, the exodus or transmission of names, iniquity, blood, and characteristics of the creature world throughout the first Three Ages of Man is indicated, and their entry into the Pisonic or Fourth age pointed to. Inasmuch,

INDICATIONS OF THE BOOK OF EXODUS. 71

however, as Moses is prohibited from crossing over into the land of Canaan as the earth in the Pisonic age,—that is, the land of Canaan as after the Deluge,—so the allegoric stand-point of verses 37, 38 finds place in the overlap of the Gihonic and Pisonic ages, the same being indicated by the six hundred thousand men on foot; for of this number one hundred thousand may be apportioned to each of the six semidivisions of these ages, in harmony with the allegorical pertaining of Moses; but the simple historical stand-point pertains to the Pisonic or Fourth age in time subsequent to the Deluge of Noah.

XII. 40, 41. " Now the sojourning of the children of Israel, who dwelt in Egypt, *was* four hundred and thirty years.

41. " And it came to pass at the end of the four hundred and thirty years, even the selfsame day it came to pass, that all the hosts of the Lord went out from the land of Egypt."

These four hundred and thirty years are accounted for as follows: from the advent of the Messiah the Prince (see Gen. xiv. 18) to the exodus (see Gen. xv. 13), four hundred years; from Abraham's departure from Haran (see Gen. xii. 4) to the advent of the Messiah the Prince, twenty-five years. Abraham, at the time of this advent (see Gen. xv. 4; Rom. iv. 19-22) being about one hundred years old, thus leaving five years from the time of the promise given Abraham in Ur of the Chaldees (see Gen. xi. 27-32; xii. 1-5; xv. 7; xxi. 1-3) to his departure from Haran, thus making in all the four hundred and thirty called for by the text; Abraham, in consequence, was seventy years old when he received the great command to leave Ur of the Chaldees.

At the end of the sojourn it is stated that "all the hosts of the Lord went out from the land of Egypt." Who were they? Simply the loins, the progeny of Jacob, Abraham's grandson? By no means; for they are called hosts, not host. If they are hosts then the indication steals forth that the two bands (see Gen. xxxii. 10) into which Jacob was divided are the hosts that came out from Egypt; for (see Gen. xlvi. 1-15) the Messiah as Jacob the Seed of Jacob went down into Egypt, sojourned there (see Deut. xxvi. 5), and became there a nation, "great, mighty, and populous."

The Messiah as the Seed of Jacob, having become a multitude, now comes forth bearing with him the names of those who existed far beyond the day of the fourth Adam (see Diagrams 7, 8). These are the people (see iii. 13, 14) of whom Moses was in ignorance; they are the people of the ages of man under the veil who worshipped their God under his great name "*I am.*" These are the people of whom even Abraham was in ignorance, as stated in Isa. lxiii. 16, "Doubtless thou *art* our Father, though Abraham be ignorant of us," and doubtless they are the substance brought forth by the Seed, as called for in Gen. xv. 14; while the children of Israel otherwise spoiled the Egyptians of their gold, their silver, and their raiment.

The four hundred years of affliction, which God assured Abraham should befall his seed (see Acts vii. 17-36), have now expired; while the triumphal march of the children of Israel shows that the Messiah as the Seed of Abraham, although battle-worn, bruised, and

INDICATIONS OF THE BOOK OF EXODUS. 73

afflicted (see Isa. lii. 9-14), possesses the gate of his enemies. Truly was it said (Ps. cxiv. 1, 2), " When Israel went out of Egypt, the house of Jacob from a people of strange language; Judah was his sanctuary, *and* Israel his dominion ;" for Israel the Seed of Jacob, who is called in the house of Judah, at this very time has dominion over Israel the House of Man; and as the Subjugator rules over the thrones of the Adversary and his powerful ally Lucifer, the destroying angel. The simple history of the sojourning of the children of Israel, as allegory, shadows the bringing forth of the people from the Egypt of the past (see Digram 8).

In Diagram 8, spaces a, a indicate the Four Ages of Man; b, b indicate the Four Ages by the land shown Abraham (see Gen. xii. 1-7); c, c indicate eight divisions in the Four Ages, and the apportionment of the four hundred and thirty years sojourning; d, d indicate time; e, e indicate the Messianic year; f, f indicate the years from the creation of the fourth Adam to the Deluge of Noah; g, g indicate the years of the First, Second, and Third ages of man.

In the allegoric sense Egypt shadows both the Second and Third ages of man, which ages are divided in the midst thereof, thus giving rise to four semidivisions. The semidivisions of the Fourth age are divided into six minor divisions, the first of which is the epoch extending from the creation of the Fourth race to the Deluge of Noah, and hence corresponds with the overlap of the Third and Fourth ages.

From the conditions expressed by the text, the sojourning of the children of Israel will, as allegory, apply to the five divisions of time from the creation of the

Ex. xii. 40, 41, considered as allegory.

DIAGRAM 8.

THE SOJOURNING OF THE CHILDREN OF ISRAEL.

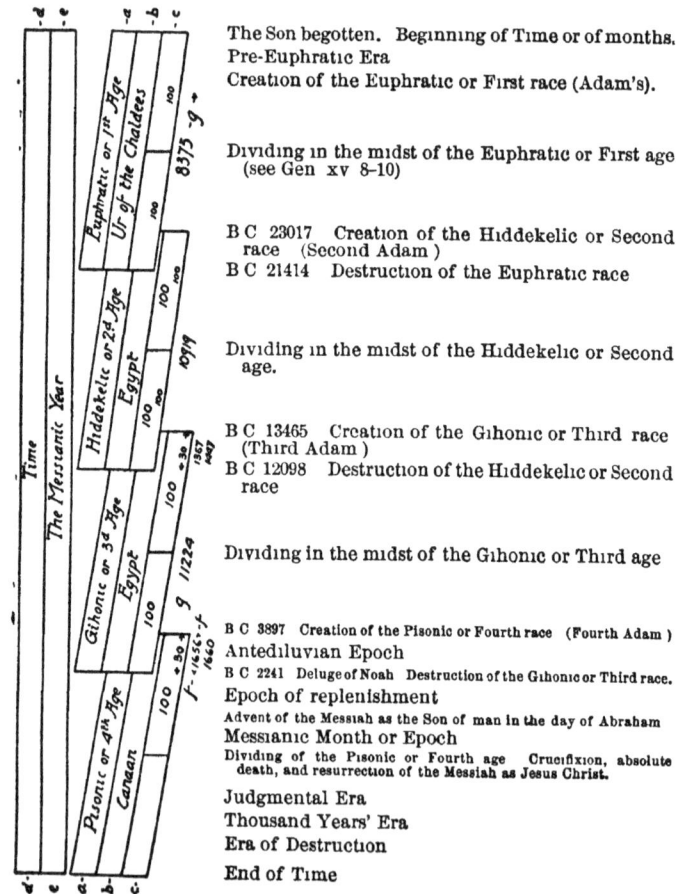

The Son begotten. Beginning of Time or of months.
Pre-Euphratic Era
Creation of the Euphratic or First race (Adam's).

Dividing in the midst of the Euphratic or First age (see Gen xv 8–10)

B C 23017   Creation of the Hiddekelic or Second race (Second Adam)
B C 21414   Destruction of the Euphratic race

Dividing in the midst of the Hiddekelic or Second age.

B C 13465   Creation of the Gihonic or Third race (Third Adam)
B C 12098   Destruction of the Hiddekelic or Second race

Dividing in the midst of the Gihonic or Third age

B C 3897   Creation of the Pisonic or Fourth race   (Fourth Adam)
Antediluvian Epoch
B C 2241   Deluge of Noah   Destruction of the Gihonic or Third race.
Epoch of replenishment
Advent of the Messiah as the Son of man in the day of Abraham
Messianic Month or Epoch
Dividing of the Pisonic or Fourth age   Crucifixion, absolute death, and resurrection of the Messiah as Jesus Christ.
Judgmental Era
Thousand Years' Era
Era of Destruction
End of Time

INDICATIONS OF THE BOOK OF EXODUS 75

Hiddekelic race to the Deluge; wherefore, inasmuch as the sojourning comprehended four hundred and thirty years, so let these years be apportioned to the five divisions of time thus indicated.

By this apportionment (see Diagrams 8, 18) one hundred years pertain to each of the semidivisions of the Second and Third ages, whereby the odd thirty years will pertain to a proportionate part of the first semi-division of the Fourth age. At the end of this proportionate part the people of Egypt as the Second and Third ages, and the overlapping portion of the Fourth, came out of this Egypt by the transmission of their names, iniquity, blood, and characteristics to the remnant that escaped the general destruction of the Deluge.

If the people of these ages really had existence, and if the years of these ages are thus approximately set forth, then the proportion of the Second and Third ages to the proportionate part of the first half of the Fourth, or time from the creation of the Pisonic race to the Deluge, should be as four hundred years are to thirty years.

The years of the Second age (see Diagram 8) are ten thousand nine hundred and nineteen, the years of the Third age are eleven thousand two hundred and twenty four; the sum of which is twenty-two thousand one hundred and forty-three; therefore as 400 : 30 : : 22143 : 1660, or to the years from the creation of the Fourth race to the Deluge of Noah. By the above proportion these years number one thousand six hundred and sixty, while by the direct chronology of the book of Genesis they number one thousand six hundred and fifty-six; hence the closeness of the approxi-

76 INDICATIONS OF THE BOOK OF EXODUS.

mation strongly supports the indications set forth that the ages of man under the veil really had existence. The allegory, however, admits of other apportionments; for the sojourning and exodus may also be construed to indicate the transmission of the debt of the First and Second ages to the Third, in which case, by apportioning one hundred years each to the four semidivisions of the First and Second ages, the thirty years that remain would pertain to the overlap of the Second and Third ages (see small digits or numbers in Diagram 8, spaces c, c).

The years of the First age from the creation of the Euphratic race (see Diagram 8, spaces g, g) are eight thousand three hundred and seventy-five; the years of the Second age, as before, are ten thousand nine hundred and nineteen, the sum of which is nineteen thousand two hundred and ninety-four. Therefore, by proportion, as 400 : 30 : : 19294 : 1447, or the overlapping years of the Second and Third ages. These years as otherwise given aggregate, by approximation, one thousand three hundred and sixty-seven; hence the approximations are confirmative of the indications as set forth.

The allegory of the sojourning admits of still further apportionment; for by it (see Diagram 9) the actual physical presence of the Messiah as the Son of man, and as the Redeemer, may be brought to notice in full harmony with the preceding indications.

In Diagram 9, spaces a, a indicate the Four Ages of Man; b, b indicate the Four Ages by the land through which Abraham passed in his journey from Ur of the Chaldees to Canaan; c, c indicate longevity of the Four

Ex. xii. 40, 41, *considered as allegory.*

DIAGRAM 9.

THE MESSIAH AS THE SON OF MAN AND AS THE REDEEMER.

	Creation of a body for the Word of God in and as the very beginning of the creation of God
1st day	First day —Creation of light Creation of the earthy
2d day	Second day —Creation of the firmament
3d day	Third day —Creation of vegetation
4th day	Fourth day —Creation of sun, moon, and stars.
5th day	Fifth day —Creation of fishes and fowl
6th day	Sixth day —Creation of cattle, creeping thing, and beast of the earth

The Son begotten   Beginning of Time.
War in heaven } Pre-Euphratic Era
Satan cast out into the earth }
Creation of the Euphratic or First race   (First Adam)

Euphratic or 1st Age — Ur of the Chaldees — 10249 years — 100

Dividing in the midst of the Euphratic age (see Gen. xv 7-10)

Creation of the Hiddekelic or Second race   (Second Adam)
Destruction of the Euphratic or First race

Hiddekelic or 2d Age — Egypt — 10919 years — 100

Dividing in the midst of the Hiddekelic age.

Creation of the Gihonic or Third race   (Third Adam)
Destruction of the Hiddekelic or Second race

Gihonic or 3d Age — Egypt — 11224 years — 100

Dividing in the midst of the Gihonic age

Creation of the Pisonic or Fourth race   (Fourth Adam)
Antediluvian Epoch
Deluge of Noah   Destruction of the Gihonic or Third race
Epoch of replenishment (see Gen ix 1)
Advent of the Messiah as the Son of man in the day of Abraham
Messianic Month or Epoch
Dividing of the Pisonic age   Crucifixion, absolute death, and resurrection of the Messiah as Jesus Christ
Judgmental Era
Thousand Years' Era
Era of Destruction

Approximate end of Time

77

Ages as through the male; d, d indicate apportionment of the four hundred and thirty years' sojourning to the Four Ages; e, e indicate apportionment of the four hundred and thirty years' sojourning to four semidivisions of the Four Ages; f, f indicate time; g, g indicate the Messianic year.

The Messiah entered upon his labors in his great personalities as the Seed of Abraham, as the Son of man, and as the Redeemer, in the day of Abraham (see Gen. xiv. 18–20; St. John viii. 56–58; Gal. iii. 16). The day of Abraham in which the Messiah thus made his advent (see page of Landmarks) was in the year B.C. 1827, or about eighteen hundred and sixty years before his crucifixion, absolute death, and resurrection as Jesus Christ.

When the Messiah thus became the Son of man he took upon himself the names and iniquity of the people which had been transmitted from the past ages, and hence these names were, from that time, "raised up among their brethren;" wherefore an exodus of names from the valley of the shadow of death in its pertaining to the Egypt of the past is indicated. In this light let four hundred years of the sojourning be apportioned to the four semidivisions from the dividing of the Hiddekelic age to the dividing of the Pisonic age, when, in harmony with the apportionments of Diagram 8, the odd thirty years will pertain to and indicate the years from the dividing of the Pisonic age to the time of the advent of the Messiah in the day of Abraham, or to the day of the exodus of the names of the brethren which were raised up from the valley of the shadow of death by the Messiah.

INDICATIONS OF THE BOOK OF EXODUS. 79

Now, the years of the Hiddekelic age, as through the male (see Diagram 9, spaces c, c), number ten thousand nine hundred and nineteen, one-half of which will be five thousand four hundred and fifty-nine ; the years of the Gihonic age number eleven thousand two hundred and twenty-four; and one-half of the Pisonic age numbers three thousand nine hundred and thirty. The sum of these years is twenty thousand six hundred and thirteen; wherefore, inasmuch as these years are shadowed by four hundred years of the sojourning, and as the odd thirty years shadow the epoch from the dividing of the Pisonic age to the advent of the Messiah as the Son of man in the day of Abraham, so, by proportion, as 400 : 30 : : 20613 : 1545, or to the years from the advent of the Messiah as the Son of man to the dividing of the Pisonic age. If, however, this period shall be redeemed, then (see Lev. xxvii. 9–13, 31) let the fifth part thereof be added thereto; wherefore, as Christ the Messiah came to redeem this land from its bondage, so let the redemptive fifth be added to the estimate already obtained, when the years from the advent of the Messiah as the Son of man in the day of Abraham to the dividing of the Pisonic age will be eighteen hundred and fifty-four as against the eighteen hundred and sixty otherwise given (see page of Landmarks).

By the apportionment as thus given only a part of the land is brought into notice in connection with the redemptive labors of the Messiah, but inasmuch as the whole land must be considered, so let the four hundred years' sojourning be apportioned to the Four Ages of Man (see Diagram 9, spaces d, d), when the odd thirty

80 INDICATIONS OF THE BOOK OF EXODUS.

years will shadow the epoch from the end of the Pisonic age back to the general exodus of the children of Israel from their bondage in the valley of the shadow of death, which exodus took place shortly after the crucifixion, absolute death, and resurrection of the Messiah as Jesus Christ (see St. Matt. xxvii. 50–53).

The Euphratic age (see Diagram 9, spaces c, c) numbers ten thousand four hundred and forty-nine years; the Hiddekelic age numbers ten thousand nine hundred and nineteen years; the Gihonic age numbers eleven thousand two hundred and twenty-four years; and the Pisonic age numbers seven thousand eight hundred and sixty years; the sum of which is forty thousand four hundred and fifty-two. Inasmuch, therefore, as four hundred years of the sojourn shadow the longevity of the Four Ages, and as the odd thirty shadow the epoch from the resurrection of the Messiah to the end of the Pisonic age, or to the end of time, so, by proportion, as 400 : 30 : : 40452 : 3033, or to time from the resurrection of the Messiah as Jesus Christ to the end of time. But if, as before, this land shall be redeemed, then (see Lev. xxvii. 9–13, 31) let the fifth part thereof be added to the estimate already obtained, when the years from the resurrection of the Messiah to the end of the Pisonic age, or to the end of time, will be three thousand six hundred and thirty-nine as against the three thousand nine hundred and thirty of the chronology of the book of Daniel.

Thus the four hundred and thirty years' sojourn of the children of Israel relates to and bears upon the history of many hosts; for many hosts lie hidden in the vale from which exodus must be made that they be not lost to the Son's inheritance.

XIII. 1, 2. "And the Lord spake unto Moses, saying,

2. "Sanctify unto me all the firstborn, whatsoever openeth the womb among the children of Israel, *both* of man and of beast: it *is* mine."

This sanctification of the first-born seems to indicate the instrumentality of Pharaoh as a sign and wonder from the Lord of hosts in Israel. Pharaoh was raised up, and his heart was hardened, that the power of the Lord might be made manifest throughout all the earth; from which the indication follows that great hosts other than men of Adam's race are present, for neither Pharaoh nor the children of Israel (see Ps. cvi. 7) understood the wonders done in Egypt. The plagues which came upon Pharaoh, however, were not unjustly cast upon him, for they really were a consequent of his unity to the Kingdom of Evil; therefore if, of the first-born, the little ones were not spared, because of existing sin, it follows that the adversarial hosts unto whom the sign was given cannot escape when the plagues shall come over them. Now, although, in the rendering of the sign, many of the smitten first-born were babes and little children, they will certainly be restored again; and in Jerusalem (Zech. viii. 5), "The streets of the city shall be full of boys and girls playing in the streets thereof."

The sanctifying of all the first-born, both of man and beast, points also to instrumentality on the part of the creature world that reaches throughout the Four

f

Ages of Man, and, further, that the sanctification of the creature, whether man or beast, seals them as holy unto the Lord.

XIII. 11, 12. "And it shall be when the Lord shall bring thee into the land of the Canaanites, as he sware unto thee and to thy fathers, and shall give it thee,

12. "That thou shalt set apart unto the Lord all that openeth the matrix, and every firstling that cometh of a beast which thou hast; the male *shall be* the Lord's."

Figuratively, when the children of Israel enter into the promised land,—that is, the land of Canaan as the earth in the Fourth age,—the Adversary will be driven out from before them; and therefore, who can distinguish between the Israelites as the progeny of Jacob and any other class of the Lord's people, that they should thus set apart their first-born unto the Lord? The text carries with it the indication that the firstborn of Pharaoh also will be included, where it is stated (verses 14–16), "And it shall be when thy son asketh thee in time to come, saying, What *is* this? that thou shalt say unto him, By strength of hand the Lord brought us out from Egypt, from the house of bondage:

"And it came to pass, when Pharaoh would hardly let us go, that the Lord slew all the firstborn in the land of Egypt, both the firstborn of man, and the firstborn of beast: therefore I sacrifice to the Lord all that openeth the matrix, being males; but all the firstborn of my children I redeem.

"And it shall be for a token upon thine hand, and for frontlets between thine eyes: for by strength of hand the Lord brought us forth out of Egypt."

It is clearly evident that the great strength exhibited by the Lord was not in his overthrow of the man Pharaoh, but, rather, that it was in the overthrow of the Adversary; the history of which is brought to light through the simple history of Pharaoh; therefore when, in the future, the song of Zion shall be sung, Pharaoh himself can sing, "I sacrificed my firstborn to the Lord when he delivered me out of the house of bondage; and it shall be for a token upon his hand, and for a frontlet between his eyes." The object of the blindness which came upon Pharaoh is indicated by Paul when he says (Rom. xi. 25), "For I would not, brethren, that ye should be ignorant of this mystery, lest ye should be wise in your own conceits, that blindness in part is happened to Israel" [Israel, by the change of name from Jacob, representing many nations], "until the fulness of the Gentiles be come in;" by which the general instrumentality of man in the labors of Zion becomes manifest. The sacrifice of the first-born (see verses 1, 2) sanctifies them unto the Lord, and if sanctified unto the Lord, then, whether man or beast, such sanctification must be considered after the death of the sacrifice (see xxix. 32, 33), lest oblivion be the result of such sanctification.

XIV. 1–18. "And the Lord spake unto Moses, saying,

2. "Speak unto the children of Israel, that they turn and encamp before Pi-hahiroth, between Migdol and the sea, over against Baal-zephon: before it shall ye encamp by the sea.

3. "For Pharaoh will say of the children of Israel,

They *are* entangled in the land, the wilderness hath shut them in.

4. "And I will harden Pharaoh's heart, that he shall follow after them; and I will be honoured upon Pharaoh, and upon all his host; that the Egyptians may know that I *am* the Lord. And they did so.

5. "And it was told the king of Egypt that the people fled: and the heart of Pharaoh and of his servants was turned against the people, and they said, Why have we done this, that we have let Israel go from serving us?

6. "And he made ready his chariot, and took his people with him:

7. "And he took six hundred chosen chariots, and all the chariots of Egypt, and captains over every one of them.

8. "And the Lord hardened the heart of Pharaoh king of Egypt, and he pursued after the children of Israel: and the children of Israel went out with a high hand.

9. "But the Egyptians pursued after them, all the horses *and* chariots of Pharaoh, and his horsemen, and his army, and overtook them encamping by the sea, beside Pi-hahiroth, before Baal-zephon.

10. "And when Pharaoh drew nigh, the children of Israel lifted up their eyes, and, behold, the Egyptians marched after them; and they were sore afraid: and the children of Israel cried out unto the Lord.

11. "And they said unto Moses, Because *there were* no graves in Egypt, hast thou taken us away to die in the wilderness? wherefore hast thou dealt thus with us, to carry us forth out of Egypt?

INDICATIONS OF THE BOOK OF EXODUS. 85

12. "*Is* not this the word that we did tell thee in Egypt, saying, Let us alone, that we may serve the Egyptians? For *it had been* better for us to serve the Egyptians, than that we should die in the wilderness.

13. "And Moses said unto the people, Fear ye not, stand still, and see the salvation of the Lord, which he will shew to you to day: for the Egyptians whom ye have seen to day, ye shall see them again no more for ever.

14. "The Lord shall fight for you, and ye shall hold your peace.

15. "And the Lord said unto Moses, Wherefore criest thou unto me? speak unto the children of Israel, that they go forward:

16. "But lift thou up thy rod, and stretch out thine hand over the sea, and divide it: and the children of Israel shall go on dry *ground* through the midst of the sea.

17. "And I, behold, I will harden the hearts of the Egyptians, and they shall follow them: and I will get me honour upon Pharaoh, and upon all his host, upon his chariots, and upon his horsemen.

18. "And the Egyptians shall know that I *am* the Lord, when I have gotten me honour upon Pharaoh, upon his chariots, and upon his horsemen."

In Diagram 10, spaces a, a indicate the Four Ages of Man; b, b indicate the land shown Abraham, of which Canaan shadows the earth in the Fourth age; c, c indicate the apportionment of the six hundred chosen chariots; d, d indicate time; e, e indicate the pertaining of Israel as a father of many nations.

86 INDICATIONS OF THE BOOK OF EXODUS.

Ex. xiv., considered as allegory.

DIAGRAM 10.

PHARAOH PURSUES THE ISRAELITES.

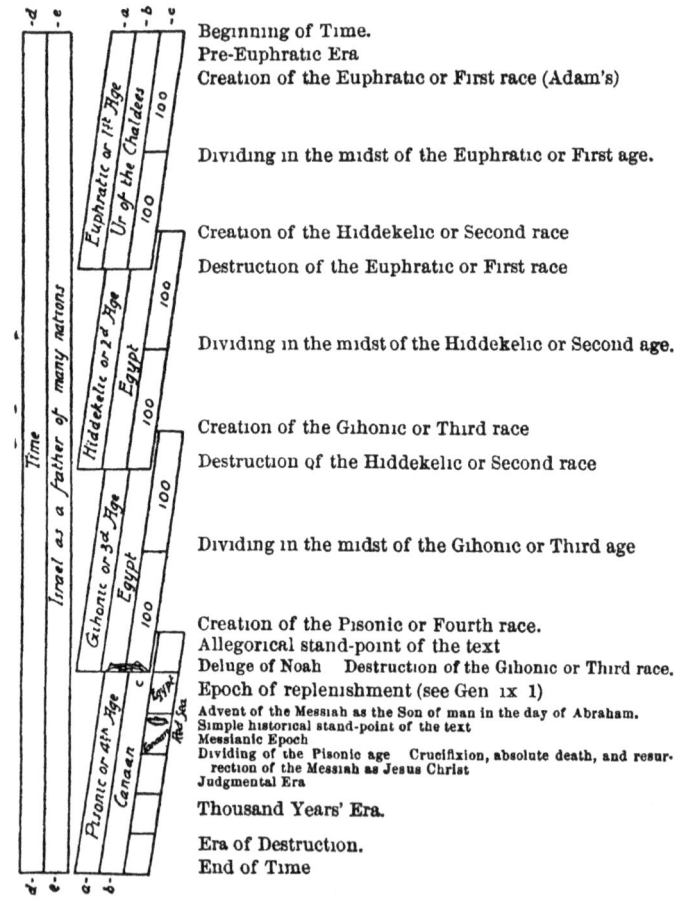

By the allegory of the sojourning of the children of Israel (see Diagrams 8, 9) the people of the past ages of man, or the people of the three ages of man under the veil, were, through the transmission of iniquity, blood, and characteristics, brought out from thence into the Fourth age,—that is, into the overlap of the Gihonic and Pisonic ages; hence while the simple historical stand-point of the test is in the Messianic Epoch, or in time subsequent to the Deluge of Noah, the allegorical stand-point is in the overlap of the Gihonic and Pisonic ages (see Diagram 10).

Pharaoh shadows Lucifer, the angel Death; wherefore, inasmuch as, by the simple history, Pharaoh said of the children of Israel, "They *are* entangled in the land, the wilderness hath shut them in," and as he shall follow after them, so by this history as shadow, from the allegorical stand-point of the text, Lucifer will say of the people, "They *are* entangled in the land, the wilderness hath shut them in," and he shall follow after them; for in the overlap of the Gihonic and Pisonic ages (see Gen. vi., vii.) the people became very transgressive, and the clouds of the overwhelming Deluge were lowering over their heads; hence Lucifer will pursue them as fiercely at this time as he pursued them in the past ages, and will further say (see verse 5), "Why have we let Israel go?" In this light the six hundred chosen chariots (see Diagram 10, spaces *c, c*) shadow the six semidivisions of the three ages of man under the veil, to which the Israelites— through Jacob as a father of many nations—pertain even as the six hundred thousand footmen (see Num. xi. 21) shadow the same.

These chariots not only shadow epochs of the past, but they point to the transgressive condition of the people through which Lucifer, or Pharaoh, claims them as his bondmen. Accordingly, as by the simple history, Pharaoh, the Egyptians (see verse 9), pursued after the children of Israel, and overtook them encamped by the sea, before Pi-hahiroth, before Baal-zephon, so, by this history as allegory, the pursuit of the children of Israel by Lucifer and his host throughout the first three ages of man is indicated, and that the camp of Israel is near the mouth of the river Gihon, which mingles with the waters of the river Euphrates, the river of the north (see meanings of Pi-hahiroth and Baal-zephon).

When the children of Israel beheld the Egyptian host (see verses 10, 11) they were sore afraid, and they said unto Moses, "Because *there were* no graves in Egypt, hast thou taken us away to die in the wilderness?" for, as allegory, unless a redeemer arise Lucifer will surely prevail against the transgressor; hence the epoch in which the people now stand is as barren of a subjugator as were the three ages preceding it.

By verses 13, 14, Moses said unto the people, "Fear ye not, stand still, and see the salvation of the Lord, which he will shew to you to day," and also, "The Lord shall fight for you, and ye shall hold your peace;" hence the deliverance of the people will come from the Lord, and the Lord himself will be the Redeemer of the people and the Subjugator of Lucifer.

The command is given (see verse 15) that the children of Israel go forward, by which the lapsing of years is indicated. By verse 16 Moses shall lift up his rod, and stretch out his hand over the sea, and divide it; and the children of Israel shall go on dry *ground* through the midst of the sea. This verse, as allegory, points to the passage of the children of Israel—those pertaining to the past ages of man—through the valley of the shadow of death.

Verses 17, 18, as allegory, indicate the overwhelming of Lucifer, and of all his host, in the valley of the shadow of death, through which (see Rev. xx. 7–10) they shall know (see verse 18) that the Lord is God.

XIV. 19, 20. "And the Angel of God, which went before the camp of Israel, removed and went behind them; and the pillar of the cloud went from before their face, and stood behind them:

20. "And it came between the camp of the Egyptians and the camp of Israel; and it was a cloud and darkness *to them*, but it gave light by night *to these:* so that the one came not near the other all the night."

The cloud thus coming between the camp of the Egyptians and the camp of Israel shadows conditions pertaining to the two armies, for (see Isa. ix. 1, 2) light may shine upon them that dwell in the land of the shadow of death, while, as for Lucifer and his host (see Isa. viii. 22), "They shall look unto the earth; and behold trouble and darkness, dimness of anguish; and *they shall be* driven to darkness."

XIV. 21, 22. "And Moses stretched out his hand over the sea: and the Lord caused the sea to go *back* by a strong east wind all that night, and made the sea dry *land*, and the waters were divided.

22. "And the children of Israel went into the midst of the sea upon the dry *ground:* and the waters *were*

a wall unto them on their right hand, and on their left."

By the records given in Gen. i., God created the heaven and the earth; he established light, and he instituted motion; he brought forth the sun, moon, and stars, and bid them to their places; he clothed the earth with verdure, and he created animal life; therefore, be these records truth or fiction, they invest their God with absolute command over all forms of matter, and over all essences, be they material or spiritual. If the records are truth, then this position must be accorded as truth; if the records are fiction, then this position must be accorded as fiction; but if the position be not accorded either as truth or as fiction, then no elucidation can follow, for God must be accorded God as called for by the text, be the text truth or fiction.

By the text, therefore, the God which created the heaven, the earth, and the sea, commanded the sea and the wind, and a passage was opened in the midst of it, through which the children of Israel passed dry shod, and with a wall of water on either hand.

The immutability of God's counsel otherwise, as witnessed in the government of the inanimate creature, makes the statement of the text almost incredible, almost beyond belief, for the fixedness of his revealed laws is visible on every side; yet it is clear that the power which creates must rule and be supreme, or automatism, not conception, would become the ruling principle of development. These great exhibitions of power were given by the Most High as signs and wonders to the hosts which fell before man was brought forth; and therefore the necessity is not absolute that man should understand them, or the causes thereof, in their fulness; but, on the contrary, a veil was thrown over the work to screen it from his eyes, from which the indication follows that natural laws may exist whereby even the sea may be parted and a passage opened in the midst of it, even as already indicated by the separation of aggregate matter into the detached masses forming the great Astral System.

Of the two great Powers brought to notice, one, the Righteous, advances, produces, or projects itself, as it were, in straight lines, whereby the strength and beauty of progress is traceable; but the other, the Evil one, although apparently starting from the same base, and apparently governed by a ruling principle of parallelism as established through the entering in of the First Covenant, almost insensibly commences to diverge, and describes the beautiful, the graceful, yet delusive curve of the parabola, thus bearing with it, to a house of destruction, thousands of victims filled with mistaken joy.

The plagues that came upon Pharaoh form a portion of the burden of the Fourth age, through which the power and majesty of the Most High are made manifest to all hosts, that they may turn from death to life; for by the fall of Pharaoh the overthrow of the Evil Element is almost unquestionably prefigured.

The waters of the sea having been parted (see verses 21, 22), the children of Israel entered therein, with a wall of water on either hand, by which, as allegory, the dwelling of the host of Israel in the land of the shadow of death is indicated. The history of the exodus, however, points to the deliverance of this

92   INDICATIONS OF THE BOOK OF EXODUS.

people from their captivity (see verse 14) through the Lord, who shall fight their battles for them.

XIV. 23-25. "And the Egyptians pursued, and went in after them to the midst of the sea, *even* all Pharaoh's horses, his chariots, and his horsemen.

24. "And it came to pass, that in the morning watch the Lord looked unto the host of the Egyptians through the pillar of fire and of the cloud, and troubled the host of the Egyptians.

25. "And took off their chariot wheels, that they drave them heavily: so that the Egyptians said, Let us flee from the face of Israel; for the Lord fighteth for them against the Egyptians."

In Diagram 11, spaces a, a indicate the Four Ages of Man; b, b indicate the Four Ages by the land through which Abraham passed in his journey from Ur of the Chaldees to Canaan; c, c indicate the Four Ages as four days; d, d indicate the Four Ages as four days divided into evenings and mornings; e, e indicate the Four Ages as four days divided into their eight watches; f, f indicate time; g, g indicate pertaining of Israel as the father of many nations.

In Diagram 11 the Four Ages are represented as four days (see, also, Diagrams 2, 3). The scriptural day commences at sundown, or about six o'clock in the evening, and is divided into two chief divisions of twelve hours each, even as the Four Ages are divided in the midst thereof (see Gen. xv. 7-10). The semi-divisions of the day are divided into four watches of three hours each; wherefore the three hours from sundown, or from the sixth hour until the ninth hour, constitute the first watch; the hours from nine to twelve,

INDICATIONS OF THE BOOK OF EXODUS. 93

Ex. xiv., considered as allegory.
DIAGRAM 11.
THE MORNING WATCH.

Beginning of Time
Pre-Euphratic Era
Creation of the Euphratic or First race (Adam's)

The morning watch.
The Euphratic age divided in the midst thereof
(see Gen xv 7-10)

Creation of the Hiddekelic or Second race

Destruction of the Euphratic or First race

The morning watch
The Hiddekelic age divided in the midst thereof.

Creation of the Gihonic or Third race.

Destruction of the Hiddekelic or Second race

The morning watch
The Gihonic age divided in the midst thereof

Creation of the Pisonic or Fourth race.
Allegorical stand-point of the text
Deluge of Noah   Destruction of the Gihonic or Third race.
Epoch of replenishment (see Gen ix 1)
Advent of the Messiah as the Son of man in the day of Abraham
Messianic Epoch   Morning watch.   The righteous Naboth slain
Advent of the Messiah as Elisha.   Overthrow of Lucifer
Dividing of the Pisonic age   Crucifixion, absolute death, and resurrection of the Messiah as Jesus Christ
Judgmental Era

Thousand Years' Era

Era of Destruction
Final overthrow of Lucifer.
End of Time

midnight, constitute the second watch; the hours from midnight until three o'clock constitute the third watch; and the hours from three o'clock until six constitute the fourth or morning watch. In continuation, the hours from six o'clock until nine, from nine until twelve, noon, from noon until three, and from three until six, constitute the first, second, third, and fourth watches of the remaining half of the day.

In the allegorical apportionment of these watches to the Four Ages (see Diagram 11, spaces c, c; e, e) the morning watch culminates at the dividings in the midst thereof; from which the indication arises (see verses 24, 25) that great disaster befell the earth at or about the time of these divisions.

By Gen. i. 5, 8, the evening and the morning were the first creative day, and the evening and the morning were the second creative day; wherefore (see Diagram 11, spaces d, d) let the Four Ages be divided into their evenings and mornings, when it will be seen that the morning of one age overlaps the evening of the succeeding age, from which the indication follows that (see verses 24, 25) great tribulation came upon the earth at or about the time of these overlaps, and that, from the simple historical stand-point of the text, the overthrow of Pharaoh and the Egyptians shadows history pertaining to the confusion of the adversarial host in the overlap of the Gihonic and Pisonic ages, and, also, to the history which culminated so disastrously in the great Deluge of Noah, but by which Lucifer became powerless in the land of the shadow of death. Moreover, in the allegoric sense, the final overthrow of Lucifer is indicated as fulfilling at or about the end of the Pisonic age.

XIV. 26–28. "And the Lord said unto Moses, Stretch out thine hand over the sea, that the waters may come again upon the Egyptians, upon their chariots, and upon their horsemen.

27. "And Moses stretched forth his hand over the sea, and the sea returned to his strength when the morning appeared; and the Egyptians fled against it; and the Lord overthrew the Egyptians in the midst of the sea.

28. "And the waters returned, and covered the chariots, and the horsemen, *and* all the host of Pharaoh that came into the sea after them; there remained not so much as one of them."

Thus, through the destruction of Pharaoh and the Egyptians, the overthrow of Lucifer and his host, and their descent into the land of the shadow of death, is indicated; and, hence, as not one man remained of Pharaoh's host that went down into the sea, so the complete overthrow of the Evil Kingdom is indicated through this history as allegory.

XIV. 29–31. "But the children of Israel walked upon dry *land* in the midst of the sea; and the waters *were* a wall unto them on their right hand, and on their left.

30. "Thus the Lord saved Israel that day out of the hand of the Egyptians; and Israel saw the Egyptians dead upon the sea shore.

31. "And Israel saw that great work which the Lord did upon the Egyptians: and the people feared the Lord, and believed the Lord, and his servant Moses."

96 INDICATIONS OF THE BOOK OF EXODUS.

By these verses, as allegory, the people of the past ages of man that lay in the land of the shadow of death came up out of that land; which condition was realized when their names, iniquity, blood, and characteristics were transmitted through the Deluge of Noah into the Pisonic age.

XV. 1. "Then sang Moses and the children of Israel this song unto the Lord, and spake, saying, I will sing unto the Lord, for he hath triumphed gloriously: the horse and his rider hath he thrown into the sea."

The song of Moses and the children of Israel takes up the grand theme of the overthrow of Lucifer the angel Death (see Rev. vi. 7, 8). As, therefore, Pharaoh and his horse perished in the midst of the sea, so will Death, and the horse upon which he rides, be cast into the sea and perish (see Diagram 11).

The horse upon which Death rides (see Rev. vi. 8) is the Pale horse or the Fourth race of men (Adam's); hence the overwhelming of the Fourth race, or the casting of the Pale horse into the sea, brings with it the sure destruction of Death. Were this not so,— that is, should the Fourth race be destroyed and Death go free,—then the Law would lack in equity. Inasmuch, however (see Isa. xi. 4), as the Law does not lack in equity, all hosts must come under its rulings; wherefore, through the Law, Death also, the last enemy (see I. Cor. xv. 26), as prefigured by the overthrow of Pharaoh, will be destroyed; and if destroyed then (see Ezek. xxviii. 18, 19) never again will he, as Death, rise into existence, and hence the triumph of the Lord is, and ever will be, most glorious.

XV. 2. "The Lord *is* my strength and song, and he is become my salvation: he *is* my God, and I will prepare him a habitation; my father's God, and I will exalt him."

Thus, although the Fourth race of men shall be destroyed through the ruling of the Law, yet, through the Lord (see xiv. 14), who fights and wins the great battle of life, the people are redeemed from death, and the Lord is become the God of their salvation. Prepare ye, therefore, a habitation for the Living Bread, that, through regeneration, the God of life may dwell within you; prepare ye a habitation for the Living Bread, that (see I. Cor. xv. 54) the corruptible may put on incorruption, that mortality may put on immortality, and that Death be swallowed up in victory.

XV. 3–8. "The Lord *is* a man of war: the Lord *is* his name.

4. "Pharaoh's chariots and his host hath he cast into the sea: his chosen captains also are drowned in the Red sea.

5. "The depths have covered them: they sank into the bottom as a stone.

6. "Thy right hand, O Lord, is become glorious in power: thy right hand, O Lord, hath dashed in pieces the enemy.

7. "And in the greatness of thine excellency thou hast overthrown them that rose up against thee: thou sentest forth thy wrath, *which* consumed them as stubble.

8. "And with the blast of thy nostrils the waters were gathered together, the floods stood upright as a heap, *and* the depths were congealed in the heart of the sea."

The right hand of the Lord (see Ps. cx.; lxxxix.

34–36; cxxxii. 11; St. Luke xx. 41–44) is the Word of God as the begotten Son of God, and as the Son of man. The Son of God made his advent as the Son of man (see Gen. xiv., xv.; St. John viii. 54–56) in the day of Abraham, at and from which time he, for four hundred years (see Gen. xv. 13, 14; Isa. lii. 11–15), suffered excessive affliction, but from which he came forth (see Gen. xxii. 15–18) possessed of the gate of his enemies.

The song of Moses and the children of Israel, as shadow, evidently takes cognizance of these wonderful labors of the Messiah, whereby the failure of the adversarial host in their demonstrations against the Messiah are made manifest; for Satan, notwithstanding his bitter persecution, could not point to one misstep on the part of the Messiah through which Lucifer could hold him captive in the dark valley of death. As, therefore, the children of Israel came through the waters of the Red Sea in safety, so the Messiah passed through the Deluge, and came forth from the land of the shadow of death bearing with him countless names pertaining to the past ages of man, the spoils which Lucifer deemed securely sealed to himself.

XV. 9, 10. "The enemy said, I will pursue, I will overtake, I will divide the spoil; my lust shall be satisfied upon them; I will draw my sword, my hand shall destroy them.

10. "Thou didst blow with thy wind, the sea covered them: they sank as lead in the mighty waters."

Thus Lucifer, not satisfied with the exhibitions of power given by the Almighty, thought still to prevail against the Messiah, or, at least, to secure a partial triumph for himself through a division of the spoils.

The Messiah, however (see I. Kings xxi. 3-6), will give up no part of his inheritance; hence the names he bears with him will never revert to Lucifer that Lucifer should confirm their everlasting captivity.

XV. 11-13. "Who *is* like unto thee, O Lord, among the gods? who *is* like thee, glorious in holiness, fearful *in* praises, doing wonders?

12. "Thou stretchedst out thy right hand, the earth swallowed them.

13. "Thou in thy mercy hast led forth the people *which* thou hast redeemed: thou hast guided *them* in thy strength unto thy holy habitation."

The holy habitation of the Lord (see Col. i. 13-18; Rev. iii. 14; St. John vi. 47-58; Heb. x. 5-7) doubtless is the body that was prepared for the Messiah in and as the very beginning of the creation of God, and which body became the Living Bread when, later, the Word of God as the Messiah invested it with life. Unto this holy habitation, therefore,—even though the earth (see verse 12) swallow up the natural body,—the spirit of man is and will be guided, and, from the simple historical stand-point, as the text clearly indicates, already has been guided unto it through the strength of the Messiah, and of the Lord who goes before him. Being guided unto the holy habitation, however, is not all; for (see St. Mark xiv. 22; St. John vi. 53, 54) the body of the Messiah must be eaten that eternal life may ensue.

In this light indications follow that those guided unto the holy habitation of the Lord became redeemed through the eating thereof, or otherwise, through the eating of the Living Bread that came down from heaven, and that, through the eating, the redeemed will grow unto a holy temple in the Lord (see Eph. ii. 20–22).

The ministration of this Bread (see Gen. xiv. 18–20; Deut. xxxiii. 8, 9; Ps. cx. 4; Heb. vii. 14–17; St. Mark xiv. 22) is cared for by the priesthood of Melchizedek, the Fulfilling Power of the Infinite Majesty; hence the overthrow of Lucifer and the release of his captives is made sure. If such be not the case, whence arises (see verse 1) the glorious triumph of the Lord? or who is the man Pharaoh that he should measure his strength with the strength of the Lord, that the Lord should glory in his overthrow? The man Pharaoh is simply as nothing in the hand of the Lord; hence the simple history clustering around Pharaoh is parable and dark saying, the same indication being evidently set forth in Psalm lxxviii.

XV. 14–19. "The people shall hear, *and* be afraid: sorrow shall take hold on the inhabitants of Palestina.

15. "Then the dukes of Edom shall be amazed; the mighty men of Moab, trembling shall take hold upon them; all the inhabitants of Canaan shall melt away.

16. "Fear and dread shall fall upon them; by the greatness of thine arm they shall be *as* still as a stone; till thy people pass over, O Lord, till the people pass over, *which* thou hast purchased.

17. "Thou shalt bring them in, and plant them in the mountain of thine inheritance, *in* the place, O Lord, *which* thou hast made for thee to dwell in; *in* the sanctuary, O Lord, *which* thy hands have established.

18. "The Lord shall reign for ever and ever.

Ex. xv. 1–19, considered as allegory.

DIAGRAM 12.

THE SONG OF MOSES AND THE CHILDREN OF ISRAEL.

Sixth day of the Creation

Creation of a body for the Word of God as the very beginning of the creation of God
Creation of light   Creation of the earth:
Creation of the firmament
Creation of vegetation
Creation of sun, moon, and stars
Creation of fishes and fowl
Creation of cattle, creeping thing, and beast of the earth
The Word is begotten as the Son of God by investing with life the body that was created in and as the very beginning of the creation of God
Pre Euphratic Era
Creation of the Euphratic or First race (Adam's)

Dividing in the midst of the Euphratic age

Creation of the Hiddekelic or Second race
Destruction of the Euphratic or First race

Dividing in the midst of the Hiddekelic age

Creation of the Gihonic or Third race
Destruction of the Hiddekelic or Second race

Dividing in the midst of the Gihonic age

Creation of the Pisonic or Fourth race.

Deluge of Noah   Destruction of the Gihonic or Third race
Advent of the Messiah as the Redeemer of man
The Messiah descends into and returns from the land of the shadow of death
Crucifixion, absolute death, and resurrection of the Messiah as Jesus Christ   Dividing of the Pisonic age
Judgmental Era,

Thousand Years' Era
Era of Destruction
End of Time

19. "For the horse of Pharaoh went in with his chariots and with his horsemen into the sea, and the Lord brought again the waters of the sea upon them; but the children of Israel went on dry *land* in the midst of the sea."

In Diagram 12, spaces a, a indicate the Four Ages of Man; b, b indicate the Four Ages by the four cardinal points of the compass; c, c indicate the Four Ages by the land through which Abraham passed (see Gen. xii. 1-7); d, d indicate chief divisions in the grand epoch extending from the beginning of the creation down to the end of time, and also the pertainings of the fifteen dukes of Esau (see Gen. xxxvi. 15-19), or, otherwise, Edom, to these divisions; e, e indicate the pertainings of the eleven dukes of Esau (see Gen. xxxvi. 40-43, or, otherwise, Edom, to the first eleven chief divisions from the beginning of the creation; f, f indicate time; g, g indicate pertaining of Palestina.

In and as the very beginning of the creation of God (see Col. i. 13-18; Rev. iii. 14), a body (see Diagram 12) was created for the Word of God that in it (see Heb. x. 5-7; Ps. xl. 6-8) the Word of God might do the will of God. Through the Word of God this body—which is a creature—has the pre-eminence in all things, and hence it is perfect and unblemishable as a created element. After the creation of the body for the Word of God the earthy (see Gen. i. 1) was created. The earthy, however, is good but not perfect, in that the first-mentioned body has the pre-eminence in all things; hence the earthy is blemishable.

Thus in the beginning two conditions of creature existence, independent of each other, are brought to notice; one of which, as a created element, is endowed with perfection, while the other is not so endowed.

From the indications thus set forth the perfect body that was prepared for the Word of God, that he might do the will of God, became (see verse 13) the holy habitation of the Lord. Wherefore, when the Word of God invested with life the body that had been created for the Word in the beginning (see Diagram 12), then, in this new experience or advent, the Word of God became and was begotten as the Son of God.

The Word of God as the Son of God is now clothed upon with a created body which, through investment of the Word, has the pre-eminence in all things; hence no power exists that can approach it for harm, or add to its excellence, other than that of Almighty God.

The body of man of Adam's race (see Gen. ii. 7) was formed out of the dust of the ground, and hence (see I. Cor. xv. 47) is of the earth, earthy. This earthy body (see I. Cor. xv. 46) is the first or natural body of man, and in it (see I. Cor. xv. 45) man was made a living soul; but (see I. Cor. xv. 44) there is a spiritual body as well as a natural body. The spiritual body, however, is greater than the natural or earthy body,—for the natural body is raised a spiritual body,—hence indications become manifest that the spiritual body raised up pertains to the body created in the beginning for the Word of God that, in it, he might do the will of God; this body having the pre-eminence in all things.

In this light (see I. Cor. xv. 45) the first man Adam, who in the day of his creation was made a living soul,

INDICATIONS OF THE BOOK OF EXODUS. 103

became a quickening spirit through his redemption, whereby (see verse 17) he was led, regenerated, or born into the holy habitation of the Lord; born into the sanctuary of the Lord; born into the body that was created for the Lord as the Word of God; born into the dwelling of the Lord. This dwelling or habitation evidently is the Tree of Life, and the Lord established it in the beginning as a suitable habitation for the creature world; hence, truly (see I. Cor. xv. 47), the first man *is* of the earth, earthy; but the second man *is* the Lord from heaven.

By verse 13 the Lord led forth the people whom he had redeemed. Who were the people thus led forth? They were (see Diagram 12, spaces *b, b*) the people of the past ages of man. How could the people that lay in the valley of the shadow of death be led forth? They are led forth through the transmission of their names, iniquity, blood, and characteristics to the children of the fourth generation or age, in harmony with the great Law of Iniquity as given in xxxiv. 6, 7. Of what advantage to the people of the past is the leading forth thus indicated? The advantage lies in the possibility of their redemption. How can they be redeemed? They can be redeemed through the transmission of their iniquity, blood, and characteristics to the Messiah when, as the Son of man, and as the Redeemer of man, he takes upon himself (see Diagram 9) the flesh of sinful man; for the iniquity is transmitted through the flesh from the fathers to the children.

At the time of the exodus of the children of Israel from Egypt, the Messiah was physically manifest as the Son of man; hence, by the laws that govern the transmission of iniquity, the people of the past ages were led unto the holy habitation of the Lord, and their names were raised up again among their brethren through the strength of the Lord when he came forth into the world as the Son of man.

Is it any wonder, therefore (see Diagram 12), that "people shall hear, *and* be afraid," and that "sorrow shall take hold on the inhabitants of Palestina"? for the people of Palestina are not only man of Adam's race, but the whole host of evil dwells therein; the host that strove against the creature, and thought to have held it captive forever. Is it any wonder that the dukes of Edom shall be amazed (see Diagram 12, spaces *d, d*) when, in the final era of time, the Lord shall smite the Egyptians, and when all the people of Canaan shall melt away?

As, therefore (see verse 19), "the horse of Pharaoh went in with his chariots and with his horsemen into the sea, and the Lord brought again the waters of the sea upon them," so the complete overthrow of the adversarial host is shadowed; and as "the children of Israel went on dry *land* in the midst of the sea," so their return from the valley of the shadow of death is indicated.

Of the two counts of the dukes of Edom (see Gen. xxxvi.), one gives fifteen and the other gives eleven. Therefore let the fifteen dukes (see Diagram 12) be apportioned to fifteen chief divisions of the grand epoch from the beginning of the creation down to the end of time. Let them be apportioned according to the order given in the text of Genesis, commencing with Eliphaz and ending with Korah, when it will be

INDICATIONS OF THE BOOK OF EXODUS. 105

found that, here and there, the meanings of the proper names thus pertaining to these divisions become landmarks in the establishment of the accuracy of the divisions. Accordingly, Eliphaz (see Diagram 12, spaces *d, d*) pertains to the creative days, and Eliphaz is defined to mean "the endeavor of God;" by which creative labor is indicated.

Teman pertains to the first portion of the Pre-Euphratic era, and is defined to mean "perfect." In the beginning of this era the Word of God was begotten as the Son of God that he might do the will of God; hence perfection is called for in Teman as shadow.

Omar pertains to the second portion of the Pre-Euphratic era, and is defined to mean "he that speaks, or bitter;" hence, inasmuch as in this era Satan made war against the begotten Son, and as he, together with his angels, was cast into the earth, so the bitter enemy of the Son is called for in Omar as shadow.

Zepho pertains to the portion of the Euphratic age that witnessed the creation of man of Adam's race as a subjugatory element, and that witnessed the entering in of the Law for the government of all hosts; wherefore, inasmuch as Zepho is defined to mean "that sees and observes, that expects or covers," so the Law, with its ordination to life, and its ministration of death, sees and observes, expects a life or covers with death.

Kenaz pertains to the last portion of the Euphratic age, and is defined to mean "this nest, this lamentation;" hence, in harmony with which, the Euphratic race was swept away because of their transgression, and, through the Law, death covered them; hence, again, the lamentation.

106 INDICATIONS OF THE BOOK OF EXODUS.

Korah pertains to the first portion of the Hiddekelic age, the portion (see Diagram 12) that overlaps the North or Euphratic age. Korath is defined to mean "bald, frozen, icy." Inasmuch, therefore, as Korah overlaps into the North or Euphratic age, so an indication arises that Korah also means "bald, frozen, icy," and hence that, as shadow, it overlaps the ice-bound regions of the north, or, otherwise, that the Euphratic and Hiddekelic ages overlap in Kenaz and Korah.

Gatam pertains to the last portion of the Hiddekelic age, and is defined to mean "their lowing." Lowing (see Job vi. 5) doubtless signifies lamentation; wherefore the lowing or lamentation indicated by Gatam points to the destruction of the Hiddekelic race, even as the lamentation of Kenaz pointed to the destruction of the Euphratic race.

Amalek pertains to the first portion of the Gihonic age. In the beginning of this age the Gihonic race was created; hence, as Amalek is defined to mean "a people that licks up," so the transgression of this people is indicated. The Gihonic race was destroyed in the Deluge of Noah.

Shammah pertains to the second division of the Pisonic age, or to the division immediately succeeding the Antediluvian epoch. Shammah is defined to mean "loss, desolation, astonishment;" wherefore these conditions find place immediately after the destructive Deluge.

Jeush pertains to the fourth division of the Pisonic age, and is defined to mean "he that is devoured." The fourth division of the Pisonic age (see Diagram 12) corresponds with the Judgmental era; hence the

INDICATIONS OF THE BOOK OF EXODUS 107

overthrow of Satan, King of Evil, points to the one who, in this era, shall be devoured.

Jaalam pertains to the fifth division of the Pisonic age, and is defined to mean "who is hidden." The fifth division of the Pisonic age corresponds with the Thousand Years' era, during which the Messiah reigns, with his saints, a thousand years; hence, inasmuch as Satan is bound during these years, so he is the one who is hidden during this epoch.

Korah (the second) pertains to the sixth division of the Pisonic age. The sixth division of this age corresponds with the Era of Destruction, while the Era of Destruction brings with it the end of time. As before, Korah doubtless means "bald, frozen, icy." In this light, therefore, let the Four Ages of Man be conformed to the four walls of the great city Jerusalem; the Euphratic age (see Sketch A) constituting the north wall, the Hiddekelic age constituting the east wall, the Gihonic age constituting the south wall, and the Pisonic age constituting the west wall, when, by the conformity thus established, both the Korah of the Hiddekelic and the Korah of the Pisonic ages overlap the Euphratic age as the north, whereby the harmony of the apportionment of the fifteen dukes of Edom to the chief divisions called for by the allegory is further confirmed.

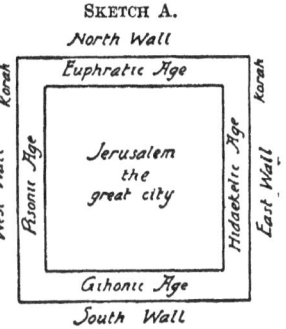

By the second count the dukes of Edom are eleven in number, as given by name. These eleven dukes, with great probability (see Gen. xxxvi. 31-43) pertain to the chief divisions, as already given, from the beginning of the creation unto that epoch of the Pisonic age in which kings really did reign over Israel. In this light (see Diagram 12 at *e, e*) the eleven dukes just fill the eleven divisions from the·beginning of the creation down to the Messianic epoch, in which the Messiah was manifest as the Son of man, and during which, by the simple history, kings commenced to reign over Israel.

Well, therefore (see verse 15), may the dukes of Edom be amazed at the wonderful labors of the Messiah as he releases the captives from the land to which they, as shadow, pertain. Thus the two counts of the dukes of Edom harmonize, and, by the harmony, two witnesses are made manifest confirmatory of the actual existence, as history, of the Four Ages of Man, and their chief divisions.

XV. 20, 21. "And Miriam the prophetess, the sister of Aaron, took a timbrel in her hand; and all the women went out after her with timbrels and with dances.

21. "And Miriam answered them, Sing ye to the Lord, for he hath triumphed gloriously: the horse and his rider hath he thrown into the sea."

Here Miriam also reiterates the song in which the Lord triumphed gloriously. The Lord's glorious triumph is not the overthrow of the man Pharaoh simply, and the bringing forth from Egypt of the mere progeny of Jacob, but it is the triumph of the Messiah over all his enemies, whereby (see Gen. xv. 13, 14; xxii. 15-18) he, the Messiah, came forth from Egypt

INDICATIONS OF THE BOOK OF EXODUS. 109

possessed of the gate of his enemies; for Lucifer is overthrown, and Satan is powerless before him.

If man is to be delivered from bondage, then the captor of man (see II. Tim. ii. 26) must be brought to the light; not merely the one who, for the moment, and who, through circumstance, reigns over his neighbor, as Pharaoh, but the one which crept into Eden and bound man to his kingdom. He is the enemy that rose up against God, he is the one whom God overthrew, and, doubtless, he is the one of whose downfall Moses and the children of Israel sing in their song of thanksgiving and joy.

XV. 22. "So Moses brought Israel from the Red sea, and they went out into the wilderness of Shur; and they went three days in the wilderness, and found no water."

The three days' journey of the children of Israel into the wilderness (see Diagrams 3, 13) indicates the Three Ages of Man which are under the veil. By their journey indication is also given that the history of the children of Israel in the wilderness (see Ps. lxxviii.) is allegory pertaining to these ages, although it may still retain bearings upon the Fourth independent of the simple history of the Fourth.

XV. 23-26. "And when they came to Marah, they could not drink of the waters of Marah, for they *were* bitter: therefore the name of it was called Marah.

24. "And the people murmured against Moses, saying, What shall we drink?

25. "And he cried unto the Lord; and the Lord shewed him a tree, *which* when he had cast into the waters, the waters were made sweet: there he made for

them a statute and an ordinance, and there he proved them,

26. "And said, If thou wilt diligently hearken to the voice of the Lord thy God, and wilt do that which is right in his sight, and wilt give ear to his commandments, and keep all his statutes, I will put none of these diseases upon thee, which I have brought upon the Egyptians: for I *am* the Lord that healeth thee."

The three days' journey into the wilderness, as already indicated (see Diagram 13), takes history back to the beginning of the First Age of Man. The tree which the Lord showed unto Moses indicates the Tree of Life (see, also, Rev. ii. 1-7), while the statute and ordinance which the Lord made indicates the Tree of the Knowledge of Good and Evil, or the entering in of the Law (see Gen. ii. 15-17). As the allegory now stands, the begotten Son, the Man for whom a body was prepared (see Diagram 12), is among the hosts of Israel; therefore he, and all hosts that pertain to and are present in the Pre-Euphratic era, come under the rulings of the statute and ordinance of the Lord as set forth and shadowed by the text, and as indicated by the charges given in the garden of Eden. By these statutes and ordinances, or by the Law, man is proved; and, therefore, by the text, the One who was begotten as the Son of God and man of Adam's race, both were proved (see Deut. xxxiii. 8, 9) in Eden even as both were proved at the waters of Marah. Of the two, man of Adam's race failed completely; and, in consequence, he is overwhelmed with all the plagues that came upon the Egyptians; the manifest fulfilment of

INDICATIONS OF THE BOOK OF EXODUS. 111

Ex. xv. 22–26, considered as allegory.

DIAGRAM 13.

THE CHILDREN OF ISRAEL AT THE WATERS OF MARAH.

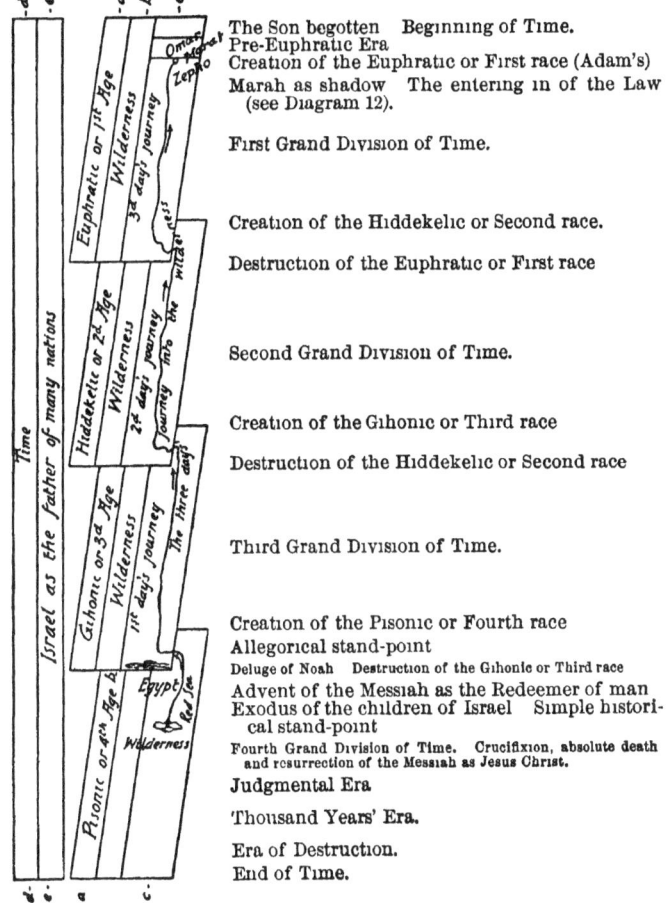

The Son begotten   Beginning of Time.
Pre-Euphratic Era
Creation of the Euphratic or First race (Adam's)
Marah as shadow   The entering in of the Law
(see Diagram 12).

First Grand Division of Time.

Creation of the Hiddekelic or Second race.

Destruction of the Euphratic or First race

Second Grand Division of Time.

Creation of the Gihonic or Third race

Destruction of the Hiddekelic or Second race

Third Grand Division of Time.

Creation of the Pisonic or Fourth race
Allegorical stand-point
Deluge of Noah   Destruction of the Gihonic or Third race
Advent of the Messiah as the Redeemer of man
Exodus of the children of Israel   Simple historical stand-point
Fourth Grand Division of Time.   Crucifixion, absolute death and resurrection of the Messiah as Jesus Christ.
Judgmental Era
Thousand Years' Era.
Era of Destruction.
End of Time.

112 *INDICATIONS OF THE BOOK OF EXODUS.*

which is seen in the afflictions that are general to the creature world.

In Diagram 13, spaces a, a indicate the Four Ages of Man; b, b indicate the first three ages as the wilderness; c, c indicate the first three ages by the three days' journey into the wilderness; d, d indicate time; e, e indicate pertaining of Israel (see Gen. xxxv. 9–12) as a father of nations.

The three days' journey into the wilderness, as allegory (see Diagram 13, spaces c, c), carries the standpoint of the text towards the beginning of the Euphratic or First age. Marah, therefore, pertains to the Euphratic age. The waters of Marah were bitter, and (see verse 23) because they were bitter the name of it was called Marah. By reference to Diagram 12, Omar also pertains to the beginning of the Euphratic age, and Omar is defined to mean "he that speaks, or bitter;" hence by Marah and Omar the same general stand-point is indicated. From this position the indication follows that the bitter waters point to or shadow the transgressive element that existed in the beginning of time, and that sought to make all things bitter; hence the people's cry "What shall we drink?"

In the epoch represented by Omar sin existed, but (see Rom. v. 13) sin was not imputed to the transgressor; for there was no law. With the creation of man of Adam's race, however (see Rom. v. 14; Gal. iii. 19), the Law entered for the government of all hosts. This Law (see Diagrams 12, 13) is shadowed by Zepho, which is defined to mean "that sees or observes," "that expects or covers;" hence the Law becomes judge.

INDICATIONS OF THE BOOK OF EXODUS. 113

The indication is manifest that the entering in of the Law creates, as it were, a new starting-point for all intelligences; which is further indicated (see verse 25) by the tree which the Lord showed Moses, and which Moses cast into the waters, whereby they were made sweet,—that is, existing or accumulated transgression was not imputed to the transgressor. This tree (see Gen. ii. 9; also charge to the people of the Euphratic age, Rev. ii. 1-7) doubtless points to the Tree of Life, the body created for the Word of God in and as the beginning of the creation of God.

That the Law entered at this time is indicated by the statute and ordinance (see verse 25) which the Lord made, and hence by the statute and ordinance, or by the Law, all hosts will be proved, heavenly (see Deut. xxxiii. 8, 9) as well as earthly. If, therefore, from this time (see verse 26) people shall keep all the Lord's commandments and statutes, then no power can touch them for harm; but if they fail, then sin will be imputed and the transgressor will come under the penalty of the Law.

XV. 27. "And they came to Elim, where *were* twelve wells of water, and threescore and ten palm trees': and they encamped there by the waters."

In Diagram 14, spaces a, a indicate the Four Ages of Man; b, b indicate (see Num. xxxiii. 9, 10) the journey of the children of Israel from Marah back to the Red Sea; c, c indicate the apportionment of the threescore and ten palm-trees according to the Decade System of Chronology; d, d indicate the apportionment of the twelve wells of water to twelve chief divisions of time; e, e indicate time; f, f allegorical pertaining of Moses.

114 INDICATIONS OF THE BOOK OF EXODUS.

Ex. xv. 27, considered as allegory.

DIAGRAM 14.

THE TWELVE WELLS OF WATER AND THE THREESCORE AND TEN PALM-TREES.

The Son begotten   Beginning of Time.
Pre-Euphratic Era
Creation of the Euphratic or First race (Adam's)
Marah as shadow (see Diagram 13).

Dividing in the midst of the Euphratic age

Creation of the Hiddekelic or Second race

Destruction of the Euphratic or First race.

Elim as shadow (see Gen xv 8, xxix 1-10 Ezek. xlvii 1-10 Rev xxii 1, 2) The twelve wells of water at Elim

Creation of the Gihonic or Third race

Destruction of the Hiddekelic or Second race

Dividing in the midst of the Gihonic age.

Creation of the Pisonic or Fourth race
Allegorical stand-point
Deluge of Noah   Destruction of the Gihonic or Third race.
Epoch of replenishment (see Gen ix 1)
Advent of the Messiah as the Son of man in the day of Abraham
Simple historical stand-point
Dividing in the midst of the Pisonic age   Crucifixion, absolute death, and resurrection of the Messiah as Jesus Christ.

Judgmental Era.
Thousand Years' Era
Era of Destruction.
End of Time.

INDICATIONS OF THE BOOK OF EXODUS. 115

On their return from Marah (see Diagram 14) the children of Israel came to Elim, where were twelve wells of water and threescore and ten palm-trees, and they encamped there. Elim is defined to mean "the rams," "the strong;" the Hiddekelic age (see Dan. viii. 1-21) is shadowed by the kings of Media and Persia; the kings of Media and Persia are shadowed by a ram with two horns; a portion of the land to be inherited by Abraham (see Gen. xv. 7-10) is shadowed by a ram also; hence the indication arises that, in the allegoric sense, Elim pertains to the Hiddekelic or Second age (see, also, Dan. ii. 36-40).

The Hiddekelic age (see Gen. ii. 14) is indicated by the east; the east (see Gen. xxix. 1-10; Neh. xii. 31-37; Ezek. xlvii. 1-10; Rev. xxii. 1, 2) is identified with the flow of water that brings life "whithersoever the rivers shall come;" hence, again, by the twelve wells of water at Elim the pertaining of Elim to the Hiddekelic age, as shadow, is further indicated.

By apportionment, the twelve wells of water (see Diagram 14) memorialize the Messianic year (see Diagram 6) or the twelve chief divisions of time. As, therefore, the people of these twelve divisions of time shall gather together in the east (see Gen. xxix. 1-10), so this gathering together is indicated by the twelve wells that find place at Elim.

The apportionment of the twelve wells is further confirmed by the harmonious apportionment of the threescore and ten palm-trees according to the Decade System of Chronology, whereby a ten is found for each of the first seven semidivisions of the Four Ages. From this position the threescore and ten palm-trees point to the seventy years' desolation of Jerusalem (see Dan. ix. 2), which extend from the fall of the first man of the Euphratic race until the Saviour Jesus Christ (see Diagram 12) shall rise from the dead; at which time he will come into his kingdom, and Jerusalem will be desolate no more.

Now, although the Saviour came into his kingdom when he rose from the dead, and bore with him at that time the souls of the redeemed to his celestial abode, it does not follow that the statute and ordinance which the Lord enacted in the garden of Eden were made void thereby. They cannot be made void, for they are the embodiment of the First Covenant, and, by the First Covenant, judgment will, finally, be rendered against the unbelieving; hence the pestilences, famines, devastations, and ills developing with the growth of years are so many evidences of the vitality of the Divine command, and of the increasing activity of its fulfilment as long as transgression shall exist.

The children of Israel left Elim (see Num. xxxiii. 11) and came to the Red Sea; wherefore the simple historical stand-point is brought down to the Red Sea; but the allegorical stand-point is brought down to the Deluge of Noah, or into the overlap of the Gihonic and Pisonic ages.

XVI. 1–4. "And they took their journey from Elim, and all the congregation of the children of Israel came unto the wilderness of Sin, which *is* between Elim and Sinai, on the fifteenth day of the second month after their departing out of the land of Egypt.

2. "And the whole congregation of the children of

INDICATIONS OF THE BOOK OF EXODUS. 117

Israel murmured against Moses and Aaron in the wilderness:

3. "And the children of Israel said unto them, Would to God we had died by the hand of the Lord in the land of Egypt, when we sat by the flesh pots, *and* when we did eat bread to the full; for ye have brought us forth into this wilderness, to kill this whole assembly with hunger.

4. "Then said the Lord unto Moses, Behold, I will rain bread from heaven for you; and the people shall go out and gather a certain rate every day, that I may prove them, whether they will walk in my law, or no."

In Diagram 15, spaces a, a indicate the Four Ages of Man; b, b indicate the first two ages, as Sinai and Elim; c, c indicate the first three ages by the first three months' wandering of the children of Israel; d, d, as shadowed, indicate the wilderness into or through which the children of Israel passed in their journey from the Red Sea back to the wilderness of Sin; e, e indicate time; f, f, allegorical pertaining of Moses to the first three ages of man.

The children of Israel (see Diagram 13) journeyed from the Red Sea to Marah, and from Marah (see Diagram 14) they returned to the Red Sea again; now, however, they journey from the Red Sea to the wilderness of Sin, doubtless stopping at Elim on the way thither. The wilderness of Sin lies between Elim and Sinai; wherefore the indication comes forth that inasmuch as Elim (see Diagram 14) shadows the Hiddekelic age, so Sinai, as being beyond Elim (see Diagram 15), shadows the Euphratic or First age, and hence that the allegorical stand-point is carried to the overlap of these two ages.

118 INDICATIONS OF THE BOOK OF EXODUS.

Ex. xvi. 1–4, considered as allegory.

DIAGRAM 15.

THE JOURNEY FROM THE RED SEA TO THE WILDERNESS OF SIN.

The Son begotten   Beginning of Time.
Pre-Euphratic Era
Creation of the Euphratic or First race (Adam's).
 The Law enters into the Euphratic race.

The earth in the Euphratic age.

Creation of the Hiddekelic or Second race
Allegorical stand-point of the wilderness of Sin   The Law enters into the Hiddekelic race
Destruction of the Euphratic or First race

The earth in the Hiddekelic age

Creation of the Gihonic or Third race.
Destruction of the Hiddekelic or Second race.

The earth in the Gihonic age

Creation of the Pisonic or Fourth race
Allegorical stand-point as from the Deluge
Deluge of Noah   Destruction of the Gihonic or Third race.
Epoch of replenishment (see Gen ix 1)   [ham
Advent of the Messiah as the Son of man in the day of Abra-
Simple historical stand point as from the Red Sea
The earth in the Pisonic age   Crucifixion, absolute death, and resurrection of the Messiah as Jesus Christ.
Judgmental Era.

Thousand Years' Era.

Era of Destruction.
End of Time

In this light, therefore, the newly-created Hiddekelic race will be proved (see verse 4) even as the Euphratic race was proved at the waters of Marah (see Diagram 13), from which the indication is given that the Law has entered into this people also.

Verse 4 indicates, further, that the people will be proved by the bread that shall rain from heaven. This bread (see, also, Gen. i. 29, 30) is given them for food, but flesh (see Num. xi. 4–6) was not thus granted them. Should, therefore, the people eat flesh, then they would transgress the Law and (see xv. 26) the plagues of the Egyptians would come upon them.

In the charge to the people of the Hiddekelic age (see Rev. ii. 12–17) the promise is made, " To him that overcometh will I give to eat of the hidden manna ;" hence, when the children of Israel (see verses 13–15) saw the bread which had rained from heaven, they called it manna,—doubtless thinking it the hidden manna,—for they knew not what it was. Moses, however, did not call it manna, but said, " This *is* the bread which the Lord hath given you to eat."

Of the two mannas thus brought to notice, one shadows the earthy body, and the other, or the hidden manna, is the body that was created for the Word of God in and as the beginning of the creation of God; wherefore (see St. John vi. 49–51), " if any man eat of this bread,"—doubtless the hidden manna,—" he shall live for ever," and (see Rev. ii. 17) shall receive a new name, " which no man knoweth saving he that receiveth *it*." The sojourning of the children of Israel in the wilderness of Sin, at this time, evidently points to the entering in of the Law to the Hiddekelic race.

XVI. 8. "And Moses said, *This shall be,* when the Lord shall give you in the evening flesh to eat, and in the morning bread to the full; for that the Lord heareth your murmurings which ye murmur against him: and what *are* we? your murmurings *are* not against us, but against the Lord."

This episode, in which the people lusted after flesh, indicates history relating to the Second or Hiddekelic age; and, as this age is indicated by the second month of the departure from Egypt, so the fifteenth day indicates the approximate time, in the world's history, when the gratification of this lust for flesh culminated in a great plague.

The children of this age bear with them the blood and characteristics of the preceding race (see Diagram 15), and, consequently, form and constitute the mixed multitude called for in Num. xi. 4, as follows: "And the mixed multitude that *was* among them fell a lusting: and the children of Israel also wept again, and said, Who shall give us flesh to eat?" In the beginning of this age (see verses 4, 5) man was forbidden to eat flesh or animal food, but the text discloses an unrighteous desire on the part of the people to disregard the Divine command; therefore, to prove them, the Lord rained manna upon them in bounteous measure, and also sent an abundance of flesh that they might eat their fill.

By Num. xi. 32, 33, "And the people stood up all that day, and all *that* night, and all the next day, and they gathered the quails: he that gathered least gathered ten homers: and they spread *them* all abroad for themselves round about the camp.

"And while the flesh *was* yet between their teeth,

INDICATIONS OF THE BOOK OF EXODUS. 121

ere it was chewed, the wrath of the Lord was kindled against the people, and the Lord smote the people with a very great plague." Thus the transgressive condition of the people of this age is set forth in their disregard of the Divine command; for they chose the flesh for food instead of the bread.

Of this people and this plague it is further stated (Num. xvi. 45–49), " Get you up from among this congregation, that I may consume them as in a moment. And they fell upon their faces.

" And Moses said unto Aaron, Take a censer, and put fire therein from off the altar, and put on incense, and go quickly unto the congregation, and make an atonement for them: for there is wrath gone out from the Lord; the plague is begun.

" And Aaron took as Moses commanded, and ran into the midst of the congregation; and, behold, the plague was begun among the people: and he put on incense, and made an atonement for the people.

" And he stood between the dead and the living; and the plague was stayed.

" Now they that died in the plague were fourteen thousand and seven hundred, besides them that died about the matter of Korah."

It may be stated here that, by the allegoric rendering of the chronology of Num. xvi., the fourteen thousand and seven hundred which died of the plague indicate the year 14,700 from the creation of the Euphratic race, and, therefore, the plague occurred at or about the dividing of the Second age. The particular line of chronology thus indicated is also taken up in Dan. vi. 1, 2. Moreover, where this history is further recorded in Psalm lxxviii. 31-34, "The wrath of God came upon them, and slew the fattest of them, and smote down the chosen *men* of Israel.

"For all this they sinned still, and believed not for his wondrous works.

"Therefore their days did he consume in vanity, and their years in trouble.

"When he slew them, then they sought him: and they returned and inquired early after God."

By these verses the indication is plainly seen that the plague occurred in the midst of their age; for afterwards, when their days had run out, they were slain; they having perished in the great Hiddekelic famine which nearly depopulated the earth about the year 19,765 of the Grand Era of Time, or about the year 12,098 B.C.

XVI. 36. "Now an omer *is* the tenth *part* of an ephah."

This indicates or memorializes that as the omer of manna, which is the tenth part of an ephah, shall be eaten (see xvi. 16), so (see Isa. vi. 13) the tenth "shall return, and shall be eaten: as a teil tree, and as an oak, whose substance *is* in them, when they cast *their leaves:* so the holy seed *shall be* the substance thereof" (see, also, xvi. 33).

XVII. 1-7. "And all the congregation of the children of Israel journeyed from the wilderness of Sin, after their journeys, according to the commandment of the Lord, and pitched in Rephidim: and *there was* no water for the people to drink.

2. "Wherefore the people did chide with Moses, and said, Give us water that we may drink. And Moses

INDICATIONS OF THE BOOK OF EXODUS. 123

said unto them, Why chide ye with me? wherefore do ye tempt the Lord?

3. "And the people thirsted there for water; and the people murmured against Moses, and said, Wherefore *is* this *that* thou hast brought us up out of Egypt, to kill us and our children and our cattle with thirst?

4. "And Moses cried unto the Lord, saying, What shall I do unto this people? they be almost ready to stone me.

5. "And the Lord said unto Moses, Go on before the people, and take with thee of the elders of Israel; and thy rod, wherewith thou smotest the river, take in thine hand, and go.

6. "Behold, I will stand before thee there upon the rock in Horeb; and thou shalt smite the rock, and there shall come water out of it, that the people may drink. And Moses did so in the sight of the elders of Israel.

7. "And he called the name of the place Massah, and Meribah, because of the chiding of the children of Israel, and because they tempted the Lord, saying, Is the Lord among us, or not?"

By these verses the drought accompanying the great Hiddekelic famine is indicated; and, therefore, the hidden history involved by the text occurred (see Diagram 16) about the year 19,765 of the Grand Era of Time, or, as already indicated, about the year 12,098 B.C. By verse 6, Moses, in obedience to the Divine command, smote the rock, and water was supplied, whereby the entire destruction of the people was prevented. Previous to the drought at Meribah, however (see Diagram 16), the Gihonic race had been created, and hence, like unto the Euphratic and Hiddekelic races, it also was proved at Meribah (see Deut. xxxiii. 8); but the failure of these people to fulfil the commandments and statutes of the Lord is indicated, xxxiii. 3, 4, "For I will not go up in the midst of thee; for thou *art* a stiffnecked people: lest I consume thee in the way.

"And when the people heard these evil tidings, they mourned: and no man did put on him his ornaments."

XVII. 8–16. "Then came Amalek, and fought with Israel in Rephidim.

9. "And Moses said unto Joshua, Choose us out men, and go out, fight with Amalek: to morrow I will stand on the top of the hill with the rod of God in mine hand.

10. "So Joshua did as Moses had said to him, and fought with Amalek: and Moses, Aaron, and Hur went up to the top of the hill.

11. "And it came to pass, when Moses held up his hand, that Israel prevailed: and when he let down his hand, Amalek prevailed.

12. "But Moses' hands *were* heavy; and they took a stone, and put *it* under him, and he sat thereon; and Aaron and Hur stayed up his hands, the one on the one side, and the other on the other side; and his hands were steady until the going down of the sun.

13. "And Joshua discomfited Amalek and his people with the edge of the sword.

14. "And the Lord said unto Moses, Write this *for* a memorial in a book, and rehearse *it* in the ears of Joshua: for I will utterly put out the remembrance of Amalek from under heaven.

INDICATIONS OF THE BOOK OF EXODUS 125

Ex. xvii, considered as allegory.

DIAGRAM 16

THE JOURNEY FROM THE WILDERNESS OF SIN TO REPHIDIM.

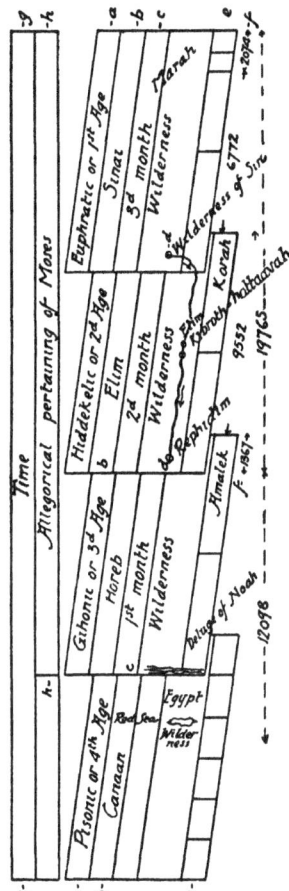

The Son begotten   Beginning of Time.
Pre-Euphratic Era
Creation of the Euphratic or First race (Adam's).
Marah as shadow   The Law enters into the Euphratic race
Dividing in the midst of the Euphratic age

Creation of the Hiddekelic or Second race
Wilderness of Sin as shadow   Massah   The Law enters into the Hiddekelic race
Destruction of the Euphratic race (see Num xvi 1-40).

Dividing in the midst of the Hiddekelic age   Kibroth-hattaavah as shadow

Creation of the Gihonic or Third race
Rephidim as shadow.
Destruction of the Hiddekelic race by drought and famine   Meribah   The Law enters into the Gihonic race.

Dividing in the midst of the Gihonic age.

Creation of the Pisonic or Fourth race.
Allegorical stand-point as from the Deluge of Noah   Destruction of the Gihonic race
Epoch of replenishment (see Gen ix 1)   [Abraham
Advent of the Messiah as the Son of man in the day of
The simple historical stand point as from the Red Sea.
Advent of the Messiah as Jesus Christ the Son of the Virgin
Dividing in the midst of the Pisonic age   Crucifixion, absolute death, and resurrection of the Messiah as Jesus Christ
Judgmental Era.
Thousand Years' Era.
Era of Destruction.
End of Time.

11*

15. "And Moses built an altar, and called the name of it Jehovah-nissi:

16. "For he said, Because the Lord hath sworn *that* the Lord *will have* war with Amalek from generation to generation."

In Diagram 16, spaces a, a indicate the Four Ages of Man; b, b indicate the Four Ages, as Sinai, Elim, Horeb, and Canaan; c, c indicate the first three ages by the first three months' wandering of the children of Israel; d, d indicate the wilderness through which the children of Israel journeyed,—that is, from the wilderness of Sin to Rephidim; e, e indicate chief divisions of time, and also the pertainings of Korah and Amalek (dukes of Edom, see Diagram 12) to two of these divisions; f, f indicate the years from the beginning of time down to the destruction of the Hiddekelic race; g, g indicate time; h, h, allegorical pertaining of Moses.

Inspection of Diagrams 12, 16 will show that, through the dukes of Edom, Amalek pertains to the first portion of the Gihonic age, while the absence of water at Rephidim, for both men and cattle, points to the great drought that culminated in the destruction of the Hiddekelic race; wherefore the allegorical standpoint of the text is carried from the wilderness of Sin, or from the overlap of the Euphratic and Hiddekelic ages to the overlap of the Hiddekelic and Gihonic ages.

The plague which came upon the Hiddekelic race occurred, as already indicated, at or about the dividing of the age to which this people belonged; but, inasmuch as transgression still followed them, they perished (see Ps. lxxviii. 31–34; Gen. xli. 56; Isa. iii. 1–4;

Jer. v. 14–18) by drought and famine when their days as a nation had run out.

The destruction of the Euphratic race (see Diagram 16) is made manifest through the history of Korah (see Num. xvi. 1–40). This people was swept away (see Num. xi. 1–3; Isa. iii. 14–26; Jer. iv. 19–31) through the agency of volcanic eruption and earthquake.

The war between Joshua and Amalek, as now shadowed, took place in the overlap of the Hiddekelic and Gihonic ages, and points to the exceeding great power of the Adversary over the hosts of Israel that are in bondage to him, while death through drought and famine threatens them on every side. The Subjugator, however, is there, the Man for whom a body was prepared suitable and fitting for the overthrow of the Serpent is there, and he will not permit the entire annihilation of the fallen race of man that the promises made Abraham as a father of nations (see Gen. xii. 1–3; xxii. 15–18) should become valueless. By the smiting of the rock, as already indicated, and the consequent flow of water, as shadow, a remnant was made to escape the almost universal death; through which remnant the debts of the people were transmitted until, in the Fourth age, they were paid by the Subjugator when he revealed himself as the Redeemer.

Amalek, therefore, indicates the Power of Evil in the beginning of the Gihonic age, and (verse 16) "the Lord hath sworn *that* the Lord *will have* war with Amalek from generation to generation," which decree, evidently, is further set forth (Gen. iii. 15), "And I will put enmity between thee and the woman, and between thy seed and her seed." This war, therefore, will exist from generation to generation, or during the Four Ages of Man; but the end will come, and the Lord the Subjugator will reign with his saints a thousand years, in proof of his triumph and of the discomfiture of Amalek, even as (see Gen. xxii. 15–18) the Lord hath sworn that the seed of Abraham shall possess the gate of his enemies.

XVIII. 1–12. " When Jethro, the priest of Midian, Moses' father in law, heard of all that God had done for Moses, and for Israel his people, *and* that the Lord had brought Israel out of Egypt;

2. " Then Jethro, Moses' father in law, took Zipporah, Moses' wife, after he had sent her back,

3. " And her two sons; of which the name of the one *was* Gershom; for he said, I have been an alien in a strange land :

4. " And the name of the other *was* Eliezer; for the God of my father, *said he, was* mine help, and delivered me from the sword of Pharaoh :

5. " And Jethro, Moses' father in law, came with his sons and his wife unto Moses into the wilderness, where he encamped at the mount of God:

6. " And he said unto Moses, I thy father in law Jethro am come unto thee, and thy wife, and her two sons with her.

7. " And Moses went out to meet his father in law, and did obeisance, and kissed him; and they asked each other of *their* welfare; and they came into the tent.

8. " And Moses told his father in law all that the Lord had done unto Pharaoh and to the Egyptians for

Ex. xviii. 1-12, considered as allegory

DIAGRAM 17.

JETHRO'S MEETING WITH MOSES AFTER THE EXODUS.

The Word begotten as the Son of God, as the Living Bread, and as the Tree of Life   Beginning of Time
Pre-Euphratic Era
Creation of the Euphratic or First race (Adam's)
Marah as shadow   The Tree of Life placed in the garden of Eden

Sinai shadows the earth in the Euphratic age

Creation of the Hiddekelic or Second race
Allegorical stand-point of the wilderness of Sin
Destruction of the Euphratic or First race by volcanic eruption and earthquake (see Num xvi 1-40, Jer iv 19-31). Mass

Elim shadows the earth in the Hiddekelic age
Kibroth-hattaavah as shadowed by the text

Creation of the Gihonic or Third race.
Rephidim   Meribah   The rock in Horeb as shadowed by the text
Destruction of the Hiddekelic or Second race by drought and famine

Horeb shadows the earth in the Gihonic age

Creation of the Pisonic or Fourth race   Destruction of the Gihonic or Third race
Allegorical stand-point as from the Deluge
Deluge of Noah as shadowed by the Red Sea.   The Red Sea as shadowing the Deluge of Noah

Advent of the Messiah as the Redeemer   The exodus   Crucifixion, absolute death, and resurrection of the Messiah
Simple historical stand-point as from the Red Sea
Canaan shadows the earth in the Pisonic age
Judgmental Era

Thousand Years' Era

Era of Destruction
End of Time.

INDICATIONS OF THE BOOK OF EXODUS 129

Israel's sake, *and* all the travail that had come upon them by the way, and *how* the Lord delivered them.

9. "And Jethro rejoiced for all the goodness which the Lord had done to Israel, whom he had delivered out of the hand of the Egyptians.

10. "And Jethro said, Blessed *be* the Lord, who hath delivered you out of the hand of the Egyptians, and out of the hand of Pharaoh; who hath delivered the people from under the hand of the Egyptians.

11. "Now I know that the Lord *is* greater than all gods: for in the thing wherein they dealt proudly *he was* above them.

12. "And Jethro, Moses' father in law, took a burnt offering and sacrifices for God: and Aaron came, and all the elders of Israel, to eat bread with Moses' father in law before God."

In Diagram 17, spaces *a, a* (see Gen. ii. 10–14) indicate the Four Ages of Man; *b, b* (see Gen. xii. 1–7; xiii. 14–17) indicate the land shown and promised Abraham; *c, c* indicate the Four Ages as Sinai, Elim, Horeb, and Canaan (see Diagrams 15, 16, 17); *d, d* indicate the pertainings of Jethro's children to chief divisions of time (see Diagram 2); *e, e* indicate the wilderness through which the children of Israel wandered (see Diagrams 3, 14) both as simple history and as allegory; *f, f* indicate the pertainings of Korah and Amalek, dukes of Edom (see Diagram 2), to two chief divisions of time; *g, g* indicate time; *h, h* indicate pertaining of Jethro, priest of Midian (see Diagrams 2, 3), to time as a whole; *i, i* indicate pertaining of Moses (see Diagrams 1, 2); *k* points to the simple historical

i

130 INDICATIONS OF THE BOOK OF EXODUS.

position of the children of Israel, both before and after the exodus. This position, as simple history pertaining to the Pisonic age, shadows history pertaining to the ages of man under the veil. The Red Sea shadows the Deluge of Noah.

Diagram 17 gives clear indications that the sojourning of the children of Israel in Egypt, the exodus, and their subsequent wanderings in the wilderness, as simple history, becomes allegory through which light is shed bearing upon the past ages of man. When, therefore, Moses (see verse 8) told Jethro, his father-in-law, "all that the Lord had done unto Pharaoh and to the Egyptians for Israel's sake, *and* all the travail that had come upon them by the way, and *how* the Lord delivered them," and when Jethro said (see verse 10), "Blessed *be* the Lord, who hath delivered you out of the hand of the Egyptians, and out of the hand of Pharaoh; who hath delivered the people from under the hand of the Egyptians," so, through this simple history (see Diagram 17), the bringing forth of the people of the past ages of man is indicated, and hence that Lucifer, the angel Death, is not sole monarch of the position.

The Red Sea shadows the Deluge of Noah; wherefore the crossing of the Red Sea, as shadow, indicates that the names, iniquity, blood, and characteristics of those which lay in the valley of the shadow of death, pertaining to the past ages of man, have been safely passed through the Deluge of Noah, and are mingled with the escaping remnant of that great day of the Lord; the proof being indicated by the wanderings of the children of Israel in the wilderness shortly after

INDICATIONS OF THE BOOK OF EXODUS. 131

they had crossed the Red Sea (see, also, Eccl. i. 9-11).

In this light the three days' journey in the wilderness (see xv. 22) from the Red Sea to the waters of Marah points (see Diagram 13) to an historic ray that reaches to or about the time the Euphratic or First race was created, and at or about which time the Law entered for the government of all hosts; hence by the entering of the Law (see xv. 23-25) the people were proved. Moses, however, by the simple history, is chosen (see iii. 10-12) to bring forth the children of Israel out of Egypt; wherefore, in harmony with this history, and with the shadow as given by the crossing of the Red Sea, Moses went at the first (see Diagram 13) to the people of the Euphratic age, and (see Diagram 14) he returned with them (see Num. xxxiii. 9, 10) to the Red Sea as simple history and as shadow; for Judah, who pertains to the Euphratic age (see Ezek. xlviii. 30, 31), shall (see Num. ii. 9) set out first.

From the Red Sea (see xvi. 1-4; Num. xxxiii. 9-11) they journeyed to the wilderness of Sin, in the second month after their departing out of Egypt (see Diagram 15). The second month, in this portion of the allegory, shadows the Hiddekelic age; but the wilderness of Sin, evidently, is beyond Elim,—Elim (see Diagram 14) shadowing the Hiddekelic age,—while Sinai is beyond the wilderness of Sin.

By xix. 1, the children of Israel came into the wilderness of Sinai in the third month after their departure from Egypt; wherefore, as the second month shadowed the Hiddekelic age, so, by harmony (see

Diagram 13), the third month shadows the Euphratic age; hence Sinai also shadows the Euphratic age.

From this position the indication is well marked that the wilderness of Sin, as shadow, points to the overlap of the Euphratic and Hiddekelic ages, at or about which time the Law entered in for the government of the Hiddekelic race (see xvi. 4), and hence by the Law they were proved; but their murmurings (see xvi. 7) point to their discontent and to their transgressive state.

Moses, as shadow, gathered this people also, and (see Diagram 16) he came to Rephidim (see xvii. 1) and pitched there. At Rephidim the people thirsted for water, and there was none, whereby an indication arises that Rephidim shadows the overlap of the Hiddekelic and Gihonic ages. This indication is confirmed by the fight between Joshua and Amalek, for (see Diagram 12) Amalek, duke of Edom, pertains to that portion of the Gihonic age overlapping the Hiddekelic. The Hiddekelic age (see xvii. 7) is also known as Massah and Meribah; wherefore the indication follows that as (see Deut. xxxiii. 8, 9) the holy one was proved at Massah, so the children of Israel also were proved at Meribah. As, therefore, both the Euphratic and Hiddekelic races were proved by the statutes and commandments of the Lord, the one at Marah and the other in the wilderness of Sin as shadow, so now the Law enters into the Gihonic race that they may be proved also. Inasmuch, however, as this people did dispute and tempt the Lord at Meribah, so their transgressive state is indicated, and will be imputed, even as transgression was imputed to the two preceding races.

In the light that Horeb shadows the Gihonic age, then the smiting of the rock by Moses can, as shadow (see Diagram 17), pertain to the overlap of the two ages in question.

Moses gathered this people also, and, together with the Hiddekels, he brought them to the mount of God, —which mount (see iii. 1) is Horeb,—or, doubtless (see Diagrams 13, 14, 17), down to the sea that shadows the Deluge of Noah. Through this sea or Deluge they must pass that their names be raised up again among their brethren in the Fourth age.

Thus the journeys indicated by Diagrams 13, 14, 15, 16 combine into one continuous line of march (see Diagram 17), by which Moses (see xxxiii. 12–17) comprehended the people whom he was commanded to bring up, and of whom he told Jethro his father-in-law. Is it any wonder that Jethro rejoiced for all the goodness which the Lord had done for Israel? No; for Jethro, priest of Midian (see Diagrams 2, 17), pertains to time as a whole, while his children pertain to the chief divisions thereof; hence, as the children are brought out, so the rejoicing of Jethro finds place (see, also, Isa. lxiii).

XVIII. 13–27. "And it came to pass on the morrow, that Moses sat to judge the people: and the people stood by Moses from the morning unto the evening.

14. "And when Moses' father in law saw all that he did to the people, he said, What *is* this thing that thou doest to the people? Why sittest thou thyself alone, and all the people stand by thee from morning unto even?

15. "And Moses said unto his father in law, Because the people come unto me to inquire of God:

16. "When they have a matter, they come unto me; and I judge between one and another, and I do make *them* know the statutes of God, and his laws.

17. "And Moses' father in law said unto him, The thing that thou doest *is* not good.

18. "Thou wilt surely wear away, both thou, and this people that *is* with thee: for this thing *is* too heavy for thee; thou art not able to perform it thyself alone.

19. "Hearken now unto my voice, I will give thee counsel, and God shall be with thee: Be thou for the people to God-ward, that thou mayest bring the causes unto God:

20. "And thou shalt teach them ordinances and laws, and shalt shew them the way wherein they must walk, and the work that they must do.

21. "Moreover thou shalt provide out of all the people able men, such as fear God, men of truth, hating covetousness; and place *such* over them, *to be* rulers of thousands, *and* rulers of hundreds, rulers of fifties, and rulers of tens:

22. "And let them judge the people at all seasons: and it shall be, *that* every great matter they shall bring unto thee, but every small matter they shall judge: so shall it be easier for thyself, and they shall bear *the burden* with thee.

23. "If thou shalt do this thing, and God command thee *so*, then thou shalt be able to endure, and all this people shall also go to their place in peace.

24. "So Moses hearkened to the voice of his father in law, and did all that he had said.

25. "And Moses chose able men out of all Israel, and made them heads over the people, rulers of thousands, rulers of hundreds, rulers of fifties, and rulers of tens.

26. "And they judged the people at all seasons: the hard causes they brought unto Moses, but every small matter they judged themselves.

27. "And Moses let his father in law depart; and he went his way into his own land."

In Diagram 18, spaces a, a' indicate the Four Ages of Man; a', a'' indicate the creative days (the creative days are indicated by the number 2); b, b' indicate the Four Ages by four numerals; b', b'' indicate the creative days; c, c' indicate the eight semidivisions of the Four Ages; c', c'' indicate the creative days; d, d' indicate ten divisions of the Four Ages from the creation of the Euphratic race down to the end of time; d', d'' indicate two epochs from the creation of the Euphratic race back to the beginning of the creation of God; e, e' indicate twelve divisions or epochs from the creation of the Euphratic race down to the end of time; e', e'' indicate eight epochs from the creation of the Euphratic race back to the beginning of the creation; f, f' indicate time; f', f'' indicate the epoch from the beginning of time back to the beginning of the creation; g, g' indicate pertaining of Jethro, priest of Midian (see Diagrams 2, 3); g', g'' indicate possible pertaining of Jethro to the creative days; h, h' indicate pertaining of Moses and his two sons; h', h'' possible pertaining of Moses to the creative days.

Diagram 18 indicates the chief divisions of the grand epoch extending from the beginning of the creation down to the end of time, each of which, as allegory,

136 INDICATIONS OF THE BOOK OF EXODUS.

Ex. xviii. 13–27, considered as allegory.

DIAGRAM 18.

THE DECADE SYSTEM OF CHRONOLOGY.

Creation of a body for the Word of God in and as the very beginning of the creation of God (see Col i 13–18, Rev iii 14)

1st day — First day — Creation of light.
2nd day — Second day — Creation of the firmament.
3rd day — Third day — Creation of vegetation
4th day — Fourth day — Creation of sun, moon, and stars.
5th day — Fifth day — Creation of fishes and fowl.
6th day — Sixth day — Creation of cattle, creeping thing, and beast of the earth

The Son begotten Beginning of Time
Pre Euphratic Era divided in the midst
Creation of the Euphratic or First race (Adam's)

Dividing in the midst of the Euphratic age

Creation of the Hiddekelic or Second race

Destruction of the Euphratic race

Dividing in the midst of the Hiddekelic age.

Creation of the Gihonic or Third race.

Destruction of the Hiddekelic race

Dividing in the midst of the Gihonic age

Creation of the Pisonic or Fourth race
Antediluvian Epoch
Deluge of Noah   Destruction of the Gihonic race
Era of replenishment (see Gen ix 1)
Advent of the Messiah as the Redeemer of man
Messianic Epoch   [Jesus Christ.
Crucifixion, absolute death, and resurrection of the Messiah as
Judgmental Era
Advent of the Messiah as King of the Thousand Years' Era
Thousand Years' Era
End of the thousand years' reign.
Era of Destruction
End of Time

may be a ruler of thousands, a ruler of hundreds, a ruler of fifties, or a ruler of tens. By the ruling thus indicated, the Decade System of Chronology is brought to notice, whereby, through the numerals of scriptural text, history pertaining to the various epochs may be located and established.

Inspection of Diagram 18 will show that inasmuch as four general chronological lines are given, so the indication follows that should any epoch or chief division of any one line be considered as the ruler of a thousand, then one thousand would pertain to each chief division in that line. Should, however, any one epoch or chief division be considered the ruler of a hundred, then one hundred would pertain to and shadow each epoch or chief division of the line to which it belongs, independent of the actual years or longevity of such epochs; wherefore the same rule will apply to these epochs as rulers of fifties, and as rulers of tens.

A fractional portion of a hundred or thousand, fifty or ten, may proportionately pertain to a fractional portion of an epoch in its line (see Diagrams 8, 9), but the ruler of a hundred cannot be held as a ruler of a thousand in the solution of an allegory; for the allegoric value of an epoch once fixed by the Decade System, the same must pertain to each full epoch in that line during the particular allegoric rendering under consideration.

One piece of simple history, as allegory, can have several solutions, or one episode may contain several distinct historic rays, in which case a given epoch may, in one solution or ray, be a ruler of thousands, in another it may be a ruler of hundreds, in another it

138 *INDICATIONS OF THE BOOK OF EXODUS.*

may be a ruler of fifties, and in another a ruler of tens, so that each ray or solution have its own chronological line and its proper significance, and, also, that confusion be avoided.

Wherefore (see Diagram 18), should space 12 be given a numerical value of 1,—whether as one year, one month, one day, or one joined to some other magnitude,—then this value will pertain to each space in the line e, e', e'' for the allegoric rendering under consideration. Should any other numerical value be given to space 12, one thousand for instance, then, as before, one thousand must be given to each space or epoch throughout the line e, e', e'' to which it pertains, the same system applying to all chronological lines thus established.

A further inspection of Diagram 18 will show that the numerical harmony of the several lines of chronology is undisturbed by contact the one with the other; hence, by the relations thus existing, many historic rays converge, as it were, to given points, whereby the resulting unity of diverse labors is made manifest.

Thus the burden of Moses in his pertaining to the ages of man (see diagram 18) is divided up between rulers of thousands, rulers of hundreds, rulers of fifties, and rulers of tens; through which matters pertaining to individual ages and epochs will be brought to notice in a manner both comprehensive and simple.

The chief divisions thus indicated are not only shadowed by numerals, but (see Diagrams 2, 12, 16, 17) they are shadowed also by the sons and daughters of men, who (see Isa. viii. 18) are given " for signs and for

Ex. xix. 1-18, considered as allegory.

DIAGRAM 19.

THE JOURNEY FROM REPHIDIM TO SINAI.

Creation of a body for the Word of God in and as the very beginning of the creation of God (see Col 1 18-18, Rev iii. 14)
First day —Creation of light.
Second day —Creation of the firmament.
Third day —Creation of vegetation
Fourth day —Creation of sun, moon, and stars
Fifth day —Creation of fishes and fowl
Sixth day —Creation of cattle, creeping thing, and beast of the earth
The Son begotten Beginning of Time.
Pre-Euphratic Era
Creation of the Euphratic or First race (Adam's)
Mount Sinai as shadow

The earth in the Euphratic age

Creation of the Hiddekelic or Second race

Destruction of the Euphratic or First race

The earth in the Hiddekelic age

Creation of the Gihonic or Third race.

Destruction of the Hiddekelic or Second race

The earth in the Gihonic age.

Creation of the Pisonic or Fourth race
Mount Horeb as shadow   Allegorical stand-point of from the Deluge
Deluge of Noah as shadowed by the Red Sea   Destruction of the Gihonic or Third race

wonders in Israel from the Lord of hosts, which dwelleth in mount Zion."

XIX. 1-6. "In the third month, when the children of Israel were gone forth out of the land of Egypt, the same day came they *into* the wilderness of Sinai.

2. "For they were departed from Rephidim, and were come *to* the desert of Sinai, and had pitched in the wilderness; and there Israel camped before the mount.

3. "And Moses went up unto God, and the Lord called unto him out of the mountain, saying, Thus shalt thou say to the house of Jacob, and tell the children of Israel;

4. "Ye have seen what I did unto the Egyptians, and *how* I bare you on eagles' wings, and brought you unto myself.

5. "Now therefore, if ye will obey my voice indeed, and keep my covenant, then ye shall be a peculiar treasure unto me above all people: for all the earth *is* mine:

6. "And ye shall be unto me a kingdom of priests, and a holy nation. These *are* the words which thou shalt speak unto the children of Israel."

In Diagram 19, spaces a, a indicate the Four Ages of Man; b, b indicate the Four Ages as Sinai, Elim, Horeb, and Canaan (see Diagrams 15, 16, 17); c, c indicate the first three ages by the first three months after the departure from Egypt; d, d indicate and memorialize the first three ages by the three days' sanctification (see verses 10, 11); e, e indicate journeyings of the children of Israel in the Four Ages as the wilderness; f, f indicate time; g, g indicate pertaining of Moses;

h, h indicate pertaining of Aaron as Moses' spokesman.

The exodus of the children of Israel from Egypt shadows the exodus or bringing forth from the past ages of man (see Diagram 17) of people pertaining to these ages. The first three months' wandering of the children of Israel in the wilderness (see Diagrams 13, 14, 15, 16, 17) shadows the gathering together of these people by Moses, whereby they were safely brought through the Deluge of Noah—as shadowed by the crossing of the Red Sea—into the Pisonic or Fourth age; where, eventually, their names, iniquity, blood, and characteristics fell upon the body of the Messiah as the Son of man.

The journey thus indicated (see Diagram 17) points to the redemption of man of Adam's race. The redemption of man of Adam's race, however, comprehends but a small portion of the redemptive labors of the Messiah, the Lord having said (see verse 5) "for all the earth *is* mine;" hence redemption will extend to all the earth, lest Satan secure a partial triumph in the casting down forever of some good thing.

After the people of the past ages of man had been gathered together by Moses, and were passed through the Deluge of Noah,—whereby their redemption became assured,—indications are given (see verses 1, 2) that, by the journey from Horeb to Mount Sinai, the allegoric stand-point (see Diagram 19) is again carried into the Euphratic or First age at or about the time man of Adam's race was created. Why should the allegoric stand-point thus have been transferred? It doubtless was thus transferred that one great portion of man's mission as an instrumentality in the purpose of God might be made manifest.

The redemption of man of Adam's race was indicated by the exodus of the children of Israel from Egypt, and by the crossing of the Red Sea, whereby the names, iniquity, blood, and characteristics of those which lay in the valley of the shadow of death were transmitted to the people of the Pisonic age, and from the people of the Pisonic age they were re-transmitted to the Messiah as the Son of man.

These indications are further confirmed (see verse 4) where the statement is made, "Ye have seen what I did unto the Egyptians, and *how* I bare you on eagles' wings, and brought you unto myself;" for the Lord brought the people unto himself through the eating of the Living Bread,—which Bread came down from heaven in the day of Abraham,—whereby they were regenerated or born into, and hence were unmistakably brought unto the Lord.

The day of Abraham is in the Pisonic age; wherefore, even though the allegoric stand-point of the text is in or towards the beginning of the Euphratic age, the reference to the Pisonic or Fourth age is made manifest by the "eagles' wings" upon which the redeemed were borne unto the Lord. That the term "eagles' wings" really points to the Pisonic age is indicated in Ezek. i. 4–10; x. 8–14, 20–22; Dan. iv. 32, 33; Rev. iv. 7; vi. 7, 8.

Sinai pertains to the Euphratic age; therefore let Mount Sinai be established (see Diagram 19) upon the line that separates man of Adam's race from the Pre-Euphratic era,—for man of Adam's race as an actual existence does not extend beyond this line,—when the indication arises that the commands of the Lord as given from Mount Sinai will pertain to the whole human family, or to man of Adam's race generally.

What are the commands of the Lord as given at this time? They are these (see verses 5, 6), "Now therefore, if ye will obey my voice indeed, and keep my covenant, then ye shall be a peculiar treasure unto me above all people: for all the earth *is* mine:

"And ye shall be unto me a kingdom of priests, and a holy nation. These *are* the words which thou shalt speak unto the children of Israel."

The plan of the redemption of man of Adam's race having been made manifest in the eating of the Living Bread that came down from heaven, by which the spirit of man is regenerated or born into the Living Bread, so man of Adam's race, after such regeneration, becomes fitted as a priest, as a kingdom of priests, and as a holy nation unto the Lord.

Of what value to the Lord is such a kingdom of priests? The value of such a kingdom lies in the conditions expressed by the great Law of Iniquity. By this Law names, iniquity, blood, and characteristics are transmitted from generation to generation until they shall fall upon the body of the Messiah as the Redeemer,—not the Redeemer of man of Adam's race only, but as the Redeemer of and for the creature world, both heavenly and earthly, animate and inanimate.

For the Redeemer a pure unblemishable body was created in and as the very beginning of the creation of God; later, the earth or matter otherwise was created;

INDICATIONS OF THE BOOK OF EXODUS. 143

and later still the spirit of the living creature (host not being considered) was born into the earthy body.

The body that was created for the Word of God or the Redeemer, in and as the very beginning of the creation of God, is as perfectly fitted for a habitation of the living creature as the earthy body is fitted for a habitation of the living creature; nay (see Col. i. 18), even more so; for pre-eminence in all things gives pre-eminence in this also. But, that all hosts may be proved as to who alone can order, govern, subdue, protect, provide, and deliver, that none suffer or go hungry, the living creature was born into the earthy or natural body at the first. The general failure of the creature world as a governing element is witnessed by the general tribulation besetting the creature; hence were no redemption or regeneration provided, the individual excellence of an intelligence could never rise above tribulation or reach perfection.

Redemption and regeneration, however, have been provided for, in that the spirit of the living creature can be transferred from the earthy body, with which it was clothed in the day it was brought forth, into the pure unblemishable body that was created for the Word of God in and as the very beginning of the creation of God; hence the excellence of the creature intelligence can and does reach perfection through the redemption and regeneration thus provided.

It is stated (St. John vi. 53–57), "Then Jesus said unto them, Verily, verily, I say unto you, Except ye eat the flesh of the Son of man, and drink his blood, ye have no life in you.

"Whoso eateth my flesh, and drinketh my blood,

hath eternal life; and I will raise him up at the last day.

"For my flesh is meat indeed, and my blood is drink indeed.

"He that eateth my flesh, and drinketh my blood, dwelleth in me, and I in him.

"As the living Father hath sent me, and I live by the Father; so he that eateth me, even he shall live by me;" hence, by the eating of the body that was created for the Word of God in the beginning of the creation of God, the spirit of the eater dwells in it, or is regenerated or born into it, and thus becomes holy.

In this light, therefore, through regeneration, man of Adam's race becomes a holy nation unto the Lord; and inasmuch (see Gen. xii. 1–7; xiii. 14–17) as the promise is made to Abraham, and to the seed of Abraham, so the choosing of man of Adam's race as a kingdom of priests is indicated, in that (see Gen. xiv. 18–20; Ex. xxix. 32, 33; St. Mark xiv. 22; St. Matt. xv. 21–28) they partake of the body of the Redeemer in a direct manner, thereby becoming temples of the Lord's body.

Through the institution of the kingdom of the priests thus indicated a system of indirect regeneration for the creature world becomes manifest that will reach "unto the utmost bound of the everlasting hills;" for (see xxix. 33) "they shall eat those things wherewith the atonement was made, to consecrate *and* to sanctify them."

Thus the command of the Lord that was given to the children of Israel from the top of Sinai will, through the children of Israel as a kingdom of priests, and a holy nation, reach to the great beyond of man of Adam's race; wherefore (see Diagram 19), when Moses shall return again to Horeb he will bear with him (see x. 26) the rich fruits that pertain to the six creative days.

When the command of the Lord was given from Sinai that the children of Israel should be a peculiar treasure to the Lord above all people, and that they should be a kingdom of priests, and a holy nation unto the Lord, the condition was imposed that, to enter into these promises, they should keep the Lord's covenant. Wherefore, had the Word of God as the begotten Son not been present, had not the Son as the first-born among many brethren been present (see Diagram 19), then these promises would have fallen to the ground as valueless edicts because of the general failure of man of Adam's race. But through the presence of the Son as the first-born among many brethren, and through his actual participation in the involved labors, the promises became sealed to the people through his fulfilment of God's covenant; hence the priesthood of man is openly confirmed at the Last Supper (see St. Mark xiv. 22), when "Jesus took bread, and blessed, and brake *it*, and gave to them, and said, Take, eat; this is my body."

Through the ministrations of the priesthood of Melchizedek man becomes the temple of the body that was created for the Word of God in the beginning of the creation of God in a direct manner,—Jesus having been made a priest forever after the order of Melchizedek; whence it follows (see xxix. 32, 33) that as Aaron and his sons shall eat those things wherewith the atonement was made, but that a stranger shall not eat thereof, and as (see St. Matt. xv. 22–28) the daughter of the woman of Canaan was healed,—although the children's bread, evidently, was not sent directly to such,—that regeneration finds fulfilment also in an indirect manner, even as the crumbs are eaten that fall from the master's table. Indirect regeneration, therefore, as already indicated, can find fulfilment through man of Adam's race as a priesthood, and as a holy nation; hence the universal preying of the animal kingdoms, the one upon the other, becomes filled with a wonderful import that finds expression in the priesthood of man.

XIX. 7, 8. "And Moses came and called for the elders of the people, and laid before their faces all these words which the Lord commanded him.

8. "And all the people answered together, and said, All that the Lord hath spoken we will do. And Moses returned the words of the people unto the Lord."

Thus the people signified their willingness to accept the covenant of the Lord.

XIX. 10–13. "And the Lord said unto Moses, Go unto the people, and sanctify them to day and to morrow, and let them wash their clothes,

11. "And be ready against the third day: for the third day the Lord will come down in the sight of all the people upon mount Sinai.

12. "And thou shalt set bounds unto the people round about, saying, Take heed to yourselves, *that ye go not* up into the mount, or touch the border of it: whosoever toucheth the mount shall be surely put to death:

13. "There shall not a hand touch it, but he shall

surely be stoned, or shot through; whether *it be* beast or man, it shall not live: when the trumpet soundeth long, they shall come up to the mount."

The extreme sacredness of Mount Sinai is indicated by the above verses, so that if beast or man but touch it they shall surely die. From this mount came forth the First Covenant or Law, and hence, from the sacredness of the mount, the sacredness of the First Covenant, and the irrevocability of the penalty which follows the breaking of this covenant, is indicated. The standpoint of the text, as shadowed by the third month after the departure of the children of Israel from Egypt, is in the Euphratic age, while the three days' sanctification memorializes the first three ages, wherefore the covenant of the Lord from Sinai becomes a manifest vital ruling from the first creation of man of Adam's race, and not from the day of Moses only. The existence of the covenant before the day of Moses is clearly indicated (Rom. v. 13, 14), " For until the law sin was in the world: but sin is not imputed when there is no law.

" Nevertheless death reigned from Adam to Moses." If death reigned from Adam to Moses, it certainly follows that sin was imputed from the Adam of the Euphratic race, and if sin was imputed at that time, then the First Covenant or Law must have entered at or about the time this Adam was created. Hence the First Covenant or Law must have been in force before the simple history of the exodus was recorded; and, if it was in force before the exodus was recorded, then, inasmuch as "death reigned from Adam to Moses," it must have been made with the whole house of Adam (see Diagrams 13, 15, 16), whatever bearings it may have had upon other hosts.

The covenant from Sinai (see Gal. iv. 24) "gendereth to bondage," for the righteousness of the hearers (see verses 7, 8) depends upon their own strength; but the history of man shows clearly enough that they were altogether too weak to resist the aggressive evil which reared itself against them.

In the light (see Gal. iv. 24) that Sinai represents the First Covenant or Law,—then the charge (xix. 12, 13), "Take heed to yourselves, *that ye go not* up into the mount, or touch the border of it: whosoever toucheth the mount shall be surely put to death:

"There shall not a hand touch it, but he shall surely be stoned, or shot through; whether *it be* beast or man, it shall not live," is given also to the Adversary and his host, and to all hosts pertaining to the Pre-Euphratic era. This charge, however, was unheeded by the Adversary; for he disregarded the sacredness of Sinai as the Law, he tempted and caused the fall of man, as recorded in Gen. iii., while the only-begotten Son, the First-born himself, suffered the extremes of tribulation, suffering, and even death (see Isa. liii.; I. Kings xxi. 1–16) at his hands.

XIX. 21–25. "And the Lord said unto Moses, Go down, charge the people, lest they break through unto the Lord to gaze, and many of them perish.

22. "And let the priests also, which come near to the Lord, sanctify themselves, lest the Lord break forth upon them.

23. "And Moses said unto the Lord, The people

cannot come up to mount Sinai: for thou chargedst us, saying, Set bounds about the mount, and sanctify it.

24. "And the Lord said unto him, Away, get thee down, and thou shalt come up, thou, and Aaron with thee: but let not the priests and the people break through to come up unto the Lord, lest he break forth upon them.

25. "So Moses went down unto the people, and spake unto them."

This charge seems to relate to man immediately after the fall, at which time (see Gen. iii. 24) he was driven out of Eden; while a flaming sword, which turned every way, was placed there to keep the way of the Tree of Life; for not only man, but the whole host of evil sought the fruit of this Tree that the bounds of time might be removed.

In the light (see Gal. iv. 25) that Sinai bears upon the whole House of Man, then the bounds set about it indicate the limits of the Four Ages into which time is divided. Should, however, the people break through these bounds and partake of the Tree of Life, time would become limitless, and the people would be united forever to a kingdom abounding with pain and tribulations of all kinds; hence the Tree of Life is guarded with great care. It is not unlikely, however, but that some protection was thrown around the Tree of Life from the beginning (see Deut. xxxiii. 8), lest man should, at the first, partake of the fruit thereof and thus live forever. Should man, at the first, partake of the Tree of Life, and then eat of the Tree of the Knowledge of Good and Evil, the plan for the overthrow of Evil would be vitiated, if not made altogether void. Why? Because sin was in the world (see Rom.

150 INDICATIONS OF THE BOOK OF EXODUS.

v. 13) until the law,—but sin was not imputed when there is no law,—and the Law entered that the offence might abound; hence through the offence sin is imputed, and where sin is imputed death reigns. Should, therefore, man first partake of the Tree of Life, then, notwithstanding the offence, death could not reign over the transgressor; hence sin would become established forever, unless some destructive element other than death was brought forth to overwhelm it. The text becomes evidence that the great mission of Lucifer, the destroying angel, is the absolute destruction of the Kingdom of Evil; hence the bringing forth of so powerful a creature by the creative Power; hence again (I. Cor. xv. 26), "The last enemy *that* shall be destroyed *is* death;" and also, as indicated in Ezek. xxviii. 18, 19, Death shall be destroyed by his own attribute; for the decree recorded in Ezek. xxviii. 18, 19, "Therefore will I bring forth a fire from the midst of thee, it shall devour thee, and I will bring thee to ashes upon the earth in the sight of all them that behold thee.

"All they that know thee among the people shall be astonished at thee; thou shalt be a terror, and never *shalt* thou *be* any more," almost unquestionably stands against Lucifer (see Isa. xiv. 3-23) as the angel Death.

Of the two charges given Moses from the top of Sinai (see verses 11-13, 21-25), one may pertain to man of Adam's race (see situation of Mount Sinai, Diagram 19), and the other to the dwellers of the Pre-Euphratic era; hence, by these charges, hosts other than man of Adam's race are brought under the ruling of the commands and statutes given from Sinai.

INDICATIONS OF THE BOOK OF EXODUS. 151

XX. 4, 5. "Thou shalt not make unto thee any graven image, or any likeness *of any thing* that *is* in heaven above, or that *is* in the earth beneath, or that *is* in the water under the earth :

5. "Thou shalt not bow down thyself to them, nor serve them : for I the Lord thy God *am* a jealous God, visiting the iniquity of the fathers upon the children unto the third and fourth *generation* of them that hate me."

In these verses the great Law of Iniquity is given forth, through the operation of which the debt of the fathers will be transmitted from the fathers upon the children unto the third and fourth generation. Three of these generations are under the veil, and they indicate the first three ages of man, while the fourth generation indicates the Fourth age. The descent of iniquity indicates the activity of the Ten Commandments from the First age (see Diagram 19), and, doubtless, they form a portion of the instructions given the fathers of the various races of men in the days of their creations, under the name of the Tree of the Knowledge of Good and Evil.

XXI., XXII., XXIII. These chapters contain various laws and ordinances for the government of the children of Israel, thereby defining the Tree of the Knowledge of Good and Evil. They may, to a certain extent, also be considered as an analysis of the Ten Commandments. In this form, as simple history pertaining to the Pisonic age, they were given forth and made with the children of Israel after the exodus, as stated in Deut. v. 2, 3, "The Lord our God made a covenant with us in Horeb.

" The Lord made not this covenant with our fathers,

but with us, *even* us, who *are* all of us here alive this day." The Ten Commandments, however, were issued before this particular version of the covenant was made and defined, even as indicated in Deut. v. 22, " These words the Lord spake unto all your assembly in the mount out of the midst of the fire, of the cloud, and of the thick darkness, with a great voice; and he added no more. And he wrote them in two tables of stone, and delivered them unto me." After these words—doubtless the Ten Commandments—had been spoken by the Lord, and which the people heard from Sinai, the covenant in Horeb was made and delivered through Moses; for the children of Israel feared the voice of the Lord; from which it follows (see Diagram 19) that although this covenant was made with the children of Israel after the exodus, the Ten Commandments do not, of necessity, take their rise from that time. Moreover (see **xx.** 18–20), the Ten Commandments were given forth that by them the people might be proved, and that they sin not. The people were proved (see Diagram 13) at Marah, they were proved (see Diagram 15) at the wilderness of Sin, and they were proved (see Diagram 16) at Meribah, whence the indication becomes marked that the Ten Commandments embodied the Law that was established with each of the four races of men in the day of their creation.

XXIV. 1–8. "And he said unto Moses, Come up unto the Lord, thou, and Aaron, Nadab, and Abihu, and seventy of the elders of Israel; and worship ye afar off.

2. "And Moses alone shall come near the Lord:

DIAGRAM 20.

THE BLOOD OF SPRINKLING.

Creation of a body for the Word of God as the very beginning of the creation of God (see Col 1 13-18, Rev iii. 14)
First day —Creation of light
Second day —Creation of the firmament
Third day —Creation of vegetation.
Fourth day —Creation of sun, moon, and stars
Fifth day —Creation of fishes and fowl
Sixth day —Creation of cattle, creeping thing, and beast of the earth
The Son begotten   Beginning of Time
Pre-Euphratic Era
Creation of the Euphratic or First race (Adam's)
Mount Sinai as shadow

The earth in the Euphratic age.

Creation of the Hiddekelic or Second race

Destruction of the Euphratic or First race

The earth in the Hiddekelic age

Creation of the Gihonic or Third race.

Destruction of the Hiddekelic or Second race

The earth in the Gihonic age.

Creation of the Pisonic or Fourth race
Mount Horeb as shadow   Allegorical stand-point as from the Deluge
Deluge of Noah as shadowed by the Red Sea   Destruction of the Gihonic or Third race
Epoch of replenishment (see Gen ix 1)
Advent of the Messiah as the Redeemer of man
The exodus as shadow   The Red Sea as shadowing the Deluge
Simple historical stand point as from the Red Sea
The earth in the Pisonic age   Crucifixion, absolute death, and resurrection of the Messiah as Jesus Christ
Judgmental Era.

Thousand Years' Era
Era of Destruction
End of Time

but they shall not come nigh; neither shall the people go up with him.

3. "And Moses came and told the people all the words of the Lord, and all the judgments: and all the people answered with one voice, and said, All the words which the Lord hath said will we do.

4. "And Moses wrote all the words of the Lord, and rose up early in the morning, and builded an altar under the hill, and twelve pillars, according to the twelve tribes of Israel.

5. "And he sent young men of the children of Israel, which offered burnt offerings, and sacrificed peace offerings of oxen unto the Lord.

6. "And Moses took half of the blood, and put *it* in basins; and half of the blood he sprinkled on the altar.

7. "And he took the book of the covenant, and read in the audience of the people: and they said, All that the Lord hath said will we do, and be obedient.

8. "And Moses took the blood, and sprinkled *it* on the people, and said, Behold the blood of the covenant, which the Lord hath made with you concerning all these words."

In Diagram 20, spaces a, a indicate the Four Ages of Man; b, b indicate the Four Ages as Sinai, Elim, Horeb, and Canaan; c, c indicate pertainings of the seventy elders of Israel to the first seven semidivisions of the Four Ages (Decade System); d, d indicate pertainings of Moses, Aaron, Nadab, and Abihu to the four chief divisions of the Euphratic age; e, e indicate appertainings of the twelve tribes of Israel to the Four Ages (see Ezek. xlviii. 30-34), and also the pertaining of the twelve pillars, as memorials of the twelve tribes, to the Four Ages; f, f indicate time; g, g indicate pertaining of Moses to the first three ages of man.

By Diagram 20, spaces d, d (see, also, verse 2), Moses has a special pertaining to the first portion of the Pre-Euphratic era; Aaron has a special pertaining to the second portion of the Pre-Euphratic era; Nadab and Abihu pertain to the two divisions of the Euphratic age from the creation of man of Adam's race, while Sinai is indicative of the Euphratic age; hence the allegoric stand-point is in the Euphratic age.

The altar under the hill shadows the earth during the Four Ages, the twelve pillars very probably shadow the appertainings of the twelve tribes of Israel to the Four Ages as a kingdom of priests, upon which the earth is borne up; as, therefore, burnt-offerings and sacrifice of peace-offerings were offered upon the altar constructed by Moses, so, through these ministrations, as shadows, the labors and tribulations that shall develop and pertain to the Four Ages of Man are indicated.

Of the blood of the sacrifice one-half was sprinkled on the altar. In the light, therefore, that the altar shadows the earth,—the four sides of the altar shadowing the Four Ages,—then the blood sprinkled upon it becomes a memorial and witness in the earth that this blood was violently shed through some direct or indirect cause.

The blood that Moses sprinkled upon the people doubtless was the half that remained of the sacrifice. Why should the people thus have been sprinkled with the blood of the sacrifice? The indications are that it was to make the mission of man as a kingdom of priests and a holy nation (see xix. 3–6) steadfast and

INDICATIONS OF THE BOOK OF EXODUS 155

sure in the eyes of all hosts; for this blood or life (see Gen. ix. 4–6) will be required.

As, therefore, the blood of the sacrifice fell upon the people as a kingdom of priests and a holy nation, so, through the ministrations of the people as a kingdom of priests and a holy nation, regeneration may, at some time, pertain to the creature whose blood (see Heb. ix. 25) rested upon them.

If (see xxix. 32, 33) Aaron and his sons shall eat those things wherewith atonement was made to consecrate and to sanctify them, then the indication follows that after man, as a kingdom of priests and a holy nation, shall have eaten of the Lord's body, or the body that was created for the Word in the beginning of the creation of God, that regeneration will, through some prescribed channel, fall to the creature that has been so consecrated and sanctified; for (see Heb. ix. 11, 12) "Christ being come a high priest of good things to come, by a greater and more perfect tabernacle, . . . having obtained eternal redemption *for us.*" The redemption of man, therefore, must obtain through the great and perfect tabernacle that was prepared for Christ the Word of God in and as the very beginning of the creation of God, whereby the imperfect or earthy body will be left behind forever. From this position indications follow that, as with man, the spirit of the creature world is transferred from the earthy body, and is regenerated or born into the pure unblemishable body that was created and prepared for Christ as the Word of God, and hence that, after regeneration, their redemption (see Heb. x. 20) is made sure by the blood of Christ when he gave his life (see St. John iii. 16, 17) for the life of the world.

Indications further follow (see Eph. ii. 11-22; Col. ii. 15-19) that Christ, in the pure unblemishable body that was prepared for him, really is "the Head, from which all the body by joints and bands having nourishment ministered, and knit together, increaseth with the increase of God." As, therefore, the creature world is regenerated or born into the body that was created for the Word of God in and as the very beginning of the creation of God,—which body is entirely suitable for the purpose,—so "all the building fitly framed together groweth unto a holy temple in the Lord," and thus "increaseth with the increase of God."

XXIV. 16. "And the glory of the Lord abode upon mount Sinai, and the cloud covered it six days: and the seventh day he called unto Moses out of the midst of the cloud."

The six days during which the cloud rested upon Mount Sinai memorialize the six semidivisions of the three ages under the veil, and the seventh day indicates the epoch—viz., the first half of the Fourth age—in which the Messiah came forth for the redemption (see Heb. ix. 14, 15) of the transgressions that were under the First or Old Testament.

XXV. 10-22. "And they shall make an ark *of* shittim wood: two cubits and a half *shall be* the length thereof, and a cubit and a half the breadth thereof, and a cubit and a half the height thereof.

11. "And thou shalt overlay it with pure gold, within and without shalt thou overlay it, and shalt make upon it a crown of gold round about.

12. "And thou shalt cast four rings of gold for it,

INDICATIONS OF THE BOOK OF EXODUS. 157

and put *them* in the four corners thereof; and two rings *shall be* in the one side of it, and two rings in the other side of it.

13. "And thou shalt make staves *of* shittim wood, and overlay them with gold.

14. "And thou shalt put the staves into the rings by the sides of the ark, that the ark may be borne with them.

15. "The staves shall be in the rings of the ark: they shall not be taken from it.

16. "And thou shalt put into the ark the testimony which I shall give thee.

17. "And thou shalt make a mercy seat *of* pure gold: two cubits and a half *shall be* the length thereof, and a cubit and a half the breadth thereof.

18. "And thou shalt make two cherubim *of* gold, *of* beaten work shalt thou make them, in the two ends of the mercy seat.

19. "And make one cherub on the one end, and the other cherub on the other end: *even* of the mercy seat shall ye make the cherubim on the two ends thereof.

20. "And the cherubim shall stretch forth *their* wings on high, covering the mercy seat with their wings, and their faces *shall look* one to another; toward the mercy seat shall the faces of the cherubim be.

21. "And thou shalt put the mercy seat above upon the ark; and in the ark thou shalt put the testimony that I shall give thee.

22. "And there I will meet with thee, and I will commune with thee from above the mercy seat, from between the two cherubim which *are* upon the ark of

the testimony, of all *things* which I will give thee in commandment unto the children of Israel."

In Diagram 21, spaces *a, a* indicate the Four Ages of Man; *b, b* indicate the Four Ages as Sinai, Elim, Horeb, and Canaan; *c, c* indicate the first seven semi-divisions of the Four Ages by the seven days (see xxiv. 15, 16) the cloud rested upon Mount Sinai; *d, d* indicate the first three ages by the three half-cubits' breadth of the Ark of the Covenant; *e, e* indicate time; *f, f* indicate and comprehend the time, or times, in which the Law entered in for the government of all hosts; *g, g* indicate pertaining of the Ark of the Covenant to time as comprehending the issue of the Law; *h, h*, as the two staves, indicate and shadow the presence of the two Faithful Witnesses.

By Diagram 21, spaces *d, d*, the three half-cubits' breadth of the Ark pertain to the first three ages of man. During the days of these ages—the Gihonic or third, ending with the Deluge of Noah—four consecutive races of men were created by the Almighty Power, and given place and mission. These four races constitute the human family, or man of Adam's race; and, with the advent of each race, the Law entered that they might be proved in regard to their fitness as subjugators, providers, protectors, and rulers; hence the Ark of the Covenant takes up and shadows (see Heb. viii. 4, 5) conditions pertaining to the calling and mission of man.

In the beginning of the Euphratic age (see Diagram 21) the Son was begotten, and (see Lev. xxvii.; Rev. xii.) with the begetting of the Son time begins. The Son (see Rom. viii. 29; Gen. i. 26, 27; Rev. xii. 1–5, 17) is the first-born among many brethren; wherefore,

INDICATIONS OF THE BOOK OF EXODUS 159

Ex. xxv 10-22, considered as allegory.

DIAGRAM 21.

THE ARK OF THE COVENANT.

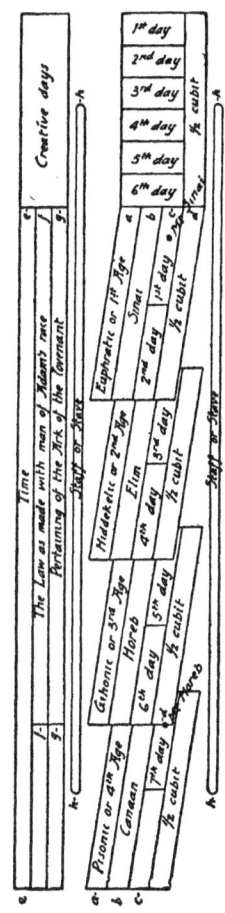

Creation of a body for the Word of God as the very beginning of the creation of God (see Col 1 13-18, Rev iii 14)
First day —Creation of light
Second day —Creation of the firmament
Third day —Creation of vegetation.
Fourth day —Creation of sun, moon, and stars
Fifth day —Creation of fishes and fowl
Sixth day —Creation of cattle, creeping thing, and beast of the earth
The Son begotten   Beginning of Time
Pre-Euphratic Era
Creation of the Euphratic or First race (Adam's)
The Law enters in to the Euphratic race (see Diagram 13)
Dividing in the midst of the Euphratic age.

Creation of the Hiddekelic or Second race   The Law enters in to the Hiddekelic race (see Diagram 15)
Destruction of the Euphratic or First race

Dividing in the midst of the Hiddekelic age.

Creation of the Gihonic or Third race. The Law enters in to the Gihonic race (see Diagram 16)
Destruction of the Hiddekelic or Second race

Dividing in the midst of the Gihonic age

Creation of the Pisonic or Fourth race   The Law enters in to the Pisonic race (see Gen ii 10-17)
Deluge of Noah   Destruction of the Gihonic or Third race
Epoch of replenishment (see Gen ix 1)
Advent of the Messiah as the Son of man in the day of Abraham
Messianic Epoch
Dividing in the midst of the Pisonic age   Crucifixion, absolute death, and resurrection of the Messiah as Jesus Christ.
Judgmental Era
Thousand Years' Era.
Era of Destruction
End of Time.

as the Law is over the brethren, so the Law is over the first-born also, and he must come under the ruling thereof.

The presence of the begotten Son in the various ages of man is indicated by the staves upon which the Ark and all its precious appointments are borne; hence (see verse 15), as these staves shall not be removed from their assigned places, so (see Diagram 21) the Son cannot be taken from under the Law that entered in for the government of all hosts (see, also, Rev. xi. 3, 4).

In the light that the staves shadow the two Faithful Witnesses, then the Ark itself may shadow man of Adam's race as a holy nation; and if a holy nation, then (see xix. 3–6) as a kingdom of priests also, by which—gold within, gold without, and a golden crown to grace all—the instrumentality of man in the ministration of the pure, unblemishable body of the Messiah is made manifest.

To whom shall the kingdom of priests thus indicated minister? They doubtless shall minister, either directly or indirectly, to the hosts of creatures that pertain to the six creative days; for, in conformity with values already assigned (see Diagrams 18, 21), let the creative days be represented by a half-cubit, and let the Pisonic age be represented by a half-cubit, when the grand epoch from the beginning of the creation of God unto the end of time will be represented by five half-cubits. The length of the Ark is just five half-cubits; wherefore, by five half-cubits of length, and by five half-cubits of breadth, a perfect square is shadowed or brought to notice that indicates a perfect unit of labor as established upon it as a base.

INDICATIONS OF THE BOOK OF EXODUS. 161

The Mercy-seat is five half-cubits in length and three half-cubits in breadth, and is placed above upon the Ark; hence it pertains in a particular manner to the same periods of time as the Ark itself. But, however, that the mercy of the Lord may reach to all, the staves (see I. Kings viii. 7-9) can be and are drawn out (see, also, Diagram 21), by which the labors of the two Faithful Witnesses—of whom (see Rev. i. 5) Jesus Christ the Messiah is one—will reach from the beginning of the creation of God unto the end of time.

The pertaining of the Mercy-seat further points to the priesthood of man; for, through the revealed or manifest ministrations of the priesthood of Melchizedek (see Gen. xiv. 18-20; St. Mark xiv. 22), man of Adam's race is a direct partaker of the "hidden manna," the Living Bread that came down from heaven, whereby he becomes the temple of the "hidden manna," or Living Bread, and hence, as such, is priest and minister of holy things; hence, again, through man as a kingdom of priests the "hidden manna" may be partaken of by other hosts than man of Adam's race, that redemption may fall to them as well as to those who first fell asleep in the valley of the shadow of death, yet after the manner of Christ, who said (see St. Mark xiv. 22), "Take, eat; this is my body."

Sketch B indicates the relative positions of the Ark of the Covenant, the Mercy-seat, and the two cherubim. As a shadow of heavenly things they symbolize the Trinity in the labors for the overthrow of Evil and for the redemption of the fallen. By it the visible manifestation of two Persons of the Trinity is indicated; but the Father, whom no man hath seen at any time, dwells between the cherubim, an invisible, all-powerful God.

Since, by the death of the Saviour Jesus Christ, the First Covenant is made old, the figure further indicates that the way into the holiest is free to all through his blood, and that Jesus stands there ready and willing to receive all who may come unto him, and to appear in the presence of God to make intercession for them. Behold the empty Mercy-seat; behold the attitude of blessing; behold the mute, the powerful, appeal for all to come and " enter into the holiest by the blood of Jesus"! By the figure, Jesus Christ is waiting. Who will come?

Sketch B.

The Ark of the Covenant.

XXV. 23-30. "Thou shalt also make a table *of* shittim wood : two cubits *shall be* the length thereof, and a cubit the breadth thereof, and a cubit and a half the height thereof.

24. "And thou shalt overlay it with pure gold, and make thereto a crown of gold round about.

25. "And thou shalt make unto it a border of a handbreadth round about, and thou shalt make a golden crown to the border thereof round about.

26. "And thou shalt make for it four rings of gold,

INDICATIONS OF THE BOOK OF EXODUS 163

and put the rings in the four corners that *are* on the four feet thereof.

27. "Over against the border shall the rings be for places of the staves to bear the table.

28. "And thou shalt make the staves *of* shittim wood, and overlay them with gold, that the table may be borne with them.

29. "And thou shalt make the dishes thereof, and spoons thereof, and covers thereof, and bowls thereof, to cover withal: *of* pure gold shalt thou make them.

30. "And thou shalt set upon the table shewbread before me always."

In Diagram 22, spaces a, a indicate the Four Ages of Man; b, b indicate the Four Ages as Sinai, Elim, Horeb, and Canaan; $c, c,$ by half-cubits, indicate pertaining of table for shewbread to the Hiddekelic and Gihonic ages; d, d (see, also, Diagram 18) indicate twelve chief divisions of the Four Ages in two sets of six each; e, e indicate time; f, f indicate pertaining of table for shewbread to time; g, g indicate pertaining of the two staves as the two Faithful Witnesses.

The table for shewbread is one cubit in breadth and two cubits in length; therefore let the chronological system applied to the Ark of the Covenant be applied to the table for shewbread, when it will be found (see Diagram 22) that one half-cubit will pertain to the Hiddekelic age and one half-cubit to the Gihonic age.

The staves upon which the table is borne doubtless project, even as those of the Ark projected, and hence, should they be drawn out they would reach from the beginning of the Euphratic age down to the end of the Pisonic age, and thus would cover time from the be-

164 INDICATIONS OF THE BOOK OF EXODUS.

Ex. xxv. 23–30, considered as allegory.

DIAGRAM 22.

THE TABLE FOR SHEWBREAD.

Creation of a body for the Word of God as the very beginning of the creation of God (see Col i. 13–18, Rev iii 14)

1st day — First day —Creation of light   Creation of the earthy.

2nd day — Second day —Creation of the firmament

3rd day — Third day —Creation of vegetation.

4th day — Fourth day —Creation of sun, moon, and stars.

5th day — Fifth day —Creation of fishes and fowl.

6th day — Sixth day —Creation of cattle, creeping thing, and beast of the earth. The Word of God invests the body that was created for the Word of God in the beginning, thereby endowing it with life, and so the Word becomes the begotten Son of God   The body thus invested with life is, with little or no doubt, the Living Bread that shall be eaten (see St John vi 51–56) that, by the eating thereof, the creature world may be regenerated or born into it, and thus through regeneration, have eternal life   The begetting of the Son marks the beginning of Time
Creation of the Euphratic or First race (Adam's)
First Grand Division of Time

Creation of the Hiddekelic or Second race

Destruction of the Euphratic or First race.

Second Grand Division of Time

Creation of the Gihonic or Third race

Destruction of the Hiddekelic or Second race

Third Grand Division of Time.

Creation of the Pisonic or Fourth race
Allegorical stand-point as from the Deluge.
Deluge of Noah   Destruction of the Gihonic or Third race.
Epoch of replenishment (see Gen ix 1)
Advent of the Messiah as the Son of man in the day of Abraham
Simple historical stand point as from the Red Sea
Messianic Epoch
Fourth Grand Division of Time   Crucifixion, absolute death, and resurrection of the Messiah as Jesus Christ
Judgmental Era.
Thousand Years' Era.
Era of Destruction
End of Time.

ginning to the end. The two staves doubtless indicate the two Faithful Witnesses.

Further, the table is two cubits, or four half-cubits, in length; wherefore,—in conformity with the chronological system set forth by Diagram 18 (see, also, Diagram 21),—let the Euphratic age be represented by a half-cubit, and let the Pisonic age be represented by a half-cubit, when it will be seen that the table for shewbread, together with the staves thereof, point to a perfect square, which, as in the case of the Ark of the Covenant, indicates a perfect unit of labor as established upon it as a base.

The perfect square thus shadowed is further indicated by the cakes of shewbread, twelve in number (see Lev. xxiv. 5, 6), that shall be set upon it. The shewbread is placed in two rows, six in each row; hence they memorialize the twelve chief divisions of time (see Diagram 22, spaces d, d) as in two sets of six each.

What is the unit of labor shadowed by this square, or to what does it relate? The indications are that it relates to the body of the Son of God, as the Living Bread, from the begetting of the Son unto the end of time. The labor involved is the regeneration of the creature world, whereby, through regeneration, or by being born again, the creature world is made partaker of the eternal life that pertains to the body created for the Word of God.

XXV. 31–37. " And thou shalt make a candlestick *of* pure gold : *of* beaten work shall the candlestick be made : his shaft, and his branches, his bowls, his knops, and his flowers, shall be of the same.

32. " And six branches shall come out of the sides

of it; three branches of the candlestick out of the one side, and three branches of the candlestick out of the other side:

33. "Three bowls made like unto almonds, *with* a knop and a flower in one branch; and three bowls made like almonds in the other branch, *with* a knop and a flower: so in the six branches that come out of the candlestick.

34. "And in the candlestick *shall be* four bowls made like unto almonds, *with* their knops and their flowers.

35. "And *there shall be* a knop under two branches of the same, and a knop under two branches of the same, and a knop under two branches of the same, according to the six branches that proceed out of the candlestick.

36. "Their knops and their branches shall be of the same: all of it *shall be* one beaten work *of* pure gold.

37. "And thou shalt make the seven lamps thereof: and they shall light the lamps thereof, that they may give light over against it."

SKETCH C.
The Golden Candlestick

In the candlestick (see Sketch C) the four bowls, which are upon the top of the shaft, indicate the Four Ages of Man during which the labors of the two Faithful Witnesses were continued (see Diagrams 21, 22) for the overthrow of Evil and for the redemption of the fallen. The seven lamps within the four bowls indicate the first seven semidivisions of time, or of the Four Ages, throughout which the First Covenant was the ruling principle for the government of all hosts. The three branches on the one side, and the three branches on the other side, indicate the two Faithful Witnesses,—in whom dwelleth all the fulness of the Godhead bodily,—and, doubtless, they are those indicated in Zech. iv. 12-14, as follows: "What *be these* two olive branches, which through the two golden pipes empty the golden *oil* out of themselves? . . .

"Then said he, These *are* the two anointed ones, that stand by the Lord of the whole earth;" and, doubtless, they are those indicated in Rev. xi. 3, 4, "And I will give *power* unto my two witnesses, and they shall prophesy a thousand two hundred *and* threescore days, clothed in sackcloth.

"These are the two olive trees, and the two candlesticks standing before the God of the earth." The divine character and triune fulness of these two are indicated by the three branches, by the three bowls with their knops, and by the three knops joined in one at the point where the olive branches empty the golden oil out of themselves into the two golden pipes.

By the shadow the oil is poured into the bowls which are upon the ends of the branches, flowing from thence through the branches and golden pipes into the shaft of the candlestick, where it rises up, thus abundantly supplying the lamps that the light may shine over against them; but by the substance, the labors emanate

168 INDICATIONS OF THE BOOK OF EXODUS.

from the Three Persons of the Trinity who are represented in shadow by the branches which supply the candlestick with oil.

The four almond-shaped bowls on the candlestick (see Sketch D) unite with knops or bulb-like protuberances and form a beautiful flower with four petals, which, as already stated, indicated the Four Ages of Man: in a similar manner the three bowls of a branch unite and form a flower with three petals; which is indicative of the Trinity.

SKETCH D.

SKETCH E.

The shaft of the candlestick, very probably, is a square column admitting of four distinctive knops; a knop to each bowl. The base, as constructed, is indicative of the fruit of the involved labors as shadowed in Ezek. xlvii. 1-9.

Sketch E indicates three knops in one by which a knop is found under any two branches of their respective groups.

In Diagram 23, spaces a, a indicate the Four Ages of Man; b, b indicate the Four Ages as Sinai, Elim, Horeb, and Canaan; c, c indicate the Four Ages by the four bowls of the golden candlestick; d, d indicate the first seven semidivisions of the Four Ages by the seven lamps of the golden candlestick; e, e indicate the two Faithful Witnesses by the two sets of branches of the golden candlestick.

The golden candlestick constructed by Moses (see Sketch C) is (see Heb. vii. 5) a shadow of heavenly things; hence through this candlestick heavenly things

INDICATIONS OF THE BOOK OF EXODUS. 169

Ex xxv. 31-37, considered as allegory.

DIAGRAM 23.

THE GOLDEN CANDLESTICK.

Creation of a body for the Word of God as the very beginning of the creation of God (see Col. i 13-18, Rev. iii 14)
First day —Creation of light   Creation of the earthy

Second day —Creation of the firmament

Third day —Creation of vegetation

Fourth day —Creation of sun, moon, and stars

Fifth day —Creation of fishes and fowl

Sixth day —Creation of cattle, creeping thing, and beast of the earth
The Son begotten (see Rev. xii , Lev. xxvii)
Beginning of Time
Pre-Euphratic Era
Creation of the Euphratic or First race (Adam's)

Dividing in the midst of the Euphratic age (see Gen. xv. 8-10)

Creation of the Hiddekelic or Second race

Destruction of the Euphratic or First race

Dividing in the midst of the Hiddekelic age

Creation of the Gihonic or Third race.

Destruction of the Hiddekelic or Second race

Dividing in the midst of the Gihonic age

Creation of the Pisonic or Fourth race
Antediluvian Epoch
Deluge of Noah   Destruction of the Gihonic or Third race
Epoch of replenishment (see Gen ix 1)   [Abraham
Advent of the Messiah as the Son of man in the day of Messianic Epoch
Dividing in the midst of the Pisonic age   Crucifixion, absolute death, and resurrection of the Messiah as Jesus Christ the Faithful Witness   Judgmental Era
Thousand Years' Era
Era of Destruction
End of Time

H   15

can be made manifest. Wherefore (see Diagram 23) let the four bowls, as shadow, indicate the Four Ages of Man, and let the seven lamps indicate the first seven semidivisions of these ages, when it will be seen that the shaft of the candlestick with its lamps shadows man of Adam's race as an instrumentality in the purpose of God.

The two sets of branches, and the two golden pipes, point to and shadow the two Faithful Witnesses (see Zech. iv. 11-14) in the great labors for the overthrow of Evil, for the redemption of the fallen, and for the establishment of the Kingdom of Righteousness. The triune fulness pertaining to these Witnesses, as already indicated, is shadowed by the three branches, with their three bowls and their three knops that join the golden pipes.

As in the shadow (see Sketch C), the golden oil is emptied out of the branches into the golden pipes, and from thence into the candlestick, with its seven lamps, so (see Diagram 23, at e, e) the two Faithful Witnesses enter into and bear up the whole House of Man, whereby the labors for the redemption hasten towards completion through the regeneration thus indicated. The branches of the candlestick are given position in harmony with Gen. xxix. 1-8; Ezek. xlvii. 1-9, although they may with equal harmony join the House of Man in the Fourth age.

The lamps (see verse 37) shall give light over against the candlestick; hence the indication follows that, inasmuch as (see Diagram 23) the seven lamps pertain to the Four Ages of Man, so the light they shed must extend to the beyond of these ages; wherefore, by this extension, the instrumentality of man, and the priesthood of man, are still further indicated.

In the light that the two golden pipes shadow the two Faithful Witnesses, then the indication becomes well marked that the two staves, upon which the Ark of the Covenant and the table for shewbread were borne, indicate the two Faithful Witnesses also.

XXVI. 1–6. " Moreover thou shalt make the tabernacle *with* ten curtains *of* fine twined linen, and blue, and purple, and scarlet : *with* cherubim of cunning work shalt thou make them.

2. " The length of one curtain *shall be* eight and twenty cubits, and the breadth of one curtain four cubits: and every one of the curtains shall have one measure.

3. " The five curtains shall be coupled together one to another ; and *other* five curtains *shall be* coupled one to another.

4. " And thou shalt make loops of blue upon the edge of the one curtain from the selvedge in the coupling ; and likewise shalt thou make in the uttermost edge of *another* curtain, in the coupling of the second.

5. " Fifty loops shalt thou make in the one curtain, and fifty loops shalt thou make in the edge of the curtain that *is* in the coupling of the second ; that the loops may take hold one of another.

6. " And thou shalt make fifty taches of gold, and couple the curtains together with the taches: and it shall be one tabernacle."

Spaces *a, a,* Diagram 24, indicate the Four Ages of Man ; *b, b* indicate the Four Ages as Sinai, Elim,

172 *INDICATIONS OF THE BOOK OF EXODUS.*

Ex. xxvi. 1-6, considered as allegory.
DIAGRAM 24.
THE TEN LINEN CURTAINS FOR THE TABERNACLE.

1st day	Creation of a body for the Word of God as the very beginning of the creation of God (see Col 1 13-18, Rev iii. 14) First day.—Creation of light. Creation of the earthy
2nd day	Second day —Creation of the firmament.
3rd day	Third day —Creation of vegetation
4th day	Fourth day —Creation of sun, moon, and stars
5th day	Fifth day —Creation of fishes and fowl
6th day	Sixth day —Creation of cattle, creeping thing, and beast of the earth

The Son begotten (see Rev xii, Lev xxvii) Beginning of Time
Pre-Euphratic Era
Creation of the Euphratic or First race (Adam's)

Dividing in the midst of the Euphratic age

Creation of the Hiddekelic or Second race.

Destruction of the Euphratic or First race.

Dividing in the midst of the Hiddekelic age.

Creation of the Gihonic or Third race

Destruction of the Hiddekelic or Second race.

Dividing in the midst of the Gihonic age

Creation of the Pisonic race.
Antediluvian Epoch
Deluge of Noah. Destruction of the Gihonic or Third race
Epoch of replenishment (see Gen ix 1)
Advent of the Messiah as the son of man and as the Redeemer.
Messianic Epoch
Crucifixion, absolute death, and resurrection of the Messiah as Jesus Christ The Year of Jubilee enters into the redeemed through the resurrection of Jesus Christ the Messiah Dividing of the Pisonic age
Judgmental Era
Thousand Years' Era.
Era of Destruction
End of Time.

INDICATIONS OF THE BOOK OF EXODUS. 173

Horeb, and Canaan; c, c indicate the Four Ages by the four cardinal points of the compass (see Gen. ii. 10-14); d, d indicate the first seven semidivisions of the Four Ages by the seven primary colors of the rainbow (see Gen. ix. 12-16); e, e indicate pertaining of the ten linen curtains (in sets of five each) to the ten chief divisions of time (see Diagram 18); f, f indicate time; g, g indicate pertaining of the first seven breadths of linen curtains to the first seven semidivisions of the Four Ages.

In the light that the seven primary colors of the rainbow (see Gen. ix. 12-16) point to the first seven semidivisions of the Four Ages, then the indication comes forth that the purple of the text corresponds with and is identical with the violet of the rainbow; wherefore (see Diagram 24) the violet or purple will find place in the first part of the Euphratic age, the blue will find place in the first part of the Hiddekelic age, and the red or scarlet will find place in the first part of the Pisonic age. By this apportionment of colors time is indicated and covered from the begetting of the Son unto the dividing of the Pisonic age, at which time the crucifixion, absolute death, and resurrection of the Son of God as Jesus Christ the Messiah were fulfilled.

Each of these curtains was four cubits in breadth and twenty-eight cubits in length; hence the seven breadths,—which are shadowed by the seven primary colors of the rainbow,—when coupled together, will form a perfect square, which, as in the case of the Ark of the Covenant (see Diagram 21), and also in the case of the table for shewbread (see Diagram 22), indicates that a perfect unit of labor is established upon it as a

174 INDICATIONS OF THE BOOK OF EXODUS.

base. These labors, therefore, as shadowed by the ornamentation of the linen curtains, are those of the two Faithful Witnesses, whose presence is indicated by the cherubim with which they were made (see, also, Ark of the Covenant, Sketch B). Hence a perfect unit of labor is fulfilled by these two Witnesses in the period of time from the begetting of the Son unto the dividing of the Pisonic age.

The unit of labor thus indicated doubtless pertains to the redemption and deliverance of those whom Moses as shadow (see Diagrams 13, 15, 16, 17) brought out of Egypt. Wherefore as in the length of the curtains there were fifty loops, so, by them, the curtains are divided into forty-nine spaces. The seven breadths, however, form a perfect square; hence the indication comes forth (see Lev. xxv. 8–13) that the forty-nine spaces shadow the forty-nine years' durance, while the fiftieth loop points to the ushering in of the year of Jubilee to the redeemed hosts that rose with Christ (see St. Matt. xxvii. 50–53) after his absolute death and resurrection.

Inspection of Diagram 24 will show that the blue color pertains in an especial manner to the Hiddekelic age; hence, in harmony with Gen. xxix. 1–10; Neh. xii. 31–37; Ezek. xlvii. 1–9), all the curtains are coupled together with loops of blue, as a memorial that the flocks (see Gen. xxix. 1–10) will be gathered together in the east, that they may partake (see Rev. xxii. 1–6) of the water of life forever.

The golden coupling of the two sets of breadths doubtless points to some unusually sacred episode in the world's history (see Rev. iii. 7–13).

XXVI. 7–13. "And thou shalt make curtains *of* goats' *hair* to be a covering upon the tabernacle: eleven curtains shalt thou make.

8. "The length of one curtain *shall be* thirty cubits, and the breadth of one curtain four cubits: and the eleven curtains *shall be all* of one measure.

9. "And thou shalt couple five curtains by themselves, and six curtains by themselves, and shalt double the sixth curtain in the forefront of the tabernacle.

10. "And thou shalt make fifty loops on the edge of the one curtain *that is* outmost in the coupling, and fifty loops in the edge of the curtain which coupleth the second.

11. "And thou shalt make fifty taches of brass, and put the taches into the loops, and couple the tent together, that it may be one.

12. "And the remnant that remaineth of the curtains of the tent, the half curtain that remaineth, shall hang over the back side of the tabernacle.

13. "And a cubit on the one side, and a cubit on the other side of that which remaineth in the length of the curtains of the tent, it shall hang over the sides of the tabernacle, on this side and on that side, to cover it."

In Diagram 25, spaces a, a indicate the Four Ages of Man; a', a'' indicate the creative days; b, b indicate the Four Ages as Sinai, Elim, Horeb, and Canaan; c, c indicate the Four Ages by the cardinal points of the compass; d, d indicate pertainings of the eleven curtains of goats' hair in sets of five and six; e, e indicate time; f, f indicate pertaining of seven and

176 INDICATIONS OF THE BOOK OF EXODUS.

Ex. xxvi. 7–13, considered as allegory.

DIAGRAM 25.

THE CURTAINS OF GOATS' HAIR.

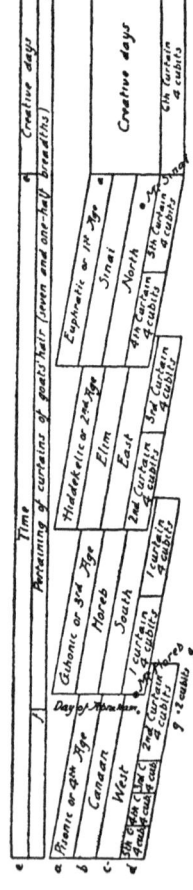

Creation of a body for the Word of God as the very beginning of the creation of God (see Col 1 13-18, Rev iii 14)
First day —Creation of light. Creation of the earthy
Second day —Creation of the firmament.
Third day —Creation of vegetation.
Fourth day —Creation of sun, moon, and stars.
Fifth day —Creation of fishes and fowls.
Sixth day —Creation of cattle, creeping thing, and beast of the earth.
The Son begotten. Beginning of Time.
Pre-Euphratic Era
Creation of the Euphratic or First race (Adam's).

Dividing in the midst of the Euphratic age.

Creation of the Hiddekelic or Second race
Destruction of the Euphratic or First race.

Dividing in the midst of the Hiddekelic age.

Creation of the Gihonic or Third race.
Destruction of the Hiddekelic or Second race

Dividing in the midst of the Gihonic age

Creation of the Pisonic race.
Antediluvian Epoch
Deluge of Noah   Destruction of the Gihonic or Third race
Epoch of replenishment (see Gen ix 1)
Abraham, the first temple of the Living Bread, born
Advent of the Messiah as the son of Abraham (see Gal iii 16, St John viii 56)   Messianic Epoch
Crucifixion, absolute death, and resurrection of the Messiah as Jesus Christ
Judgmental Era.
Thousand Years' Era.
Era of Destruction
End of Time.

INDICATIONS OF THE BOOK OF EXODUS. 177

one-half breadths, or thirty cubits' breadth of curtains; *g, g* indicate pertaining of half breadth to time from the beginning of the Pisonic age to the day of Abraham.

In Diagram 24 the ten linen curtains pertain to time from the begetting of the Son down to the end of the Pisonic age; the eleven curtains of goats' hair, however (see Diagram 25), not only cover time but they include and cover the creative days from the beginning thereof.

The curtains of goats' hair are thirty cubits in length; wherefore let thirty cubits of breadth be counted off that a perfect square be formed (see, also, Diagrams 22, 23, 24), when it will be found that this square ends at or about the time Abraham, the first temple of the Living Bread, was born.

To what does the unit of labor shadowed by this perfect square relate? It relates, in all probability, to the regeneration of the creature world; for, through the priesthood of Melchizedek (see Gen. xiv. 18–20), Abraham, with little doubt, partook of the bread brought forth by Melchizedek, which bread—in that Melchizedek was priest of the most high God, and (see Heb. vii. 1–4) was without beginning of days or end of life—must have been (see St. John vi. 32–35; viii. 56–58; Col. i. 13–18; Rev. iii. 14) of the body that was created for the Word of God in and as the very beginning of the creation of God, and which, by pre-eminence, was and is entirely suitable for the regeneration of the creature world.

When, therefore, Abraham partook of this bread his body was replenished from it, and if his body was replenished from it, then his spirit was born into it, and pertains to it, even as his spirit pertains to the replenishment derived from the consumption of his daily food.

If Abraham's spirit is born into the bread of life, then his spirit is regenerated or born into the body of the Messiah, and (see St. John vi. 56) the Messiah dwells in Abraham in his dual body.

What does Abraham simply as man represent? Abraham simply as man stands before the world (see xxxiv. 6, 7; Gen. vii. 13, 23) the bearer of other men's iniquity, blood, and characteristics, that are handed down or transmitted from father to son by the Law of Iniquity working through and in harmony with the Law of Generation (see Gen. i. 24).

Adam (see Job i. 8; Gen. i. 31) was created perfect and upright,—Job being the Adam and progenitor of the Gihonic or Third race,—hence, as such, no iniquity rested upon him through eating or through any constructive lineal descent (see Job. i. 9-10). With Abraham, however (see Job xiv. 19-22), the case is different, for the names, iniquity, blood, and characteristics of his sleeping progenitors rest upon him through the operation of the law or laws governing the same.

In this light the indication follows that when Abraham partook of the Bread of life brought forth by Melchizedek, priest of the most high God, regeneration, through the eating thereof, was extended not only to him, but to all those whose names, iniquity, blood, and characteristics had been transmitted to him from the preceding generations.

From the positions thus set forth the indication is marked that the perfect square shadowed by the seven and one-half curtains of goats' hair relates to the com-

munion of the body that was created for the Word of
God in and as the very beginning of the creation of
God. Inasmuch, therefore, as this square extends from
the beginning of the creation of God down to the day
of Abraham, so Abraham (see Gen. xiv. 18–20; xviii.
1–5) was, in all probability, the first creature commu-
nicant of the Living Bread.

The direct communion of the Living Bread by
Abraham points to the choosing of man (see xix. 3–6)
as a kingdom of priests, and a holy nation unto the
Lord. Wherefore (see verse 9) as the sixth curtain shall
be doubled in the fore-front of the tabernacle, so (see
Diagrams 24, 25) the sixth curtain—which pertains to
the creative days—can be doubled over the curtain of
the linen tabernacle that pertains to man of Adam's
race; thereby indicating that the burden of hosts pertaining to the creative days really falls upon man of
Adam's race as a kingdom of priests, and (see xix. 5)
as a peculiar treasure unto the Lord above all people.

Hence indications follow that the regeneration of
creature hosts can be positively, yet indirectly, fulfilled
through the eating of any regenerated body, for "a
little leaven leaveneth the whole lump;" but without
regeneration (see St. Matt. xxii. 11–13; St. John vi.
51–54) no soul can partake of the eternal life offered
by the King of Glory, who gave his body—the body
that was created for the Word of God in the beginning
—as a wedding garment (see St. Matt. xxii. 1–14) for
the spirit of the creature, that none (see St. Matt. xix.
6) put asunder what God hath joined together.

XXVI. 15–30. "And thou shalt make boards for
the tabernacle *of* shittim wood standing up.

16. "Ten cubits *shall be* the length of a board, and a cubit and a half *shall be* the breadth of one board.

17. "Two tenons *shall there be* in one board, set in order one against another: thus shalt thou make for all the boards of the tabernacle.

18. "And thou shalt make the boards for the tabernacle, twenty boards on the south side southward.

19. "And thou shalt make forty sockets of silver under the twenty boards; two sockets under one board for his two tenons, and two sockets under another board for his two tenons.

20. "And for the second side of the tabernacle on the north side *there shall be* twenty boards,

21. "And their forty sockets *of* silver; two sockets under one board, and two sockets under another board.

22. "And for the sides of the tabernacle westward thou shalt make six boards.

23. "And two boards shalt thou make for the corners of the tabernacle in the two sides.

24. "And they shall be coupled together beneath, and they shall be coupled together above the head of it unto one ring: thus shall it be for them both; they shall be for the two corners.

25. "And they shall be eight boards, and their sockets *of* silver, sixteen sockets; two sockets under one board, and two sockets under another board.

26. "And thou shalt make bars *of* shittim wood; five for the boards of the one side of the tabernacle,

27. "And five bars for the boards of the other side of the tabernacle, and five bars for the boards of the side of the tabernacle, for the two sides westward.

INDICATIONS OF THE BOOK OF EXODUS. 181

28. "And the middle bar in the midst of the boards shall reach from end to end.

29. "And thou shalt overlay the boards with gold, and make their rings *of* gold *for* places for the bars: and thou shalt overlay the bars with gold.

30. "And thou shalt rear up the tabernacle according to the fashion thereof which was shewed thee in the mount."

In Diagram 26, spaces a, a indicate the Four Ages of Man; b, b indicate the Four Ages as Sinai, Elim, Horeb, and Canaan; c, c indicate the Four Ages by the four short bars; d, d indicate the semidivisions of the Four Ages by the eight boards used in the construction of the west side of the tabernacle of the congregation; d', d'' indicate the creative days; e, e indicate pertaining of middle bar; f, f indicate time; g, g indicate pertaining of tabernacle (west side) to time.

By Diagram 25, one breadth of the curtain of goats' hair was doubled over the linen tabernacle, thus indicating that burdens pertaining to the creative days had fallen upon man of Adam's race. Therefore (see Diagram 26) let the burden pertaining to the creative days be considered as having fallen upon man of Adam's race, when it will be seen that, essentially, the burdens pertaining to all ages from the creation of God down to the end of time will be identified with the eight semidivisions of the Four Ages. These eight semidivisions are shadowed by the eight boards, but, inasmuch as two of these boards shall be used as corner boards, the actual breadth of the structure (see Sketch F) will be limited to

SKETCH F.

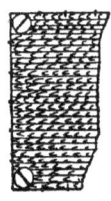

182 INDICATIONS OF THE BOOK OF EXODUS.

Ex. xxvi. 15–30, *considered as allegory.*

DIAGRAM 26.

THE TABERNACLE OF THE CONGREGATION (WEST SIDE).

Creation of a body for the Word of God as the very beginning of the creation of God (see Col 1 13–18, Rev iii 14)

First day —Creation of light   Creation of the earthy

Second day —Creation of the firmament

Third day —Creation of vegetation

Fourth day —Creation of sun, moon, and stars

Fifth day —Creation of fishes and fowl.

Sixth day —Creation of cattle, creeping thing, and beast of the earth

The Son begotten   Beginning of Time

Pre-Euphratic Era

Creation of the Euphratic or First race (Adam's)

Dividing in the midst of the Euphratic age

Creation of the Hiddekelic or Second race.

Destruction of the Euphratic or First race

Dividing in the midst of the Hiddekelic age.

Creation of the Gihonic or Third race

Destruction of the Hiddekelic or Second race.

Dividing in the midst of the Gihonic age

Creation of the Pisonic or Fourth race

Antediluvian Epoch

Deluge of Noah   Destruction of the Gihonic or Third race

Epoch of replenishment (see Gen ix 1)

Advent of the Messiah as the Son of man.

Messianic Epoch

Crucifixion, absolute death, and resurrection of the Messiah as Jesus Christ the Redeemer   Dividing of the Pisonic age   Judgmental Era begins

Thousand Years' Era

Era of Destruction

End of Time

six boards. As, therefore, two corner boards are doubled into or comprehended in the breadth thus indicated, so (see Diagram 26) the two corner boards pertaining to time can be doubled, as it were, over the six remaining semidivisions, and the burdens thereof become connected with them.

By Diagram 26, the four short bars shadow the Four Ages of Man, while the middle bar shadows the Messiah as the Redeemer; wherefore as the middle bar shall reach from end to end, so, by the shadow or middle bar (see Diagram 26), the labors of the Messiah are indicated that reach from the dividing of the Euphratic age down to the dividing of the Pisonic age.

At or about the dividing of the Pisonic age the Messiah as Jesus Christ the Redeemer died an absolute death, and rose again from the dead a living proof of his excellence and of the perfect fulfilment of his mission as the Redeemer,—the Redeemer not of man only, but the Redeemer of hosts (see Diagrams 25, 26) pertaining to days that had existence before man of Adam's race was brought forth as instrumentality in the sublime purpose of the Infinite God.

By reference to Rev. ii. 8-11, the charge to the people at the dividing of the Euphratic age is made manifest; hence this charge, "Fear none of those things which thou shalt suffer: behold, the devil shall cast *some* of you into prison, that ye may be tried; and ye shall have tribulation ten days: be thou faithful unto death, and I will give thee a crown of life," pertains also to the begotten Son, who made his advent as such in the beginning of time.

By Diagram 26, bar *e, e*, it will be seen that labors

184 INDICATIONS OF THE BOOK OF EXODUS.

Ex. xxvi. 15-30, considered as allegory.

DIAGRAM 27.

THE WOODEN TABERNACLE OF THE CONGREGATION (NORTH SIDE).

Creation of a body for the Word of God in and as the very beginning of the creation of God (see Col i 13-18, Rev iii 14)

First day —Creation of light

Second day —Creation of the firmament

Third day —Creation of vegetation

Fourth day —Creation of sun, moon, and stars

Fifth day —Creation of fishes and fowl

Sixth day —Creation of cattle, creeping thing, and beast of the earth

The Son begotten Beginning of Time
Pre-Euphratic Era divided in the midst thereof
Creation of the Euphratic or First race (Adam s)

Dividing in the midst of the Euphratic age

Creation of the Hiddekelic or Second race.

Destruction of the Euphratic or First race.

Dividing in the midst of the Hiddekelic age.

Creation of the Gihonic or Third race

Destruction of the Hiddekelic or Second race.

Dividing in the midst of the Gihonic age.

Creation of the Pisonic or Fourth race.
Antediluvian Epoch
Deluge of Noah   Destruction of the Gihonic or Third race.
Epoch of replenishment (see Gen ix 1)
Advent of the Messiah as the Son of man
Messianic Epoch
Crucifixion, absolute death, and resurrection of the Messiah as Jesus Christ   Dividing of the Pisonic age
Judgmental Era
Thousand Years' Era.
Era of Destruction
End of Time.

INDICATIONS OF THE BOOK OF EXODUS. 185

pertaining to the Messiah as the begotten Son are, in this portion of the allegory, taken up from the time the above charge was given; therefore, was the Messiah faithful unto death? Undoubtedly: for trace the Messiah's path down through the succeeding ages, down to the dividing of the Pisonic age, as shadowed by the middle bar, when evidences will become clear that the Messiah, as Jesus Christ, was faithful unto death, and that (see charge to the people of the Pisonic age, Rev. iii. 14–21) he had won the crown of life promised at the outset (see Rev. ii. 8–11) to him that should overcome.

By the unfolding of the west side of the tabernacle (see Diagram 26, spaces d, d), and of the overlapping of the curtain of goats' hair, the labors of the Messiah bear upon the grand epoch extending from the beginning of the creation of God down to the end of time. Wherefore as these labors are indicated by the breadth of the structure, so (see Diagrams 21, 22, 24, 25) the length of the wooden tabernacle will indicate the complete square upon which, as a base, these labors as a unit are identified. In this light, therefore, the north side of the tabernacle is allegorically taken up in Diagram 27.

In Diagram 27, spaces a, a indicate the Four Ages of Man; b, b indicate the Four Ages as Sinai, Elim, Horeb, and Canaan; c, c indicate the Four Ages by the four short bars; d, d indicate pertainings of the twenty boards to the twenty chief divisions from the beginning of the creation of God down to the end of time (see Diagrams 12, 18); e, e indicate pertainings of middle bars as shadowing the two Faithful Witnesses; f, f indicate time; g, g pertaining of wooden tabernacle to the grand epoch from the beginning of the creation to the end of time.

By the unfolding of the west side of the wooden tabernacle, and of the curtain of goats' hair, as shadow (see Diagram 26, spaces *d, d*), the grand epoch from the beginning of the creation down to the end of time was indicated, while the twenty boards constituting the length of the tabernacle pointed to a perfect square, upon which a perfect unit of labor was identified as a base.

This unit of labor is further manifested (see Diagram 27, spaces *d, d*) by the apportionment of the twenty boards to the twenty chief divisions into which the epoch from the beginning of the creation to the end of time (see Diagrams 12, 18, 20) is divided.

By this apportionment six boards pertain to the six creative days, two to the Pre-Euphratic era, two to the remaining divisions of the Euphratic age, two to the semidivisions of the Hiddekelic age, two to the semidivisions of the Gihonic age, and six to the six divisions of the Pisonic age.

As, therefore, the middle bars shall reach from end to end, so by them, as shadow, the presence of the two Faithful Witnesses is indicated from the very beginning of the creation of God down to the end of time. One of these Witnesses (see Heb. vii. 1–4) doubtless is Melchizedek, Priest of the most high God, King of righteousness, who was without beginning of days or end of life, in that he is made like unto the Son of God, who (see Rev. i. 5) is the faithful witness, the first-begotten of the dead, and the Prince of the kings of the earth.

INDICATIONS OF THE BOOK OF EXODUS. 187

Now, inasmuch as the body created for the Word of God, in and as the very beginning of the creation of God (see Col. i. 13-18; Rev. iii. 14; Heb. x. 5), shall be eaten as the Bread of Life, that regeneration may ensue (see St. John vi. 51-54; St. Mark xiv. 22), so the care of it must pertain to some holy one that had existence before the creation of this body.

This holy one doubtless is the Third Person of the Trinity as Melchizedek priest of the most high God, and, hence, he, in this mission, is shadowed by one of the middle bars (see Diagram 27), whereby his presence is made manifest, in the perfect square under consideration, from the very beginning of the creation of God down to the end of time.

Thus the Priest of the most high God, and the Bread of Life are traceable from the beginning; thus the two Faithful Witnesses—side by side—watch over the interests of the creature world, and guard each detail of God's great purpose from any desecrating hand. Well, therefore, may the golden boards find rest in silver sockets, well may the garnishments be "fine twined linen, blue, and purple, with cherubim of cunning work;" for that which they shadow never will grow dim, or vanish from eternity's long roll of songs.

XXVI. 31-37. "And thou shalt make a vail *of* blue, and purple, and scarlet, and fine twined linen of cunning work: with cherubim shall it be made.

32. "And thou shalt hang it upon four pillars of shittim *wood* overlaid with gold: their hooks *shall be of* gold, upon the four sockets of silver.

33. "And thou shalt hang up the vail under the taches, that thou mayest bring in thither within the vail

the ark of the testimony: and the vail shall divide unto you between the holy *place* and the most holy.

34. "And thou shalt put the mercy-seat upon the ark of the testimony in the most holy *place*.

35. "And thou shalt set the table without the vail, and the candlestick over against the table on the side of the tabernacle toward the south: and thou shalt put the table on the north side.

36. "And thou shalt make a hanging for the door of the tent, *of* blue, and purple, and scarlet, and fine twined linen, wrought with needlework.

37. "And thou shalt make for the hanging five pillars *of* shittim *wood*, and overlay them with gold, *and* their hooks *shall be of* gold: and thou shalt cast five sockets of brass for them."

By the general text a rectangular structure of boards was made for the linen tabernacle; each board ten cubits in length, and one cubit and a half in breadth. This building faced the east; twenty boards forming the north side, twenty boards the south side, and six the west side; whereby the structure would be thirty cubits in length, nine cubits in breadth, and ten cubits in height. Each corner on the west side was strengthened by a board set diagonally across it, which was secured or held in its place by rings at the top and at the bottom (see Sketch F). The sides were further strengthened by five braces or bars (see Sketch G, the central ones extending the whole length, while the short bars in pairs met, in all probability, at the centre, forming obtuse angles. Within this wooden structure the cunningly-wrought linen tabernacle, with its covering of

SKETCH G.

INDICATIONS OF THE BOOK OF EXODUS. 189

goats' hair, was placed. At the door five pillars of shittim wood were reared, to which a hanging of fine twined linen wrought with needle-work was secured. Within the tabernacle or tent four more pillars were erected, to which the veil was attached. It is very probable that an entablature rested upon these various pillars, and that the linen tabernacle, with its covering of goats' hair, was thrown over it, thus forming a rectangular space twenty-eight cubits in length, eight cubits in breadth, and ten cubits in height; for although the complement of boards calls for thirty cubits in length, it is manifest that the thickness of the boards must be taken into consideration; also the diagonal corner boards at the west side, and the pillars at the east end of the tent. The twenty-eight cubits in the length of the curtains would just reach from the floor on the one side up over the entablature, thence across and down to the floor on the opposite side. Now, inasmuch as the curtains were four cubits in breadth, it would take just seven to make a perfect square; and, therefore, commencing at the east end, these seven would occupy about all the available rectangular space enclosed by the boards and pillars. The three breadths remaining droop from the rear end of the tabernacle, whereby the designs appertaining to them are nearly hidden from view. These breadths in all probability relate to the three chief divisions of the eighth epoch or semi-division of the Four Ages, in that by the Decade System of Chronology, or system of tens, the ten curtains shadow the ten divisions of time (see Diagram 24), or, by apportionment, one curtain to each division; wherefore the first seven represent the first seven semidivisions of the Four Ages, while the remaining three represent the eighth semidivision (see, also, Diagram 18), as divided into the Judgmental Era, the Thousand Years' Era, and the short Era of Destruction, thus indicating that the ten curtains cover the ten divisions of time from the beginning thereof down to the end thereof.

By verses 31–33, the veil shall be hung upon four pillars of shittim wood, and it shall divide between the holy place and the most holy (see Sketch H), also that the veil shall be hung under the taches. By verse 3 five curtains are coupled together into one curtain, and five into another, irrespective of their peculiar fasten-

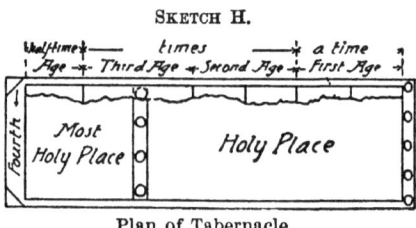

Plan of Tabernacle.

ings; but the two sets of curtains are joined together (see verses 5, 6) by the loops and the golden taches; therefore the position of the veil as established within the tent is, by the text, immediately under the taches of gold. As the veil divides the tent into the holy place and the most holy, it becomes clearly evident that the taches and curtains run parallel with the veil, as shown in the plan (see Sketch H); from which it follows that the veil and its four pillars are situated just twenty cubits within the tabernacle of wrought linen.

The rectangular space thus formed is called the holy

INDICATIONS OF THE BOOK OF EXODUS. 191

SKETCH I.

A. Wooden structure.
B. Curtains of wrought linen.
C. Curtains of goats' hair.
D. Covering of rams' skins dyed red.
E. Covering of badgers' skins.
F. Court.
G. Altar of burnt-offering.
H. Long bar.
I I. Short bars.
K. Pillars of shittim wood.
L. Hangings for court.
M. Laver.
N. Sanctuary.

Tabernacle of the Congregation (South Side).

place; while the remaining space, that within the veil, is called the most holy place. It will be found that the latter measures eight cubits longitudinally, as indicated by the two breadths of curtains, and that it measures eight cubits transversely,—for the height of the structure on one side is ten cubits, and the height on the other side is ten cubits, which leaves just eight cubits, in the length of the curtain, for the width of the most holy place,—hence the base or floor is a perfect square. The height, however, is ten cubits by measure; yet by the hidden meaning or when measured by time the enclosed space indicates a perfect cube; for the four pillars, forming one side, upon which the veil is hung, indicate the Four Ages of Man; the eight cubits of the two breadths which form another side, indicate the eight semidivisions of time; while the ten cubits in the height indicate, by the Decade System of Chronology, the ten epochs of time as already described; hence, figuratively, when measured by time the most holy place is a perfect cube; the construction of which is in full harmony with the requirements of the Sacred Records; still the perfect square that constitutes the floor of the most holy place in itself may point to a perfect unit of labor as established upon it as a base.

Chronologically considered the veil appears to have been established at the dividing of the Gihonic or Third age; and if so, it must have been a marked feature in the plan for the fulness of transgression that Evil might be overthrown. The charge given to the people of this epoch, the sixth, is recorded as follows (Rev. iii. 7–13): "And to the angel of the church in Philadelphia write; These things saith he that is holy,

INDICATIONS OF THE BOOK OF EXODUS.

he that is true, he that hath the key of David, he that openeth, and no man shutteth; and shutteth, and no man openeth.

"I know thy works: behold, I have set before thee an open door, and no man can shut it: for thou hast a little strength, and hast kept my word, and hast not denied my name.

"Behold, I will make them of the synagogue of Satan, which say they are Jews, and are not, but do lie; behold, I will make them to come and worship before thy feet, and to know that I have loved thee.

"Because thou hast kept the word of my patience, I also will keep thee from the hour of temptation, which shall come upon all the world, to try them that dwell upon the earth.

"Behold, I come quickly: hold that fast which thou hast, that no man take thy crown.

"Him that overcometh will I make a pillar in the temple of my God, and he shall go no more out: and I will write upon him the name of my God, and the name of the city of my God, *which is* new Jerusalem, which cometh down out of heaven from my God: and *I will write upon him* my new name.

"He that hath an ear, let him hear what the Spirit saith unto the churches."

By this charge it will be seen that the temptation set forth to this epoch is one of great magnitude. The temptation is not unrighteous in itself, but it is established as a proof of loyalty; therefore, "If the Lord *be* God, follow him: but if Baal, *then* follow him;" but Baal sitting in the temple of the Lord (see II. Thess. ii. 3, 4) is no proof that he has overcome, but rather that he is there as a transgressor. The open door of the charge seems, with little doubt, to indicate the veil of the tabernacle, within which no man was permitted to enter except the high priest: for (Heb. ix. 8) "the way into the holiest of all was not yet made manifest, while as the first tabernacle was yet standing." The charge also indicates the labors of the two Faithful Witnesses, which labors are rendered in figure by the cherubim with which the curtains of the tabernacle were wrought.

If the world was prohibited from entering into the most holy place, then transgression in this respect would become very sinful, and sin would be imputed far beyond all established precedents. Was this prohibition respected? No; for where the history of this age, the Third, is taken up (Dan. viii. 9-12) it is stated, "And out of one of them came forth a little horn, which waxed exceedingly great, toward the south, and toward the east, and toward the pleasant *land*.

"And it waxed great, *even* to the host of heaven; and it cast down *some* of the host and of the stars to the ground, and stamped upon them.

"Yea, he magnified *himself* even to the prince of the host, and by him the daily *sacrifice* was taken away, and the place of his sanctuary was cast down.

"And a host was given *him* against the daily *sacrifice* by reason of transgression, and it cast down the truth to the ground; and it practised and prospered;" hence the sanctity of the most holy place was disregarded in the latter part of the Third age, and the proof of disloyalty established.

The four walls in the most holy place indicate the

four walls of Jerusalem, and within the four walls the cherubim and the mercy-seat are placed; therefore through the labors of the two Faithful Witnesses during the Four Ages of Man, as a perfect cube, the way into the most holy place is made open to all; and those who shall enter therein are the "thousands of Manasseh and the ten thousands of Ephraim," upon whom is named the name of Abraham, and of Isaac, and of Jacob: for all those justified by faith shall be counted as the seed of Abraham.

The tabernacle of wood as it now stands is without a roof; for the linen tabernacle, with its covering of goats' hair, is thrown over the entablature that rests upon the pillars; therefore a covering of rams' skins dyed red was made of a suitable size and thrown over it; the ends of which, with great probability (see Sketches I, J, K), hung down outside the gold-covered boards of the structure. The linen curtains, with their coverings of goats' hair, however, were wholly within, and they formed the walls of the tabernacle proper.

At some convenient distance above the covering of rams' skins, a second covering of badgers' skins was placed. Now, inasmuch as the whole tabernacle was complete when the covering of rams' skins was placed over it, the conclusion is almost unavoidable that the covering of badgers' skins was for the purpose of protecting it from the changing conditions of weather, such as heat, rain, and other natural deteriorating causes; hence the shape and position of this covering doubtless were governed thereby (see Sketches I, J, K).

196 INDICATIONS OF THE BOOK OF EXODUS.

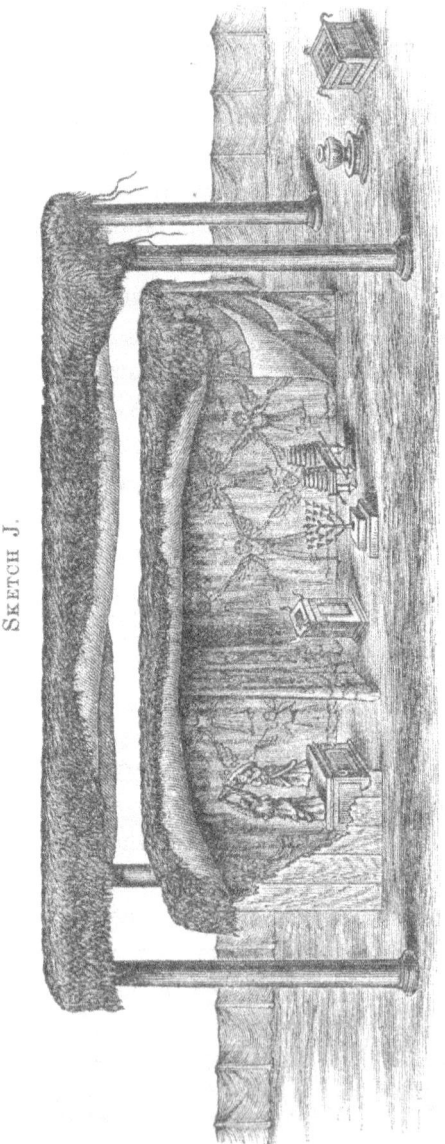

Sketch J.

Tabernacle of the Congregation (Interior).

INDICATIONS OF THE BOOK OF EXODUS. 197

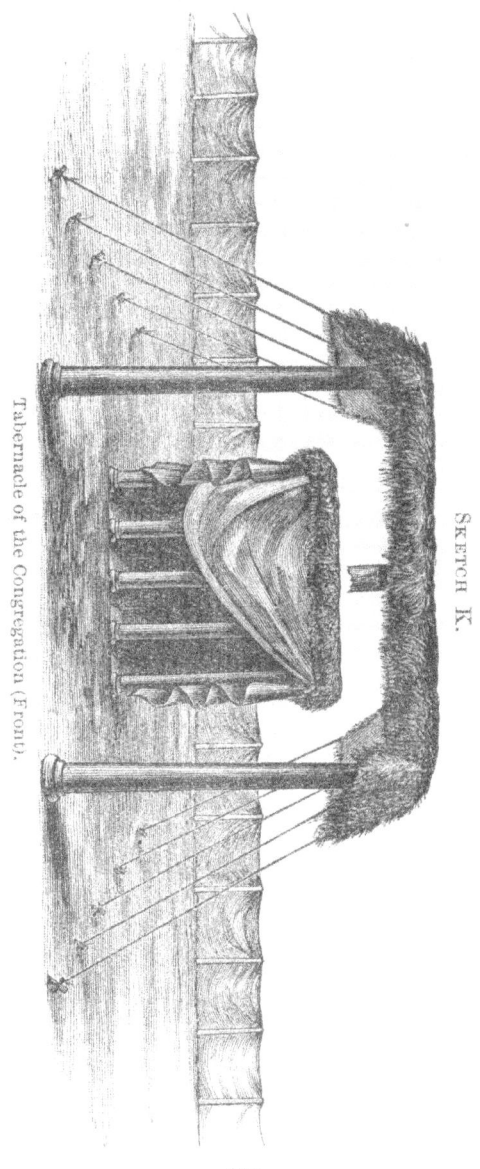

SKETCH K.

Tabernacle of the Congregation (Front).

198 INDICATIONS OF THE BOOK OF EXODUS.

XXVII. 1–8. "And thou shalt make an altar *of* shittim wood, five cubits long, and five cubits broad; the altar shall be foursquare, and the height thereof *shall be* three cubits.

2. "And thou shalt make the horns of it upon the four corners thereof: his horns shall be of the same: and thou shalt overlay it with brass.

3. "And thou shalt make his pans to receive his ashes, and his shovels, and his basins, and his flesh-hooks, and his firepans: all the vessels thereof thou shalt make *of* brass.

4. "And thou shalt make for it a grate of network *of* brass; and upon the net shalt thou make four brazen rings in the four corners thereof.

5. "And thou shalt put it under the compass of the altar beneath, that the net may be even to the midst of the altar.

6. "And thou shalt make staves for the altar, staves *of* shittim wood, and overlay them with brass.

7. "And the staves shall be put into the rings, and the staves shall be upon the two sides of the altar, to bear it.

8. "Hollow with boards shalt thou make it: as it was shewed thee in the mount, so shall they make *it.*"

In Diagram 28, spaces *a, a* indicate the Four Ages of Man; *b, b* indicate the Four Ages as Sinai, Elim, Horeb, and Canaan; *c, c* indicate the Four Ages by the four horns of the altar; *d, d* indicate fourteen chief divisions of time by the apportionment of the fourteen half-cubits of the altar (diagonal measure); *e, e* indicate the earth as shadowed by the altar of burnt-

INDICATIONS OF THE BOOK OF EXODUS. 199

Ex. xxvii. 1–8, *considered as allegory.*

DIAGRAM 28

THE ALTAR OF BURNT-OFFERING.

Creation of a body for the Word of God in and as the very beginning of the creation of God (see Col 1. 15–18, Rev. iii 14)

First day.—Creation of light

Second day —Creation of the firmament

Third day —Creation of vegetation

Fourth day —Creation of sun, moon, and stars

Fifth day —Creation of fishes and fowl

Sixth day —Creation of cattle, creeping thing, and beast of the earth
The Son begotten   Beginning of Time
War in heaven } Pre-Euphratic Era
Satan cast into the earth
Creation of the Euphratic or First race (Adam's)

The earth in the Euphratic age

Dividing in the midst of the Euphratic age

Creation of the Hiddekelic or Second race

Destruction of the Euphratic or First race

The earth in the Hiddekelic age

Dividing in the midst of the Hiddekelic age

Creation of the Gihonic or Third race

Destruction of the Hiddekelic or Second race

The earth in the Gihonic age

Dividing in the midst of the Gihonic age

Creation of the Pisonic or Fourth race
Antediluvian Epoch
Deluge of Noah   Destruction of the Gihonic or Third race
Epoch of replenishment   The earth in the Pisonic age
Advent of the Messiah as the Son of man in the day of Abraham
Messianic Epoch
Crucifixion, absolute death and resurrection of the Messiah as Jesus Christ   Dividing of the Pisonic age
Judgmental Era

Thousand Years' Era

Era of Destruction.
End of Time

offering; *f, f* indicate pertainings of the staves as the two Faithful Witnesses to the Four Ages.

Sketches L, M, of the altar of burnt-offering, are derived from the general description given in the text.

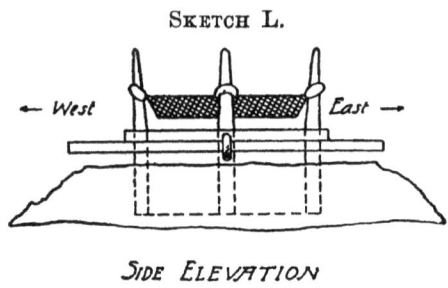

SKETCH L.

SIDE ELEVATION

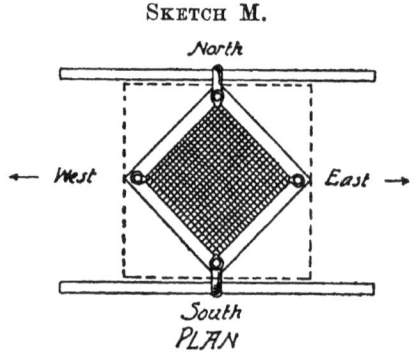

SKETCH M.

PLAN

The Altar of Burnt-Offering.

It is probable that the horns of the altar are placed one in each corner as supports for the brazen grate, and that they extend entirely through the base, the base being made hollow with boards.

The brazen grate is furnished with four rings, one at each corner; wherefore the indication becomes marked that the grate is secured or kept in position by the four rings, that are attached to the four corners thereof, slipping over the four horns of the altar. It is also probable that the fire-pans, seething-pots, and other kindred vessels used in the offering of sacrifices rest upon rods secured to the horns by rings in the same manner as the grate; the plan being both simple and effective.

The altar is borne along on staves passing through rings attached to the two sides; hence indications arise that when the altar is in position the diagonals, with the four horns thereof, point to and designate the four cardinal points of the mariner's compass (see Sketches L, M).

Figuratively, therefore (see Diagrams 1, 28), the four horns of the altar indicate the Four Ages of Man, while the altar, as a whole, shadows the earth as a great altar of sacrifice during the Four Ages as shadowed by the four rivers of Eden. Inasmuch, however, as the Redeemer entered into these waters, so the altar of burnt-offering, together with its services, shadows the labors, trials, tribulations, and physical sufferings of the Redeemer during these ages.

Hence, by these indications, the seven cubits' measure of the diagonal take in and include time from the beginning to the end thereof; wherefore (see Diagrams 21, 22, 28), the fourteen half-cubits (see, also, Diagram 18, spaces *e, e*) point to the fourteen chief divisions of time from the beginning thereof to the end thereof.

It becomes evident, from the altar of burnt-offering as allegory, that man is called as an instrumentality in the work pertaining to time; and that, as such, he will be a partaker to some extent of the sufferings of Christ; for it is only through the flesh of man that the Adversary can reach him. The bondage of man necessitates the suffering of the Redeemer,—not that suffering is called for by the plan, but that the fulness of temptation may be met and overcome; therefore if man suffered, much more has the Redeemer suffered, that his perfection be made manifest. The Lord does not institute suffering, but he permits it through the ruling of the First Covenant; the conditions of which, the First Covenant (see Gen. xxi. 22–32, xxvi. 6–33, xxxi. 44 –54) clearly showing that tribulation comes from the aggressive Evil Power.

The altar of burnt-offering is a perfect square; hence the diagonals are equal, and are perpendicular to each other; wherefore (see Sketch L, also Diagram 28), time is indicated as a perfect square upon which, as a base, a perfect unit of labor is fulfilled.

XXVII. 9–19. "And thou shalt make the court of the tabernacle: for the south side southward *there shall be* hangings for the court *of* fine twined linen of a hundred cubits long for one side:

10. "And the twenty pillars thereof and their twenty sockets *shall be of* brass; the hooks of the pillars and their fillets *shall be of* silver.

11. "And likewise for the north side in length *there shall be* hangings of a hundred *cubits* long, and his twenty pillars and their twenty sockets *of* brass; the hooks of the pillars and their fillets *of* silver.

12. "And *for* the breadth of the court on the west side *shall be* hangings of fifty cubits: their pillars ten, and their sockets ten.

13. "And the breadth of the court on the east side eastward *shall be* fifty cubits.

14. "The hangings of one side *of the gate shall be* fifteen cubits: their pillars three, and their sockets three.

15. "And on the other side *shall be* hangings fifteen *cubits:* their pillars three, and their sockets three.

16. "And for the gate of the court *shall be* a hanging of twenty cubits, *of* blue, and purple, and scarlet, and fine twined linen, wrought with needlework: *and* their pillars *shall be* four, and their sockets four.

17. "All the pillars round about the court *shall be* filleted with silver; their hooks *shall be of* silver, and their sockets *of* brass.

18. "The length of the court *shall be* a hundred cubits, and the breadth fifty everywhere, and the height five cubits *of* fine twined linen, and their sockets *of* brass.

19. "All the vessels of the tabernacle in all the service thereof, and all the pins thereof, and all pins of the court, *shall be of* brass."

By these verses the length of the court of the tabernacle is just twice the breadth, a condition that is manifest in the dimensions of the table for the shewbread.

Allegorically the limits of the court indicate epochs from the beginning of the creation of God down to the end of time. It must be kept in mind, however, that time was set apart for the accomplishment of a great purpose, and, hence, the necessity arises that its bounds or limits should be set, that a definite meaning may be given to the figures or allegories shadowing this purpose. An inspection of the court and tabernacle (see Sketch N) will show that the great journey of life, pertaining to all hosts, finds its culmination in the most holy place of the tabernacle; but to reach the most holy place, it is necessary to pass through

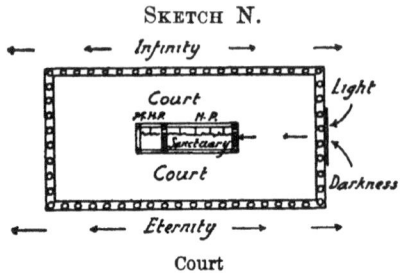

SKETCH N.

Court

and fulfil the rulings of the First Covenant, that were given for the government of all hosts, as made manifest by the sanctuary or holy place of the tabernacle. The First Covenant embodies the law of righteousness by works, and, therefore, it is manifest that only those fulfilling the requirements of the First Covenant can pass from the sanctuary into the most holy place. Indications are clear (see Diagram 20) that no man of Adam's race in himself has succeeded in passing through the sanctuary; but the only begotten Son, the Man for whom a body was prepared, he alone lived in the law in that he carried out all its provisions; whether relating to word, deed, or conscience, and, therefore, he alone, through his righteousness, can enter into the most holy place.

In Diagram 29, spaces a, a indicate the Four Ages of Man; b, b indicate the Four Ages as Sinai, Elim, Horeb, and Canaan; c, c indicate apportionment of the fifty cubits' breadth to ten chief divisions of time; d, d

INDICATIONS OF THE BOOK OF EXODUS. 205

Ex. xxvii. 9–19, considered as allegory.

DIAGRAM 29.

THE COURT OF THE TABERNACLE (EAST SIDE).

Creation of a body for the Word of God in and as the very beginning of the creation of God
First day —Creation of light

Second day —Creation of the firmament.

Third day —Creation of vegetation

Fourth day —Creation of sun, moon, and stars

Fifth day —Creation of fishes and fowl.

Sixth day —Creation of cattle, creeping thing and beast of the earth.
The Son begotten   Beginning of Time
Pre-Euphratic Era
Creation of the Euphratic or First race (Adam's).

Dividing in the midst of the Euphratic age

Creation of the Hiddekelic or Second race
Destruction of the Euphratic or First race.

Dividing in the midst of the Hiddekelic age

Creation of the Gihonic or Third race
Destruction of the Hiddekelic or Second race

Dividing in the midst of the Gihonic age.

Creation of the Pisonic or Fourth race
Antediluvian Epoch
Deluge of Noah Destruction of the Gihonic or Third race.
Epoch of replenishment (see Gen ix 1)
Advent of the Messiah as the son of man in the day of Abraham
Messianic Epoch
Dividing of the Pisonic age   Crucifixion, absolute death, and resurrection of the Messiah as Jesus Christ
Judgmental Era
Thousand Years' Era
Era of Destruction
End of Time

indicate apportionment of the ten pillars to the same ten chief divisions of time; e, e indicate time; f, f indicate pertaining of east side of the court of the tabernacle, with its gateway and sideways, to time.

Inspection of Diagram 29 will show that the east side of the court pertains to and shadows time from the beginning thereof down to the advent of the Messiah as the son of man. During this period the creature is on trial as a subjugator, but the failure of the creature in his mission is made manifest by the service that pertains to the First Covenant. By the advent of the Messiah as the son of man, however, the prevailing situation is changed, in that the Messiah takes up the subjugatory labors; hence the oblong square, or parallelogram, one hundred cubits in length and fifty cubits in breadth, that bounds the court indicates the imperfection of the labors pertaining to man simply as the creature.

In Diagram 30, spaces a, a indicate the Four Ages of Man; b, b indicate the Four Ages as Sinai, Elim, Horeb, and Canaan; c, c indicate apportionment of the hundred cubits' length of the court to the twenty chief divisions of the grand epoch from the beginning of the creation of God down to the end of time; d, d indicate apportionment of the twenty pillars to the same twenty chief divisions; e, e indicate time.

The east side of the court of the tabernacle shadowed the imperfection and failure of the creature as a subjugatory element (see Diagram 29) from the beginning of time down to the advent of the Messiah as the son of man. This period, however, is represented by the fifty cubits of breadth, by the ten pillars, and, hence, by

Ex. xxvii. 9-19, considered as allegory.

DIAGRAM 30.

THE COURT OF THE TABERNACLE (NORTH SIDE).

Creation of a body for the Word of God in and as the very beginning of the creation of God (see Col 1 13-18, Rev 111 14).

1st pillar —First day —Creation of light
2d pillar —Second day —Creation of the firmament
3d pillar —Third day —Creation of vegetation
4th pillar —Fourth day —Creation of sun, moon, and stars
5th pillar —Fifth day —Creation of fishes and fowl
6th pillar —Sixth day —Creation of cattle, creeping thing, and beast of the earth
7th pillar } War in heaven } Pre-Euphratic Era
8th pillar } Satan cast out into the earth
Creation of the Euphratic or First race (Adam's)
9th pillar . Dividing in the midst of the Euphratic age
10th pillar . . Creation of the Hiddekelic or Second race.
11th pillar . Destruction of the Euphratic or First race.
12th pillar . Dividing in the midst of the Hiddekelic age
12th pillar Creation of the Gihonic or Third race
13th pillar Destruction of the Hiddekelic or Second race
13th pillar Dividing in the midst of the Gihonic age
14th pillar. Creation of the Pisonic race
15th pillar Antediluvian Epoch
15th pillar Deluge of Noah Destruction of the Gihonic or Third race
16th pillar Epoch of replenishment (see Gen 1x 1)
17th pillar Advent of the Messiah as the Son of man
Messianic Epoch
18th pillar Crucifixion, absolute death, and resurrection of the Messiah as Jesus Christ Dividing of the Pisonic age
—The Judgmental Era.
19th pillar —The Thousand Years' Era.
20th pillar —The Era of Destruction
. End of Time

"Ask of me, and I shall give thee the heathen for thine inheritance and the uttermost parts of the earth for thy possession (Ps II 8)"

INDICATIONS OF THE BOOK OF EXODUS. 207

ten epochs or by one-half of the twenty that constitute the grand epoch from the beginning of the creation to the end of time.

The Messiah takes up the subjugatory labors from the time of his advent as the son of man; wherefore his antecedents must be considered from the time the body was prepared for him in and as the beginning of the creation suitable for the fulfilment of these labors. From the beginning of the creation of God to the end of time there are twenty chief divisions; hence as the court is one hundred cubits in length, and as it is constructed with twenty pillars, so (see Diagram 30) a perfect square is indicated upon which, as a base, the labor of the Messiah, in the fulfilment of the will of God (see Ps. xl. 5–8; Heb. x. 4–9), as a perfect unit, is brought to notice.

If man of Adam's race has failed completely in the past, is it at all likely that the future will bring forth a conqueror? No: yet, if so, the labor of Christ would be made void for righteousness, and hence life would be obtainable by the Law,—not through the labor of Christ. But if righteousness be through the Law only, and not through Christ, then no flesh can be saved, in that all fail now, and all (see Diagram 29) have failed in the past; wherefore the future gives no better promise of success. By referring to Sketch N, it will be seen that the holy place or First Covenant must be taken away, or made old, that one can enter at once into the most holy place; for none can fulfil the rulings of the First Covenant. How can the holy place or First Covenant be taken away or made old? It is made old by the establishment of a second covenant, in which righteousness is based upon the faith of Jesus Christ, the Word of God.

Now, while the Second Covenant makes the First old, the First is not made void in a single point,—for it is holy and righteous,—but, when man fails, the First-born as man (see Diagrams 29, 30) comes forward and satisfies all the demands of the First Covenant; and if all its demands are satisfied, who can question God's righteousness? Jesus Christ, the First-born, who is and was God, died, through the rulings of the First Covenant, that the penalty of man's transgressions should be paid. If, therefore, God died in fulfilment of the First Covenant, his death becomes a sign of the greatest magnitude, showing to all hosts the irrevocability of the provisions of the Law, and, hence, that through Christ alone can the sanctuary or holy place of the tabernacle be taken away, and the way into the most holy made manifest wholly free from the Law.

XXVII. 20. "And thou shalt command the children of Israel, that they bring thee pure oil olive beaten for the light, to cause the lamp to burn always."

This verse indicates that the lamp burns unceasingly, and is not permitted to go out or to be extinguished; by which the continuity of the labors of the two Faithful Witnesses (see Diagram 23) during the seven semidivisions of time are indicated.

XXVIII. 1–7. "And take thou unto thee Aaron thy brother, and his sons with him, from among the children of Israel, that he may minister unto me in the priest's office, *even* Aaron, Nadab and Abihu, Eleazar and Ithamar, Aaron's sons.

2. "And thou shalt make holy garments for Aaron thy brother, for glory and for beauty.

3. "And thou shalt speak unto all *that are* wise hearted, whom I have filled with the spirit of wisdom, that they may make Aaron's garments to consecrate him, that he may minister unto me in the priest's office.

4. "And these *are* the garments which they shall make; a breastplate, and an ephod, and a robe, and a broidered coat, a mitre, and a girdle: and they shall make holy garments for Aaron thy brother, and his sons, that he may minister unto me in the priest's office.

5. "And they shall take gold, and blue, and purple, and scarlet, and fine linen.

6. "And they shall make the ephod *of* gold, *of* blue, and *of* purple, *of* scarlet, and fine twined linen, with cunning work.

7. "It shall have the two shoulderpieces thereof joined at the two edges thereof; and *so* it shall be joined together."

The ephod seems to be a sleeveless outer garment, reaching to the waist, made all of one piece; the two edges of which are joined together in front. It is very probable that these edges were strengthened by embroidered strips or shoulder-pieces, whereby the ephod would be better adapted for sustaining the strain which might come upon it.

XXVIII. 8. "And the curious girdle of the ephod, which *is* upon it, shall be of the same, according to the work thereof; *even of* gold, *of* blue, and purple, and scarlet, and fine twined linen."

This girdle evidently is a skilfully-wrought band fixed upon or secured to the lower edge of the ephod as a waistband.

XXVIII. 9-12. "And thou shalt take two onyx stones, and grave on them the names of the children of Israel:

10. "Six of their names on one stone, and *the other* six names of the rest on the other stone, according to their birth.

11. "With the work of an engraver in stone, *like* the engravings of a signet, shalt thou engrave the two stones with the names of the children of Israel: thou shalt make them to be set in ouches of gold.

12. "And thou shalt put the two stones upon the shoulders of the ephod *for* stones of memorial unto the children of Israel: and Aaron shall bear their names before the Lord upon his two shoulders for a memorial."

Thus these two stones, which bear the names of the twelve tribes of the children of Israel, according to seniority, are placed upon the shoulders of the ephod as a memorial.

XXVIII. 13, 14. "And thou shalt make ouches *of* gold;

14. "And two chains *of* pure gold at the ends; *of* wreathen work shalt thou make them, and fasten the wreathen chains to the ouches."

These ouches, in all probability, are the settings for the two stones of onyx; upon which the names of the children of Israel were graven. It is quite probable, also, that they were secured to the shoulders of the ephod by fastenings not particularized in the text, the

INDICATIONS OF THE BOOK OF EXODUS. 211

golden chains of wreathen work being designed for another purpose.

XXVIII. 15–21. "And thou shalt make the breastplate of judgment with cunning work; after the work of the ephod thou shalt make it; *of* gold, *of* blue, and *of* purple, and *of* scarlet, and *of* fine twined linen, shalt thou make it.

16. "Foursquare it shall be *being* doubled; a span *shall be* the length thereof, and a span *shall be* the breadth thereof.

17. "And thou shalt set in it settings of stones, *even* four rows of stones: *the first* row *shall be* a sardius, a topaz, and a carbuncle: *this shall be* the first row.

18. "And the second row *shall be* an emerald, a sapphire, and a diamond.

19. "And the third row a ligure, an agate, and an amethyst.

20. "And the fourth row a beryl, and an onyx, and a jasper: they shall be set in gold in their inclosings.

21. "And the stones shall be with the names of the children of Israel, twelve, according to their names, *like* the engravings of a signet; every one with his name shall they be according to the twelve tribes."

The breastplate of judgment being doubled, forms a pocket or receptacle: it is foursquare and measures a span each way. Upon the front, doubtless, four rows of precious stones are set, by which (see Diagram 31) the Four Ages of Man are indicated through the appertainings of the twelve tribes of the children of Israel (see, also, Ezek. xlviii. 30–34).

XXVIII. 22–30. "And thou shalt make upon the

breastplate chains at the ends *of* wreathen work *of* pure gold.

23. "And thou shalt make upon the breastplate two rings of gold, and shalt put the two rings on the two ends of the breastplate.

24. "And thou shalt put the two wreathen *chains* of gold in the two rings *which are* on the ends of the breastplate.

25. "And *the other* two ends of the two wreathen *chains* thou shalt fasten in the two ouches, and put *them* on the shoulderpieces of the ephod before it.

26. "And thou shalt make two rings of gold, and thou shalt put them upon the two ends of the breastplate in the border thereof, which *is* in the side of the ephod inward.

27. "And two *other* rings of gold thou shalt make, and shalt put them on the two sides of the ephod underneath, toward the forepart thereof, over against the *other* coupling thereof, above the curious girdle of the ephod.

28. "And they shall bind the breastplate by the rings thereof unto the rings of the ephod with a lace of blue, that *it* may be above the curious girdle of the ephod, and that the breastplate be not loosed from the ephod.

29. "And Aaron shall bear the names of the children of Israel in the breastplate of judgment upon his heart, when he goeth in unto the holy *place*, for a memorial before the Lord continually.

30. "And thou shalt put in the breastplate of judgment the Urim and the Thummim; and they shall be upon Aaron's heart, when he goeth in before the Lord:

and Aaron shall bear the judgment of the children of Israel upon his heart before the Lord continually."

The doubling of the breastplate (see verse 16) brings the two ends of it together, and consequently, the two golden rings unite them at the corners. The sides are evidently closed by a system of wreathen work, whereby the breastplate as a receptacle is made complete. The two wreathen chains probably pass through the rings, and thus connect the wreathen work of the breastplate with the ouches placed upon the shoulders of the ephod; this chain evidently being the one called for in verse 14.

Two rings of gold are put upon the two ends of the breastplate in the border which is on the side of the ephod inward; hence indications arise that these rings are secured to the left border of the breastplate, and also that two other corresponding rings of gold are put upon the left side of the ephod, to which the breastplate is fastened that it may not be loosened from it. It is probable that one or both of the wreathen chains are made to disconnect from the ouches, that the ephod may be laid aside when not required for service.

In Diagram 31, spaces a, a indicate the Four Ages of Man; b, b indicate the Four Ages as Sinai, Elim, Horeb, and Canaan; c, c indicate the Four Ages through the appertainings of the twelve tribes of Israel; d, d indicate the Four Ages by the four rows of precious stones upon which the names of the twelve tribes of Israel are graven; e, e indicate time; f, f indicate the Messianic year.

The breastplate of judgment (see verse 30) is a receptacle for the Urim and the Thummim. As there-

214 *INDICATIONS OF THE BOOK OF EXODUS.*

Ex. xxviii. 15–30, considered as allegory.

DIAGRAM 31.

THE BREASTPLATE OF JUDGMENT.

Creation of a body for the Word of God in and as the very beginning of the creation of God.
First day —Creation of light
Second day —Creation of the firmament
Third day —Creation of vegetation
Fourth day.—Creation of sun, moon, and stars
Fifth day —Creation of fishes and fowl.
Sixth day —Creation of cattle, creeping thing and beast of the earth
The Son begotten   The Living Bread   The Beginning of Time
Pre-Euphratic Era
Creation of the Euphratic or First race (Adam's).

The earth in the Euphratic age

Creation of the Hiddekelic or Second race
Destruction of the Euphratic or First race.

The earth in the Hiddekelic age

Creation of the Gihonic or Third race
Destruction of the Hiddekelic or Second race.

The earth in the Gihonic age

Creation of the Pisonic or Fourth race.
Antediluvian Epoch
Deluge of Noah   Destruction of the Gihonic or Third race.
Epoch of replenishment (see Gen ix 1)
Advent of the Messiah as the Son of man
Messianic Epoch or Month
Crucifixion, absolute death, and resurrection of the Messiah as Jesus Christ the Righteous
The Judgmental Era
The Thousand Years' Era.
Era of Destruction.
End of Time

fore they, the Urim and the Thummim, shall be upon Aaron's heart when he goeth in before the Lord, and as Aaron bears the judgment of the children of Israel upon his heart before the Lord continually, the indication follows that the judgment of the children of Israel becomes identified with the Urim and the Thummim which are placed within the breastplate of judgment, whereby both are borne upon Aaron's heart when he goeth in before the Lord, clad in the priest's garments.

Allegorically, however, the breastplate of judgment (see Diagram 31) pertains in an especial manner to the Four Ages, and being a perfect square by construction, so a perfect unit of labor is indicated upon it as a base; which labor is directly connected with the Urim and the Thummim. Now, inasmuch as the body created for the Word of God in and as the very beginning of the creation of God became the Living Bread in the day the Son of God was begotten, and as the Living Bread continues to the end of time, so the probable identity of the Living Bread with the Urim and the Thummim is brought to notice.

XXVIII. 31-32. "And thou shalt make the robe of the ephod all *of* blue.

32. "And there shall be a hole in the top of it, in the midst thereof: it shall have a binding of woven work round about the hole of it, as it were the hole of an habergeon, that it be not rent."

According to Ex. xxxix. 23, this robe was of woven work, and doubtless was furnished with a flexible binding of woven work also; wherefore, the indication arises that it was seamless. The text calls for an opening in the top of it; which indicates that the robe did not extend above the curious girdle, no provision having been made for armholes. The ephod, the robe of the ephod, and the curious girdle are complete within themselves as a figure.

XXVIII. 36-38. "And thou shalt make a plate *of* pure gold, and grave upon it, *like* the engravings of a signet, HOLINESS TO THE LORD.

37. "And thou shalt put it on a blue lace, that it may be upon the mitre; upon the forefront of the mitre it shall be.

38. "And it shall be upon Aaron's forehead, that Aaron may bear the iniquity of the holy things, which the children of Israel shall hallow in all their holy gifts; and it shall be always upon his forehead, that they may be accepted before the Lord."

By verse 30, through the Urim and the Thummim, Aaron bore the judgment of the children of Israel upon his heart before the Lord continually, and, by verse 38, Aaron shall bear the iniquity of the holy things which the children of Israel shall hallow in all their holy gifts; therefore upon Aaron rest both the iniquity and the judgment of the children of Israel; for of the holy gifts, the first-born of the children of Israel shall be sanctified unto the Lord. If the judgment of the children of Israel rests upon the Urim and the Thummim, it follows that the iniquity also must rest upon them; for the offence and the judgment must be centred in one and the same individuality, that the law be fulfilled and justice unquestionably established; therefore the Urim and the Thummim indicate an atoning element.

By their gifts the children of Israel show their faith,

INDICATIONS OF THE BOOK OF EXODUS 217

and through faith their gifts are hallowed that the promises carried with the gifts may be sure unto them.

By verse 2, the garments made for Aaron are holy garments, and they are made for glory and beauty; therefore they become shadows (see Heb. viii. 4, 5) of the holy, the glorious, and the beautiful; and they indicate the same magnitudes as those set forth in the preceding figures. The curious girdle indicates the altar of sacrifice; the shoulder-pieces of the ephod indicate the horns of the altar; the two onyx stones, with the names of the children of Israel thereon, indicate the House of Man to which the promises were made; the twelve stones—four rows of three each—in the breastplate of judgment indicate the Four Ages of Man, all of which are under bondage to sin; the breastplate, itself, indicates the absolute certainty of judgment; the Urim and the Thummim indicate the one upon whom the iniquity and judgment of the House of Man shall rest; and the golden crown with its inscription, "Holiness to the Lord," indicates the holy character of the gifts and its acceptance by the Lord.

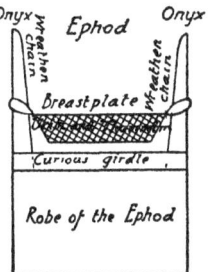

Sketch O
Mitre
Holiness to the Lord

Aaron's garments as shadowing the Altar of Burnt-Offering

Put the curious girdle on the base of the brazen altar (see Sketch O); put the breastplate of judgment, with its inestimable contents, the Urim and the Thummim, above it on the brazen grate; put the onyx stones, the memorial bearing the names appertaining to the Four Ages, upon the horns of the altar; connect the memorial with the breastplate by their wreathen chains of pure gold, and the figure of the great sacrifice is complete. Is it any wonder, therefore, that the horns of the altar are anointed with the blood of the sacrifice? Is it any wonder that the golden crown which is placed above bears the inscription, Holiness to the Lord?

As the ephod and girdle indicate the altar of sacrifice, so the robe of the ephod indicates the base which was made hollow with boards; and as, in shadow, Aaron bears the iniquity and judgment of the children of Israel upon his heart, so in reality the Messiah will bear upon himself the iniquity and judgments of the House of Man, as shadowed by the ephod of cunning work with its holy appointments.

XXIX. 1–9. "And this *is* the thing that thou shalt do unto them to hallow them, to minister unto me in the priest's office: Take one young bullock, and two rams without blemish,

2. "And unleavened bread, and cakes unleavened tempered with oil, and wafers unleavened anointed with oil: *of* wheaten flour shalt thou make them.

3. "And thou shalt put them into one basket, and bring them in the basket, with the bullock and the two rams.

4. "And Aaron and his sons thou shalt bring unto the door of the tabernacle of the congregation, and shalt wash them with water.

5. "And thou shalt take the garments, and put upon Aaron the coat, and the robe of the ephod, and the

INDICATIONS OF THE BOOK OF EXODUS 219

ephod, and the breastplate, and gird him with the curious girdle of the ephod:

6. "And thou shalt put the mitre upon his head, and put the holy crown upon the mitre.

7. "Then shalt thou take the anointing oil, and pour *it* upon his head, and anoint him.

8. "And thou shalt bring his sons, and put coats on them.

9. "And thou shalt gird them with girdles, Aaron and his sons, and put the bonnets on them: and the priest's office shall be theirs for a perpetual statute: and thou shalt consecrate Aaron and his sons."

Aaron and his sons (see xxviii. 1) are chosen by the Lord that they may minister unto the Lord in the priest's office. In the verses above given, the means whereby Aaron and his sons shall be hallowed that they may minister in the priest's office are brought to notice.

When these means are considered merely as simple historical episodes, then they point to the consecrative rites that necessarily must pertain to this priesthood that it may be distinguished simply as a priestly body. The instructions to Moses, however, as allegory, possess a value far beyond that connected with simple history; hence the allegory must supersede the simple history.

The indications are well marked (see Sketch O) that the holy garments made for Aaron shadow great magnitudes; hence it follows that, when Aaron shall have become clothed with these garments, he, as a priest ministering unto the Lord, will be identified with the magnitudes they represent.

Of the holy garments the curious girdle (see Sketch O) points to the brazen altar of burnt-offering, while the altar of burnt-offering (see Diagram 28) points to the earth as the dwelling-place of the creature. The mitre, with its inscription, points (see Lev. xxvii. 1, 2; Isa. viii. 18) to the gift and devotion of the Son of God for the life of the creature world. The breastplate of judgment points to the brazen grate; the brazen grate, in turn, points to the tribulation of the creature. The Urim and the Thummim point to the body that was prepared for the Word of God in and as the very beginning of the creation of God, which body became the Living Bread in the day the Word of God was begotten as the Son of God. The Urim and the Thummim in the breastplate of judgment as the brazen grate point to the afflictions of the Messiah as the Son of God, and as the son of man, in the redemption of the world. The wreathen chains—which doubtless are doubled—point to the four horns of the altar; the four horns of the altar point to the four races of men as instrumentalities in the great purpose of God for the redemption of the world, and for the establishment of a kingdom that shall be wholly righteous. The two onyx stones doubtless memorialize the pertainings of the twelve tribes of Israel to the creature world. The ephod with the robe thereof probably shadows the approximate ending of time.

Thus, through the holy garments and their appointments, Aaron stands revealed as a priest whose ministrations will reach throughout the Four Ages of Man. As Aaron, so his sons; wherefore the priesthood of man (see xix. 3–6) is a magnitude that bears upon the welfare of the creature world.

XXIX. 10-14. "And thou shalt cause a bullock to be brought before the tabernacle of the congregation; and Aaron and his sons shall put their hands upon the head of the bullock.

11. "And thou shalt kill the bullock before the Lord, *by* the door of the tabernacle of the congregation.

12. "And thou shalt take of the blood of the bullock, and put *it* upon the horns of the altar with thy finger, and pour all the blood beside the bottom of the altar.

13. "And thou shalt take all the fat that covereth the inwards, and the caul *that is* above the liver, and the two kidneys, and the fat that *is* upon them, and burn *them* upon the altar.

14. "But the flesh of the bullock, and his skin, and his dung, shalt thou burn with fire without the camp: it *is* a sin offering."

The four horns of the altar (see Diagram 32) indicate the Four Ages of Man, which are under bondage to sin; therefore, as the first transgression of man (see Gen. iii. 21) seems to have been the killing and eating of animals, so by the bullock of the sin-offering the transgressive action is indicated, and, also, that the blood of the animal is required at the hands of man, even as called for (Gen. ix. 4, 5), for the blood of the bullock marks the four horns symbolizing the Four Ages.

If the Four Ages of Man are marked with blood, how can they be purified? Will the blood of the sin-offering indicated above make them clean? No; for Paul says (Heb. x. 4), "*It is* not possible that the blood of bulls and of goats should take away sins."

When, however, an atonement for sin is made by the priest, the promise is given with the sacrifice (see Lev. vi. 7) that the trespass shall be forgiven; from which it becomes evident that these promises are not fulfilled at the time of the sacrifice, but that they accumulate as long as sacrifices shall be called for. Further, it is equally evident that at some time these sacrifices must cease. After such cessation the redemption of the promises given with them may as a unit of labor be carried out; the fulfilment of which condition Paul indicates (Heb. ix. 14, 15) in the death of Christ the Lord (see, also, Diagram 32).

In Diagram 32, spaces a, a indicate the Four Ages of Man; b, b indicate the Four Ages as Sinai, Elim, Horeb, and Canaan; c, c indicate the Four Ages by the four horns of the altar; d, d memorialize the blood that is violently shed throughout the Four Ages, which blood demands compensation; e, e indicate time; f, f indicate the earth as a great altar.

The promises to the Four Ages of Man are indicated by the two onyx stones upon which the names of the children of Israel are engraved, in that, as shadow, they are for a memorial to the children of Israel throughout the Four Ages. If they are for a memorial throughout the Four Ages, then the accumulated promises of forgiveness of sins pertaining to these ages must be included in the memorial. The possible redemption of these promises is indicated by the contents of the breastplate of judgment; for, by Lev. viii. 8, the Urim and the Thummim were put in the breastplate; and by Ex. xxviii. 30, 38, the Urim and the Thummim constitute an atoning element; hence this atoning element is

INDICATIONS OF THE BOOK OF EXODUS 223

Ex. xxix. 10-14, considered as allegory.
DIAGRAM 32.
THE BULLOCK OF THE SIN-OFFERING.

Creation of a body for the Word of God in and as the very beginning of the creation of God
First day —Creation of light
Second day —Creation of the firmament
Third day —Creation of vegetation.
Fourth day —Creation of sun, moon, and stars
Fifth day —Creation of fishes and fowl
Sixth day —Creation of cattle, creeping thing, and beast of the earth

The Son begotten   The Living Bread   The Urim and the Thummim
Beginning of Time
Pre Euphratic Era
Creation of the Euphratic or First race (Adam's)

The earth as the altar in the Euphratic age

Creation of the Hiddekelic or Second race
Destruction of the Euphratic or First race

The earth as the altar in the Hiddekelic age

Creation of the Gihonic or Third race
Destruction of the Hiddekelic or Second race.

The earth as the altar in the Gihonic age

Creation of the Pisonic or Fourth race

Deluge of Noah   Destruction of the Gihonic or Third race
Advent of the Messiah as the Son of man through the ministrations of the priesthood of Melchizedek (see Gen xiv 18-20)
The Messiah born of the Virgin
Crucifixion, absolute death, and resurrection of the Messiah as Jesus Christ, upon whose body rests the iniquity of the creature world
The earth as the altar in the Pisonic age   Judgmental Era
Thousand Years' Era
Era of Destruction
End of Time

Christ (see Heb. ix. 14, 15). Now, while the altar of sacrifice points to conditions appertaining to the First Covenant (see Heb. ix. 1–10) which cannot take away sins, the breastplate of judgment, with its contents, the Urim and the Thummim, does indicate the entry into the most holy place (Heb. x. 20) "By a new and living way, which he hath consecrated for us, through the vail, that is to say, his flesh" (Christ's; see Heb. x. 10). But (see St. John vi. 51; Gen. xiv. 18) Christ's flesh is the Bread of Life which came down from heaven; hence this Bread, with scarcely a doubt, is Christ the Redeemer; this Bread, with scarcely a doubt, is the Urim and the Thummim, the Atoning Element of the breastplate of judgment. If the Bread of Life is the Urim and the Thummim, who has the care of it? The care of the Bread of Life, and hence of the Urim and the Thummim, rests with Melchizedek, priest of the most high God (see Diagram 32).

That the care of the Urim and the Thummim rests with Melchizedek is indicated by Moses (Deut. xxxiii. 8–10), "And of Levi he said, *Let* thy Thummim and thy Urim *be* with thy holy one, whom thou didst prove at Massah, *and with* whom thou didst strive at the waters of Meribah;

"Who said unto his father and to his mother, I have not seen him; neither did he acknowledge his brethren, nor knew his own children: for they have observed thy word, and kept thy covenant.

"They shall teach Jacob thy judgments, and Israel thy law: they shall put incense before thee, and whole burnt sacrifice upon thine altar."

From this it is clear that the holy one is a Power

of the first order, and that, through the Thummim and the Urim, Israel shall be delivered from bondage to an evil kingdom. This deliverance can come only through the possessor of heaven and earth (see Ps. ii. 6–8); therefore it follows that Melchizedek, and the bread and wine of Gen. xiv. 18–20, indicate the same magnitudes as the holy one, and the Thummim and the Urim of Deut. xxxiii. 8–10. But who are they that have observed the word and kept the covenant? The Levites? No; for their after-history shows clearly enough that they did not. Then, if the Levites did not keep the word and the covenant, the reference of Moses must have been to the holy one and to the Thummim and the Urim; for they, as two Persons of the Trinity, have observed both the word and the covenant, and, consequently, they shall teach Jacob God's judgments, and Israel God's laws, as indicated (Heb. x. 15–17), "*Whereof* the Holy Ghost also is a witness to us: for after that he had said before [doubtless, Deut. xxxiii. 8–10],

"This *is* the covenant that I will make with them after those days, saith the Lord; I will put my laws into their hearts, and in their minds will I write them;

"And their sins and iniquities will I remember no more;" hence the holy one and the Thummim and the Urim, or the Holy One and the Living Bread,—not the Levites,—will teach Israel the law of God; for the results obtained, by the quotation from Hebrews and that from Deuteronomy, indicate one and the same thing.

It must be kept in mind that, by the Law of Iniquity, the iniquity of the people must be transmitted from father to son; but, if nothing is gained by such transmission, why should this Law have been established? It is clear enough that by the transmission of the debt payment may at some time be made. If, however, the debt be not transmitted, then the penalty of such debt must have been paid by the debtor when he laid aside his natural life (see Diagram 32), and, consequently, oblivion rolls over his head.

The Law of Iniquity unquestionably calls for the transmission of the debt, and the transmission of the debt indicates the eventual bringing forth of a redeemer. The redeemer is made manifest by the promise (see Gen. iii. 15) that the seed of woman should bruise the serpent's head. This seed as the seed of woman, by the prophecy (see Isa. vii. 10-16), shall be manifest to man after the days of Ahaz, king of Judah. But, by this same prophecy (see, also, Diagram 32), before the child borne by the Virgin shall know to refuse the evil and choose the good, the land shall be forsaken of both her kings; which evidently points to the subjugation of the Adversary before this particular advent of the Messiah as Jesus, even as called for in St. Matt. xii. 28, 29.

If the Adversary is subjugated before the prophecy to Ahaz, king of Judah, finds its fulfilment, then the indication is clear that the labors involved in such subjugation must have been hidden under the veil, and that Jesus Christ as the Subjugator filled out these labors before he was born of the Virgin; which position is further indicated by the song of Mary (see St. Luke i. 46-55), and by the words of the prophet Zacharias (see St. Luke i. 68-79). Isaiah also says in regard to work done (Isa. ix. 2–7), "The people that walked in darkness have seen a great light: they that dwell in the land of the shadow of death, upon them hath the light shined." Why is it that this light has thus shone upon the people that walked in darkness, and upon them that dwell in the land of the shadow of death? Isaiah replies, "For unto us a child is born, unto us a son is given: and the government shall be upon his shoulder: and his name shall be called Wonderful, Counsellor, The mighty God, The everlasting Father, The Prince of Peace." If this child, with his wondrous endowments, that is born in or before the day of Isaiah, is not the Messiah, the Subjugator, who is it?

If the Subjugator is the Redeemer, whom does he come to redeem? He comes to redeem transgressive man. How can he redeem transgressive man since the irrevocable penalty is over him? It is clearly evident that by the descent of man's iniquity from father to son, that his, the Redeemer's, manifestation in the flesh of man is an absolute necessity for the accomplishment thereof; for the Law cannot be revoked. If his manifestation in the flesh of man is an absolute necessity, how can it be accomplished? It is accomplished by the eating of those things wherewith atonement is made. Essential atonement, however, is made only by the Lord's body (see Diagram 32); therefore it becomes evident that the Lord's body must be eaten, even as called for in St. John vi. 47–58.

If the Lord's body is the Living Bread, then as bread it must be eaten (see St. Matt. xxvi. 26). If the Lord's body is eaten by man, then it becomes the flesh of man; and, conversely, man becomes incorporated into or regenerated into the Lord's body.

What is gained by these peculiar manifestations and transfers in the flesh? Why through them the iniquity of man is assumed, for the redeemer of man must assume man's iniquity in strict accordance with the Law governing the same. After the iniquity of man has fallen upon the Lord's body through the communion or eating thereof, how is man freed from it? As by the power of God woman was brought forth from Adam the flesh of Adam, so, by the same power, the Lord's body is brought forth from regenerated man, and hence, with the Lord, through the operation of the Law of Iniquity, are the names and debts of those which had lain for ages in the dark valley. The communion of the Lord's body, therefore, is a matter of the most vital importance; the care and ministration of which is centred in and about the priesthood of Melchizedek,— "Melchizedek, who is King of righteousness, King of peace; without father, without mother, without descent, having neither beginning of days, nor end of life; but made like unto the Son of God; abideth a priest continually."

If, as indicated in Deut. xxxiii. 8–10, the Thummim and the Urim shall teach Jacob God's judgments, and Israel God's laws, then it must be a power of the first magnitude; more especially as they have observed God's word and kept God's covenant. This Power (see Lev. viii. 8), Moses, by divine command,—doubtless through the shewbread,—put in the breastplate of judgment, whereby the ministrations of the priesthood of Melchizedek are manifest; for shewbread, as visible bread, through the priesthood of Melchizedek, can become imbued with the Living Bread, as indicated by the Urim and the Thummim in the days of the exodus, as readily as, through the same priesthood, the visible bread of the feast of the passover became imbued with it in the days of our Saviour, when he took of it, and brake it, and gave it to his disciples, saying, " Take, eat; this is my body." If the bread used at the feast of the passover became imbued with the Lord's body, or the body that was created for the Word of God in and as the very beginning of the creation of God, and which the Word invested with life, then it is a Power through which the people will be taught God's judgments and God's laws; for man's transgressions will still fall upon it, and eventually the penalty will be paid, whereby he will be forever freed from the outgrowths of an evil kingdom; moreover, by his regeneration, man will enter into the unblemishability of the body that was prepared for the " Firstborn among many brethren."

If Melchizedek is King of righteousness, then he must be God; and if the Living Bread came down from heaven, then Melchizedek must have brought it forth when he met Abraham returning from the slaughter of the kings,—for he was priest of the most high God,— and if Melchizedek brought it forth, then he is the holy one of whom Moses speaks in Deut. xxxiii. 8, by which the Living Bread became identified with the Urim and the Thummim which Moses put in the breastplate of judgment.

Now, according to the description of the breastplate of judgment, it seems clear that it was wrought with fine needle-work of many colors and beautiful designs. It was, as already stated, two spans in length and one in breadth; which, being doubled, formed a pocket or receptacle with four equal sides. The edges were closed with or by wreathen chain-work of pure gold, while the exterior was garnished with the most beautiful of precious stones; therefore (see Job xxviii. 12–23), it becomes evident that that which was placed within must have been something of far greater value; hence, as already indicated, the contents of the breastplate cannot be other than the Urim and the Thummim, the Living Bread that came down from heaven.

It seems clear that the breastplate of judgment must be the dwelling-place of the one to whom judgment was committed; and, more, that that one is the Seed, the Messiah, to whom all things were given in the day he was begotten as the Son of God; from which it further follows that the Urim and the Thummim are the Bread and Wine which were brought from heaven by Melchizedek, and which, by divine command, Moses placed in the breastplate. It does not follow, however, that the Living Bread is visible in that which Moses placed in the breastplate; but rather that, through the priesthood of Melchizedek, the visible bread—doubtless the shewbread—became imbued with the true Urim and Thummim as the Living Bread.

That, as already stated, the Urim is a Power seems clear from Num. xxvii. 21, "And he shall stand before Eleazar the priest, who shall ask *counsel* for him after the judgment of Urim before the Lord: at his word they shall go out, and at his word shall they come in, *both* he, and all the children of Israel with him, even all the congregation;" hence it is the Urim which gives judgment before the Lord, and at his word they shall come in,—not the word of Joshua, but that of the Power giving judgment,—which, according to the text, is the Urim, although the Lord is there also, as indicated in xxiii. 23.

The Trinity of the Infinite Majesty must be kept in mind continually: the Father hath no man seen at any time, but the other Persons of the Trinity are, by divine mercy, clearly manifest, or none could approach the Throne of Grace. This condition is indicated in I. Sam. xxvii. 6, as follows: "And when Saul inquired of the Lord, the Lord answered him not, neither by dreams, nor by Urim, nor by prophets." To Saul, therefore, all was silent: there was no word by the Urim; but in the case of Joshua the word was spoken or the statement would not have been made, "At his word shall they go out;" from which the indication is manifest that the Urim, the Son, and the Seed are one and the same through the body that was prepared in the beginning suitable for the labors involved in the overthrow of Evil and for the redemption of the fallen.

This body has been made manifest (see Diagram 32) as the Bread of Life, or the Living Bread, and as such it must be eaten, even as indicated in Ex. xxix. 33, "And they shall eat those things wherewith the atonement was made, to consecrate *and* to sanctify them." Again, it is stated (Ezra ii. 63), "And the Tirshatha said unto them, that they should not eat of the most holy things, till there stood up a priest with Urim and with Thummim." Nehemiah (vii. 65) also says the same thing; therefore the most holy things shall not be eaten till a priest shall stand up with Urim and with Thummim. This condition brings the concording indication that the most holy things are identified with the Urim and with the Thummim; and these accord with the body and blood of our Lord and Saviour Jesus Christ as given by the Lord to his disciples at the Last Supper. Which is the more strange, the great high priest Melchizedek bringing forth bread and wine, or the great high priest Jesus Christ—who is made a priest forever after the order of Melchizedek—bringing forth bread and wine? If the latter be true, cannot the former be possible? It is not only possible, but the Scriptures clearly call for it as an actual existing fact; wherefore the concording statement is made, "They shall eat those things wherewith the atonement was made." The great atonement was made by the body of the Redeemer, and, therefore, the body of the Redeemer must be eaten that the iniquity of man may fall upon it; that the judgment of man may surely be against it; and that the irrevocable penalty resting upon man may be paid by it; whereby the atonement is made perfect in the fulfilment of every law, order, statute, and judgment, given by the Eternal Power for the ruling of all hosts.

If, as Paul states (see Gal. iii. 16), Christ is the Seed of Abraham; and if (see St. John viii. 56) Abraham saw the day of Christ, and rejoiced and was glad, then Christ must have been present in the day of Abraham as the flesh of Abraham. Christ became the flesh of Abraham through the communion of the bread and wine brought forth by Melchizedek, whereby Abraham became possessor of heaven and earth. If Abraham

INDICATIONS OF THE BOOK OF EXODUS. 233

became possessor of heaven and earth through partaking of the bread and wine, then the inherent virtues of possession were vested in the bread and wine; and the bread and wine, however great the mystery may be, was a Power of the first magnitude, even as the Urim and the Thummim is a Power of the first magnitude. Now, inasmuch as Melchizedek (see Gen. xiv. 18) brought forth the one, and as the Lord—evidently Melchizedek also (see Num. xxvii. 21)—was before the other, the indication becomes marked that the bread and wine points to the same Power as the Urim and the Thummim, and that this Power is Christ the Seed of Abraham, for there are but three Powers of the first magnitude.

The history of the Urim and the Thummim indicates the great temporal power with which the seed of Abraham, as man, is now invested; by it he stands at the head of all Israel, and (see Num. xxvii. 21) Joshua and all the children of Israel, even all the congregation, shall both go out and come in at his word. Also by Deut. xvii. 8–12 it is indicated that the children of Israel shall not decline from their judgment either to the right hand or to the left; from which the indication is drawn that at this time the temptation of the Seed, the Messiah, is one of great temporal power, —not only temporal power, but also one involving infallibility of judgment. From the day of Abraham unto the exodus measures of extreme tribulations were experienced by the Seed, as indicated in Gen. xv. 13, but now, by the Urim and the Thummim, his history as a leader of hosts is indicated and taken up. Therefore as the Urim and the Thummim at or about this time manifestly dwell in the breastplate of judgment, they constitute the prize sought after by the Adversary that he may establish his kingdom forever; for undaunted by the unsuccessful issues of the terrible four hundred years' affliction,—from which the Seed came forth possessed of the gate of his enemies,—he seeks by prosperity and temporal power the downfall of the Messiah. His failure in this respect, however, is indicated by the overthrow of Sisera in the song of Deborah and Barak (see Judges v.) where it is stated (verses 27–30), "At her feet he bowed, he fell, he lay down: at her feet he bowed, he fell: where he bowed, there he fell down dead.

"The mother of Sisera looked out at a window, and cried through the lattice, Why is his chariot *so* long in coming? Why tarry the wheels of his chariots?

"Her wise ladies answered her, yea, she returned answer to herself,

"Have they not sped? have they *not* divided the prey; to every man a damsel *or* two; to Sisera a prey of divers colours, a prey of divers colours of needlework, of divers colours of needle-work on both sides, *meet* for the necks of *them that take* the spoil?"

What is this needle-work of divers colors on both sides but the breastplate of judgment with its hidden treasure? What is Sisera but the embodiment of evil? The struggle depicted was a struggle against the Lord; for it is said, "Curse ye Meroz, said the angel of the Lord, curse ye bitterly the inhabitants thereof; because they came not to the help of the Lord, to the help of the Lord against the mighty."

In this contest against the Lord, what prize could be of greater value to Sisera than the needle-work of divers colors on both sides? None, none! The Urim and the Thummim, the Bread of Life, are what Sisera sought after; but he failed, was overthrown, and finally was stricken by the hands of a woman.

Psalm xlv. 13, 14 further shows why Sisera sought the breastplate of judgment; for it is there stated, "The King's daughter *is* all glorious within: her clothing *is* of wrought gold.

"She shall be brought unto the King in raiment of needle-work: the virgins her companions that follow her shall be brought unto thee." This indicates redemption; for the one dwelling in the raiment wrought with gold—which raiment evidently is the breastplate of judgment—clothes the redeemed with his body, and the redeemed, therefore, dwelt with him in the raiment of needle-work; they having been consecrated through the communion by that which makes atonement. Should Sisera make a spoil of this breastplate, with its precious contents, as the Bread of Life, he would overthrow redemption and secure the establishment of his own kingdom, whereby the fallen creature would remain forever united to sin and evil.

The identity of the Urim and the Thummim with the body of the Messiah is still further indicated (Isa. xxii. 20-25), "And it shall come to pass in that day, that I will call my servant Eliakim the son of Hilkiah:

"And I will clothe him with thy robe, and strengthen him with thy girdle, and I will commit thy government into his hand: and he shall be a father to the inhabitants of Jerusalem, and to the house of Judah.

"And the key of the house of David will I lay

upon his shoulder; so he shall open, and none shall shut; and he shall shut, and none shall open.

"And I will fasten him *as* a nail in a sure place; and he shall be for a glorious throne to his father's house.

"And they shall hang upon him all the glory of his father's house, the offspring and the issue, all vessels of small quantity, from the vessels of cups, even to all the vessels of flagons.

"In that day, saith the Lord of hosts, shall the nail that is fastened in the sure place be removed, and be cut down, and fall; and the burden that *was* upon it shall be cut off; for the Lord hath spoken *it*."

The key of the house of David, with little doubt, is the Messiah as the Living Bread, wherefore, as this key shall rest upon the shoulder of Eliakim the son of Hilkiah, the indication becomes clear that it will be placed in the breastplate of judgment; the breastplate being connected with the shoulders of the priest by the two wreathen chains of pure gold as called for in Ex. xxviii. The key of the house of David, therefore, indicates the Urim and the Thummim, upon which rest the names of those lying in the dark valley waiting for release from their captivity.

The great Custodian of the Urim and the Thummim, as indicated by Moses (see Deut. xxxiii. 8, 9), is evidence sufficiently strong to establish its identity with the Living Bread, with the body of the Messiah as brought forth by Melchizedek, king of Salem; hence from all this it does not follow that the blood of the bullock which Moses put upon the four horns of the altar purified the altar, but, rather, that it was sanctified unto purification by the blood, whereby reconciliation might be made upon it (see Heb. ix. 13 ; Lev. viii. 15). The blood that is put upon the horns of the altar may also memorialize the life of the creature; hence by the shadow the instrumentality of man in the overthrow of Evil and the redemption of the creature world is indicated; for the four horns of the altar, which represent the Four Ages of Man, are sanctified unto purification that reconciliation may be made through or upon them as through a priesthood. If man was the only host which stood in need of a redeemer, this view might seem obscure, but when the great army which fell before man was brought forth, and the contemporary forms of creature life and existence are taken into consideration, a clear and well-defined purpose looms out of this seeming obscurity, sending rays of golden light in every direction, whereby the ruling of the First Covenant is made old to the creature world irrespective of host (see Isa. xxii. 24).

Verses 13, 14 stated, " And thou shall take all the fat that covereth the inwards, and the caul *that is* above the liver, and the two kidneys, and the fat that *is* upon them, and burn *them* upon the altar.

" But the flesh of the bullock, and his skin, and his dung, shalt thou burn with fire without the camp: it *is* a sin offering," by which indications are given that the inward man with all its good things shall be accepted by the Lord, but that the outward man with all its corruptions shall be done away with forever; for (see I. Cor. xv. 50) " flesh and blood cannot inherit the kingdom of God." The sin-offering is a sign to all hosts that (see Jer. xv. 19) the precious shall be taken from the vile.

XXIX. 15-18. "Thou shalt also take one ram; and Aaron and his sons shall put their hands upon the head of the ram.

16. "And thou shalt slay the ram, and thou shalt take his blood, and sprinkle *it* round about upon the altar.

17. "And thou shalt cut the ram in pieces, and wash the inwards of him, and his legs, and put *them* unto his pieces, and unto his head.

18. "And thou shalt burn the whole ram upon the altar: it *is* a burnt offering unto the Lord: it *is* a sweet savour, an offering made by fire unto the Lord."

Spaces a, a, Diagram 33, indicate the Four Ages of Man; b, b indicate the Four Ages as Sinai, Elim, Horeb, and Canaan; c, c indicate the tribulation that permeates the Four Ages; d, d indicate and memorialize the blood violently shed throughout the Four Ages; which blood demands compensation; e, e indicate time; f, f indicate the earth as a great altar of sacrifice.

This sacrifice indicates the great sea of tribulation and suffering experienced during the Four Ages of Man (see Diagrams 32, 33), which sacrifice, as an offering unto the Lord, is one remarkable savor, even as indicated in St. Mark x. 28-30 as follows: "Then Peter began to say unto him, Lo, we have left all, and have followed thee.

"And Jesus answered and said, Verily I say unto you, There is no man that hath left house, or brethren, or sisters, or father, or mother, or wife, or children, or lands, for my sake, and the gospel's,

INDICATIONS OF THE BOOK OF EXODUS 239

Ex. xxix. 15-18, *considered as allegory.*

DIAGRAM 33.

THE WHOLE RAM AS A BURNT-OFFERING, AND AS A SWEET SAVOR.

Creation of a body for the Word of God in and as the very beginning of the creation of God
First day —Creation of light
Second day —Creation of the firmament
Third day —Creation of vegetation
Fourth day —Creation of sun, moon, and stars
Fifth day —Creation of fishes and fowl
Sixth day —Creation of cattle, creeping thing, and beast of the earth
The Son begotten   Beginning of Time
Pre Euphratic Era
Creation of the Euphratic or First race (Adam's)

The earth as the altar in the Euphratic age

Creation of the Hiddekelic or Second race

Destruction of the Euphratic or First race.

The earth as the altar in the Hiddekelic age

Creation of the Gihonic or Third race.

Destruction of the Hiddekelic or Second race

The earth as the altar in the Gihonic age.

Creation of the Pisonic or Fourth race

Deluge of Noah   Destruction of the Gihonic or Third race
Advent of the Messiah as the Son of man.
The Messiah born of the Virgin
Crucifixion, absolute death, and resurrection of the Messiah as Jesus Christ
The earth as the altar in the Pisonic age   Judgmental Era.

Thousand Years' Era

Era of Destruction

End of Time

"But he shall receive a hundredfold now in this time, houses, and brethren, and sisters, and mothers, and children, and lands, with persecutions; and in the world to come eternal life."

XXIX. 19-21. "And thou shalt take the other ram; and Aaron and his sons shall put their hands upon the head of the ram.

20. "Then shalt thou kill the ram, and take of his blood, and put *it* upon the tip of the right ear of Aaron, and upon the tip of the right ear of his sons, and upon the thumb of their right hand, and upon the great toe of their right foot, and sprinkle the blood upon the altar round about.

21. "And thou shalt take of the blood that *is* upon the altar, and of the anointing oil, and sprinkle *it* upon Aaron, and upon his garments, and upon his sons, and upon the garments of his sons with him: and he shall be hallowed, and his garments, and his sons, and his sons' garments with him."

In Diagram 34, spaces *a, a* indicate the Four Ages of Man; *b, b* indicate the Four Ages by the countries through which Abraham passed in his journey from Ur of the Chaldees to Canaan; *c, c* indicate the Four Ages by the great image of Nebuchadnezzar's dream (see Dan. ii. 31-45); *d, d,* in harmony with the allegory of the great image, indicate the Four Ages through the peculiar hallowing of Aaron; *e, e* indicate and memorialize the blood that is violently shed throughout the Four Ages, which blood demands compensation; *f, f* indicate time; *g, g* indicate the earth as the great altar of sacrifice; *h, h* indicate pertaining of Aaron as priest of the Four Ages.

INDICATIONS OF THE BOOK OF EXODUS. 241

Ex. xxix. 19-21, *considered as allegory.*

DIAGRAM 34.

THE CONSECRATION OF THE FOUR AGES OF MAN.

Creation of a body for the Word of God in and as the very beginning of the creation of God
First day.—Creation of light
Second day —Creation of the firmament
Third day —Creation of vegetation
Fourth day —Creation of sun, moon, and stars
Fifth day —Creation of fishes and fowl
Sixth day —Creation of cattle, creeping thing, and beast of the earth
The Son begotten   Beginning of Time
Pre-Euphratic Era
Creation of the Euphratic or First race (Adam's)

The earth as the altar in the Euphratic age

Creation of the Hiddekelic or Second race.
Destruction of the Euphratic or First race

The earth as the altar in the Hiddekelic age

Creation of the Gihonic or Third race
Destruction of the Hiddekelic or Second race

The earth as the altar in the Gihonic age

Creation of the Pisonic or Fourth race
Antediluvian Epoch
Deluge of Noah   Destruction of the Gihonic or Third race
Epoch of replenishment (see Gen ix 1)
Advent of the Messiah as the Son of man in the day of Abraham
Messianic Epoch
The earth as the altar in the Pisonic age   Crucifixion, absolute death, and resurrection of the Messiah as Jesus Christ
Judgmental Era
Thousand Years' Era
Era of Destruction
End of Time   The Word returns to the Father

L   *q*   21

242 INDICATIONS OF THE BOOK OF EXODUS.

By the division of the great image of Nebuchadnezzar's dream into four parts (see Dan. ii.) four successive kingdoms are indicated, which, doubtless, as simple history, are found in the Assyrian, Persian, Grecian, and Roman empires. As allegory, however, these four universal empires shadow the Four Ages of Man, in which light the four divisions of the great image also shadow the Four Ages of Man. The head of gold, therefore (see Diagram 34, spaces c, c), indicates the Euphratic or First age; the breast and arms of silver indicate the Hiddekelic or Second age; the belly and thighs of brass indicate the Gihonic or Third age; and the feet and legs thereof indicate the Pisonic or Fourth. The Hiddekelic and Gihonic ages combined (see Diagrams 8, 34) are also known by the name Egypt; hence, inasmuch as the arm of the image extends from the shoulder to the thighs, so the arm—even as Egypt —indicates a pertaining to both the Hiddekelic and Gihonic ages as a unit.

Through the manner of the consecration Aaron and his sons, and their garments (see Sketch O), now become identified with the magnitudes indicated by the great image; hence the anointing of the tip of Aaron's ear points to the consecration of the Euphratic age, the anointing of Aaron's thumb (through the pertaining of the arm) points to the consecration of both the Hiddekelic and Gihonic ages, and the anointing of Aaron's great toe points to the consecration of the Pisonic age, whereby the instrumentality of man in the great purpose of God becomes manifest. The blood, therefore, that is sprinkled upon Aaron and his sons, and upon their garments, indicates (see Sketch O) the hallowing

INDICATIONS OF THE BOOK OF EXODUS. 243

of man as a kingdom of priests and a holy nation to the Lord.

By the Law of Iniquity (see xxxiv. 6, 7) the iniquity of the fathers shall be visited upon the children to the fourth generation; hence upon the fourth generation or age (see Diagram 34) the entire burden of iniquity of the Four Ages will rest. The Pisonic or Fourth age, however, is represented by the feet and legs of the great image, and by the great toe of Aaron as priest; wherefore (see St. John xiii. 3–11), " Jesus knowing that the Father had given all things into his hands, and that he was come from God, and went to God;

" He riseth from supper, and laid aside his garments; and took a towel, and girded himself.

" After that he poureth water into a basin, and began to wash the disciples' feet, and to wipe *them* with the towel wherewith he was girded.

" Then cometh he to Simon Peter : and Peter saith unto him, Lord, dost thou wash my feet?

" Jesus answered and said unto him, What I do thou knowest not now; but thou shalt know hereafter.

" Peter saith unto him, Thou shalt never wash my feet. Jesus answered him, If I wash thee not, thou hast no part with me.

" Simon Peter saith unto him, Lord, not my feet only, but also *my* hands and *my* head.

" Jesus saith to him, He that is washed needeth not save to wash *his* feet, but is clean every whit : and ye are clean, but not all.

" For he knew who should betray him; therefore said he, Ye are not all clean."

Thus the simple history of Jesus washing his disciples' feet is a great allegory bearing upon the redemption of the creature world; for (see Diagram 34) the iniquity of the creature world is transmitted through governing laws to the generation or age that is represented by the feet of the great image. The indication is manifest that, should the feet thus burdened be washed, the whole body would be clean from head to foot. When, therefore, the whole body shall have been made clean from head to foot, through the washing of the feet by the Word, then the Word will return to the Father (see I. Cor. xv. 28) that God may be all in all.

XXIX. 22–30. " Also thou shalt take of the ram the fat and the rump, and the fat that covereth the inwards, and the caul *above* the liver, and the two kidneys, and the fat that *is* upon them, and the right shoulder; for it *is* a ram of consecration:

23. " And one loaf of bread, and one cake of oiled bread, and one wafer out of the basket of the unleavened bread that *is* before the Lord:

24. "And thou shalt put all in the hands of Aaron, and in the hands of his sons; and shalt wave them *for* a wave offering before the Lord.

25. "And thou shalt receive them of their hands, and burn *them* upon the altar for a burnt offering, for a sweet savour before the Lord: it *is* an offering made by fire unto the Lord.

26. "And thou shalt take the breast of the ram of Aaron's consecration, and wave it *for* a wave offering before the Lord: and it shall be thy part.

27. "And thou shalt sanctify the breast of the wave offering, and the shoulder of the heave offering, which

INDICATIONS OF THE BOOK OF EXODUS. 245

is waved, and which is heaved up, of the ram of the consecration, *even* of *that* which *is* for Aaron, and of *that* which is for his sons:

28. "And it shall be Aaron's and his sons' by a statute forever from the children of Israel; for it *is* a heave offering: and it shall be a heave offering from the children of Israel of the sacrifice of their peace offerings, *even* their heave offering unto the Lord.

29. "And the holy garments of Aaron shall be his sons' after him, to be anointed therein, and to be consecrated in them.

30. "*And* that son that is priest in his stead shall put them on seven days, when he cometh into the tabernacle of the congregation to minister in the holy *place*."

Spaces *a, a,* Diagram 35, indicate the Four Ages of Man; *b, b* indicate the Four Ages by the countries through which Abraham passed in his journey from Ur of the Chaldees to Canaan; *c, c* indicate pertainings of sin-offering (see verses 10–14) to the grand epoch from the beginning of the creation down to the end of time; *d, d* indicate pertaining of the ram of consecration to the grand epoch from the beginning of the creation down to the end of time; *e, e* indicate time; *f, f* indicate the earth as a great altar of sacrifice.

The ram of the text is a ram of consecration; hence, by equity, it pertains to the grand epoch from the beginning of the creation of God down to the end of time. This pertaining is made manifest by the apportionment of the caul, the liver, the two kidneys, and the rump (see Diagram 35), to the grand epoch above indicated. Why should the ram have been consecrated? The reply to this question is one of great magnitude,

246 INDICATIONS OF THE BOOK OF EXODUS.

Ex. xxix. 22–30, considered as allegory.

DIAGRAM 35.

THE RAM OF CONSECRATION.

Creation of a body for the Word of God in and as the very beginning of the creation of God.
First day —Creation of light.
Second day —Creation of the firmament
Third day —Creation of vegetation
Fourth day —Creation of sun, moon, and stars.
Fifth day —Creation of fishes and fowl
Sixth day —Creation of cattle, creeping thing, and beast of the earth

The Son begotten   The Living Bread   Beginning of Time
Pre-Euphratic Era
Creation of the Euphratic or First race (Adam s)

The earth as the altar in the Euphratic age

Shoulder (see Diagram 34)   Creation of the Hiddekelic or Second race
Destruction of the Euphratic or First race

The earth as the altar in the Hiddekelic age.

Creation of the Gihonic or Third race

Destruction of the Hiddekelic or Second race

The earth as the altar in the Gihonic age

Creation of the Pisonic or Fourth race.
Antediluvian Epoch
Deluge of Noah   Destruction of the Gihonic or Third race.
Epoch of replenishment (see Gen ix 1)
Advent of the Messiah as the Son of man in the day of Abraham
Messianic Epoch
The earth as the altar in the Pisonic age   Crucifixion, absolute death, and resurrection of the Messiah as Jesus Christ
Judgmental Era
Thousand Years' Era.
Era of Destruction.
End of Time.

and doubtless involves the future existence of animal and plant life, that they may find place in the future as both material and spiritual bodies.

The possibility of the regeneration and restoration of man of Adam's race as both material and spiritual bodies (see St. Luke xxiv. 33-44) makes the possibility of the regeneration and restoration of the creature world, whether animal, plant, or mineral, entire probabilities; whereby the new heaven and new earth in all their varied forms of life and beauty (see Isa. lxv. 17-24) will be perfect, both as material and spiritual bodies.

By regeneration the life and essence of the creature world leaves the material earthy body—which will be called for no more—and is transferred into the unblemishable body that was created for the Word of God in and as the very beginning of the creation of God. This body—which has the pre-eminence in all things, whether as material or as spiritual manifestation —is as entirely suitable for the habitation of the creature irrespective of host as the blemishable earthy body is suitable for the habitation of the creature irrespective of host. Wherefore the indication follows that fruits and flowers, vines and trees, may, through regeneration, have their vitality transferred from the earthy habitation into the pure body that was created in the beginning suitable for this purpose; hence an indication further follows that inasmuch as the earthy was made out of nothing so unto nothing will it return. Not so, however, with the life of the creature world, for through regeneration the creature world, clothed with new imperishable garments, will still exist, and will people forever the realms that finite wisdom cannot measure.

The consecration of the ram denotes instrumentality on the part of the animal kingdom; hence, inasmuch as regeneration is brought about through eating (see Job iii. 23–26; St. John vi. 56) so plant life, through eating (the blood being the life, see Gen. ix. 3, 4), may be transferred to the animal that has been consecrated as such a channel, or, at least, the plant that is eaten by a consecrated channel may, through the eating, be sanctified unto purification. Wherefore, if sanctified unto purification, then regeneration at some stage of existence must surely follow.

In this light the ram of consecration becomes a magnitude that bears upon the sanctification—and hence regeneration—of numberless plants through the eating thereof. The death of the ram, however, does not make void this bearing, but it is carried forward through other channels; for (see verses 31–33) " Aaron and his sons shall eat the flesh of the ram; . . . and they shall eat those things wherewith the atonement was made, to consecrate *and* to sanctify them." When, therefore, Aaron and his sons shall have eaten the flesh of the ram of consecration, then, through the eating thereof, the flesh of the ram, with its bearings, will be further sanctified and consecrated, even as the flesh of the bullock of the sin-offering (see verse 36) is sanctified and consecrated through the eating thereof by Aaron and his sons, when they minister in the priest's office.

Indications now follow that plant life is sanctified through the consecrated eater, even though that eater

INDICATIONS OF THE BOOK OF EXODUS. 249

be an animal; and that the flesh of the animal in turn is sanctified through the consecrated eater as Aaron and his sons, ministering priests; wherefore the sanctification of the creature world—as pertaining to the earth—finds fulfilment through man of Adam's race as a kingdom of priests and a holy nation unto the Lord (see xix. 3-6).

Sanctification, however, is not regeneration, but inasmuch as sanctification is reached through man as a priesthood and a holy nation unto the Lord, so through man as "a priesthood and a holy nation unto the Lord, and as a peculiar treasure unto the Lord above all people," regeneration can pertain to the sanctified creature when, through the priesthood of Melchizedek, man himself shall have been regenerated.

The regeneration of man of Adam's race is direct, in that he directly partakes of the Living Bread or the Lord's body; for (see verse 33) "a stranger shall not eat *thereof;*" hence the regeneration of the creature otherwise is indirect (see St. Matt. xv. 21-28) in that it fulfils through regenerated man as a priesthood, and as a peculiar treasure unto the Lord above all people of the earth.

By verses 22-24 certain portions of the ram of consecration, together with one loaf of bread, one cake of oiled bread, and one wafer out of the basket of the unleavened bread that is before the Lord, shall be put in the hands of Aaron, and in the hands of his sons, for a wave-offering before the Lord. These ordinances point, with great probability, to the indirect regeneration of the creature, for the unleavened bread, the base of which is plant life, pertains to the ram of consecration. Moreover, the whole is waved in the hands of Aaron, and in the hands of his sons, whereby (see Diagram 34) a relation appertaining to both animal and plant life extends throughout the House of Man. By the waving, therefore, dedication and sanctification of the creature are implied, if not strongly indicated; hence, after dedication and sanctification, the unleavened will, at some time, become leavened, when, in the future, through the priesthood of Melchizedek, the visible bread of the communion shall have been imbued with the Living Bread, and shall have been eaten by those ministering in the priest's office. The wave-offering, doubtless, shadows the waving of the Lord's body in the service of the communion (see, also, Diagram 22).

By verse 25 the wave-offering shall be burnt upon the altar of burnt-offering; which indicates (see Diagrams 28, 33) the tribulation that shall beset the creature throughout the Four Ages. As a burnt-offering or an offering made by fire it is for a sweet savor before the Lord. Why a sweet savor before or unto the Lord? Because the tribulation thus experienced is, in a great measure, incurred in the fulfilment of God's great purpose for the establishment of the Kingdom of Righteousness. Blessed, therefore, are they who willingly offer themselves unto the mighty Mastermind that conceived the eternal purpose, wherefore, if man rejoices in self-sacrificing deeds, and crowns the martyr with a lasting fame, then such deeds and martyrdom will stir each noble impulse of the mind to recognize the attributes that brought them forth. So, also, a grateful country heeds the praise that lies concealed in laurel wreaths, and hastens honors to the wearer's brow;

much more, then, shall pain and tribulation—the fires that prove the treasure—bring forth savors pure and holy before the One that pierces through the sacrificial dross into the depths beyond.

XXIX. 31-34. "And thou shalt take the ram of the consecration, and seethe his flesh in the holy place.

32. "And Aaron and his sons shall eat the flesh of the ram, and the bread that *is* in the basket, *by* the door of the tabernacle of the congregation.

33. "And they shall eat those things wherewith the atonement was made, to consecrate *and* to sanctify them: but a stranger shall not eat *thereof*, because they *are* holy.

34. "And if aught of the flesh of the consecrations, or of the bread, remain unto the morning, then thou shalt burn the remainder with fire: it shall not be eaten, because it *is* holy."

From these words—which are the example and shadow of heavenly things (see Heb. viii. 5)—indications become evident that the body of the Redeemer must be eaten, inasmuch as absolute atonement is made only through it and by it. This condition does not refer merely to days subsequent to the absolute death of our Lord and Saviour Jesus Christ, but before those days; the Saviour himself stating, while yet alive and in the flesh, "Take, eat; this is my body." Moreover, it is scarcely probable that he would have died unless the transgression and judgment of man actually rested upon him at the time, for the law requires a fulfilment according to law, and not by substitution; hence the eating of those things wherewith absolute atonement was made becomes manifest in the priesthood of Jesus

Christ; but this manifestation in the priesthood of Melchizedek is under the veil; yet, by the lifting of the veil, the fulfilment thereof is brought to the light; through which the great harvest of iniquity is collected according to law, and judgment rendered according to law, that the penalty may be paid according to law.

It must be kept in mind that the overthrow of Evil depends upon the irrevocability of the Law; for the unbelieving will be judged by the ruling of the First Covenant; and the First Covenant cannot vanish or pass away until every point of it shall have been fulfilled. Man's redemption, however, is provided for in the eating of those things wherewith absolute atonement was made; but as the text declares, "A stranger shall not eat *thereof*, because they *are* holy," therefore the gospel (see Gal. iii. 8) which was preached unto Abraham, viz., "In thee shall all nations be blessed," was made manifest in the New Testament by the wonderful intimation (see Gal. ii. 16) that Justification by the Faith of Jesus Christ the Word of God shall be the ruling principle into which as a highway all hosts can gather that their restoration may be perfected; hence the indication is strongly marked that faith without regeneration will be baseless. How can regeneration be brought about? It is brought about through the eating of those things wherewith the absolute atonement was made, which things, clearly, are of the body that was created for the Son of God suitable for this purpose in and as the very beginning of the creation of God.

By the text Aaron and his sons shall eat the flesh of the ram, and the bread that is in the basket, by the door of the tabernacle of the congregation; hence, if Aaron and his sons have been consecrated, then the flesh of the ram and the bread will, through the eating thereof, become consecrated and sanctified. Why (see verses 26, 27) should the flesh of the ram be sanctified if nothing were gained thereby? As a mere simple rite pertaining to a singular priesthood sanctification becomes lost in form; but sanctification is not form; on the contrary, it points to some condition, state, or essential, connected with the sanctified flesh that must fulfil in the indefinite future.

Of Aaron's priesthood the text further states, "And they shall eat those things wherewith the atonement was made to consecrate *and* to sanctify them." What are the things with which the atonement is made? It is (see verse 36; Lev. i. 1–10) the burnt sacrifice of the herd, as the bullock; it is the burnt sacrifice of the flocks, as the sheep and goats. These things, therefore, —which are not of the ram of consecration,—are consecrated and sanctified through the eating thereof by Aaron and his sons.

Had this special consecration and sanctification taken place before the eating, then these rites might be considered as due to Aaron's sacred office simply, but inasmuch as the things wherewith the atonement was made are sanctified through the eating thereof by Aaron, then the sanctifying element emanates from Aaron as consecrated priest, not from the sacredness of the office, and falls upon them altogether independent of and from any previous consecration or sanctification. From this position indications arise that the consecration and sanctification by Aaron of the things wherewith the atonement was made—however great the mystery may be—seals them unto redemption. If sealed unto redemption, then the new earth—the great foundation of which is of the body that was prepared for the Word of God in the beginning—will echo with the song of birds; while trees and flowers, draped in beauty, will meet the eye, and will, on every side, grace the landscape with their welcome charms. Friends, old friends, the homes of thousands, the bread of those whose busy hum still lingers on the ear, shall new-born earth assign no dwelling-place for you? shall never more the tendril grasp the willing bough? or never more shall zephyr bear the incense sweet and pure, a grateful messenger, to waken consciousness of life unseen, that one should say where is it? It cannot be; the bald-faced rock and vacant plain would weary of their barren lot, and envy their congeners of the past. 'Tis true that newer forms of life may take the place of those quite passed away, but where is their reward? A dreamless grave will never compensate the miseries of life. Where then is God, the God of equity? He shines forth in the wondrous plan that marks redemption, restoration, for the creature world that helped to bear the burdens of the day. If the bearer meets the burden, if the worker earns his hire, why give his wages to another? That his wages will not crown another's lot is indicated where the fiat boldly stands, " And they shall eat those things wherewith the atonement was made to consecrate *and* to sanctify them ;" hence the consecration and santification of the creature of the herd and flock become evidence that the " laborer is worthy of his hire."

INDICATIONS OF THE BOOK OF EXODUS. 255

XXIX. 35-37. "And thus shalt thou do unto Aaron, and to his sons, according to all *things* which I have commanded thee: seven days shalt thou consecrate them.

36. "And thou shalt offer every day a bullock *for* a sin offering for atonement: and thou shalt cleanse the altar, when thou hast made an atonement for it, and thou shalt anoint it, to sanctify it.

37. "Seven days thou shalt make an atonement for the altar, and sanctify it; and it shall be an altar most holy: whatsoever toucheth the altar shall be holy."

Spaces a, a, Diagram 36, indicate the Four Ages of Man; b, b indicate the Four Ages as Sinai, Elim, Horeb, and Canaan; c, c indicate ten chief divisions of time, Decade System; d, d indicate the first seven semidivisions of the Four Ages by the seven days' consecration; e, e indicate the earth as a great altar; f, f indicate time; g, g indicate time by tenths, Decade System.

The seven days' consecration of Aaron and his sons point (see Diagram 36, spaces d, d) to the services and ruling of the First Covenant or Law from the beginning of time, or rather from the creation of the Euphratic race unto the crucifixion, absolute death, and resurrection of the Messiah as Jesus Christ. At or about the time of the Messiah's death (see Dan. ix. 25-27) the sacrifice and oblation shall cease; hence the seven days' consecration memorialize the first seven semidivisions of the Four Ages.

For seven days (see verse 37) an atonement shall be made for the altar. These seven days also point to or memorialize the earth as the altar during the first seven semidivisions of the Four Ages. Wherefore, as the

256 INDICATIONS OF THE BOOK OF EXODUS.

Ex. xxix. 35-37, considered as allegory.

DIAGRAM 36.

SANCTIFICATION OF THE EARTH AS THE ALTAR OF BURNT-OFFERING.

Creation of a body for the Word of God in and as the very beginning of the creation of God
First day —Creation of light.
Second day —Creation of the firmament
Third day —Creation of vegetation
Fourth day —Creation of sun, moon, and stars
Fifth day —Creation of fishes and fowl
Sixth day —Creation of cattle, creeping thing, and beast of the earth

The Son begotten. Beginning of Time
Pre-Euphratic Era
Creation of the Euphratic or First race (Adam's)
The earth as the altar sanctified in the first day

Dividing in the midst of the Euphratic age.

The earth as the altar sanctified in the second day.
Creation of the Hiddekelic or Second race
Destruction of the Euphratic or First race

The earth as the altar sanctified in the third day
Dividing in the midst of the Hiddekelic age

The earth as the altar sanctified in the fourth day.
Creation of the Gihonic or Third race
Destruction of the Hiddekelic or Second race

The earth as the altar sanctified in the fifth day
Dividing in the midst of the Gihonic age

The earth as the altar sanctified in the sixth day
Creation of the Pisonic or Fourth race
Deluge of Noah Destruction of the Gihonic or Third race

The earth as the altar sanctified in the seventh day

Crucifixion, absolute death, and resurrection of the Messiah as Jesus Christ Dividing in the midst of the Pisonic age, at or about which time the sacrifice and oblation cease (see Dan ix 25-27)
Judgmental Era
Thousand Years' Era.
Era of Destruction.
End of Time

altar of burnt-offering is sanctified and made holy, so, through it, as shadow, the sanctification of the earth during the first seven semidivisions of the Four Ages is brought to notice. The altar of burnt-offering is indicative of tribulation; hence if tribulation permeate the past ages of man, and if they were sanctified, then special mission must be accorded those who suffered, irrespective of host, that sanctification avail, and that tribulation be compensated.

The indications are manifest, however, that compensation cannot be made or brought about until after the absolute death and resurrection of the Messiah, at or about the dividing of the Pisonic or Fourth age, or (see Diagram 36) at the end of the seventh day. The fulfilment of compensation indicates a change of priesthood; hence it follows (see Heb. vii. 11–28) that a priesthood through Jesus Christ the compensating medium must supersede that indicated by Aaron; for that of Aaron, although consecrating and sanctifying continually, made nothing perfect. Still, through the labors of these days the altar, which figuratively indicates the Four Ages of Man as the four rivers of Eden, shall be an altar most holy; and as, by the text, "whatsoever toucheth the altar shall be holy," so (Ezek. xlvii. 9) "it shall come to pass *that* every thing that liveth, which moveth, whithersoever the rivers shall come, shall live; and there shall be a very great multitude of fish, because these waters shall come thither: for they shall be healed; and every thing shall live whither the river cometh."

This great result is brought about by the labors of the two Faithful Witnesses, through the priesthood of whom man (see xix. 6) shall be a kingdom of priests, a holy nation, and, also, a peculiar treasure unto the Lord above all people.

XXIX. 38–46. "Now this *is that* which thou shalt offer upon the altar; two lambs of the first year day by day continually.

39. "The one lamb thou shalt offer in the morning; and the other lamb thou shalt offer at even:

40. "And with the one lamb a tenth deal of flour mingled with the fourth part of a hin of beaten oil; and the fourth part of a hin of wine *for* a drink offering.

41. "And the other lamb thou shalt offer at even, and shalt do thereto according to the meat offering of the morning, and according to the drink offering thereof, for a sweet savour, an offering made by fire unto the Lord.

42. "*This shall be* a continual burnt offering throughout your generations *at* the door of the tabernacle of the congregation before the Lord, where I will meet you, to speak there unto thee.

43. "And there I will meet with the children of Israel, and the *tabernacle* shall be sanctified by my glory.

44. "And I will sanctify the tabernacle of the congregation, and the altar: I will sanctify also both Aaron and his sons, to minister to me in the priest's office.

45. "And I will dwell among the children of Israel, and will be their God.

46. "And they shall know that I *am* the Lord their God, that brought them forth out of the land of Egypt, that I may dwell among them: I *am* the Lord their God."

In Diagram 37, spaces *a, a* indicate the Four Ages of Man; *b, b* indicate the Four Ages as Ur of the

INDICATIONS OF THE BOOK OF EXODUS. 259

Ex. xxix. 38–46, considered as allegory.

DIAGRAM 37.

THE CONTINUAL BURNT-OFFERING.

Creation of a body for the Word of God in and as the very beginning of the creation of God.
First day — Creation of light
Second day — Creation of the firmament
Third day — Creation of vegetation.
Fourth day — Creation of sun, moon, and stars
Fifth day — Creation of fishes and fowl
Sixth day — Creation of cattle, creeping thing, and beast of the earth.
The Son begotten   Beginning of Time
Pre Euphratic Era divided in the midst
Creation of the Euphratic or First race (Adam's)
Evening — One lamb

Morning — One lamb
Dividing in the midst of the Euphratic age.
Evening — One lamb

Morning — One lamb
Creation of the Hiddekelic or Second race.

Destruction of the Euphratic or First race
Evening — One lamb.

Morning — One lamb
Dividing in the midst of the Hiddekelic age
Evening — One lamb

Morning — One lamb
Creation of the Gihonic or Third race.

Destruction of the Hiddekelic or Second race
Evening — One lamb.

Morning — One lamb
Dividing in the midst of the Gihonic age
Evening — One lamb

Morning — One lamb
Creation of the Pisonic or Fourth race

Deluge of Noah   Destruction of the Gihonic or Third race.
Evening — One lamb
Advent of the Messiah as the Son of man in the day of Abraham
Morning — One lamb
Dividing in the midst of the Pisonic age   The offering of bulls, goats, and lambs ceases with the offering of the Messiah at the end of the seventh semidivision of the Four Ages, or at the dividing of the Pisonic age   Judgmental Era
Thousand Years' Era
Era of Destruction
End of Time

Chaldees, Egypt, Egypt, and Canaan, the land shown Abraham by the Lord; c, c indicate the first seven semidivisions of the Four Ages by the seven days; d, d indicate the Grand Epoch from the beginning of the creation down to the end of time, through (see Diagrams 18, 27, 30) the tabernacle of the congregation with its twenty boards; e, e indicate the earth as a great altar of sacrifice; f, f, through the hin, indicate the Four Ages as time; g, g indicate time as divided into four parts or ages,—hence one-fourth hin shadows one of the Four Ages of Man; h, h indicate time as divided into tenths, Decade System.

The two lambs of the continual burnt-offering probably shadow the two Faithful Witnesses in their labors (see Isa. xi. 10–12) for the recovery of the people. The sacrifice of these lambs indicates the trials and sufferings of the Faithful Witnesses (see Rev. xi. 3–8; St. Matt. xvii. 10–12) in the work pertaining to the recovery during the Four Ages of Man.

The tribulations of the Faithful Witnesses in the great work pertaining to the purposes of God become evidence that the sufferings of the creature that is offered upon the altar of sacrifice also will be considered. If not, who will compensate the creature for its hapless lot? The fact that an offering made by fire is for a sweet savor unto the Lord brings with it an assurance that the sufferings of the creature shall be considered; and if considered, then the creature must be restored, or such consideration would be but an empty manifestation of something that should have followed. The continual burnt-offering, therefore, is a continual sign and memorial that the suffering of the creature world (see Diagram 37) will be considered, and that the creature world will be compensated even to restoration and life.

The sanctification of the tabernacle of the congregation points to the sanctification of the earth from the beginning of the creative eras unto the end of time; and the sanctification of the altar points to the special sanctification of the earth as an altar of burnt-offering or sacrifice (see Diagram 37) from the begetting of the Son unto the end of time.

The sanctification of Aaron and his sons to minister in the priest's office points to channels through which those things wherewith the atonement was made shall be consecrated and sanctified. These things, as already indicated, are burnt sacrifices of the herd of the flock and of fowls.

If the flesh of these animals (see verse 33) shall be consecrated and sanctified after the natural life thereof shall have passed away, then the indication is almost, if not quite, positive that restoration and life will pertain to them through indirect regeneration. The hosts, therefore, that were brought out from Egypt (see Diagrams 13, 14, 15, 16, 17, 37; also xii. 41) were, in the allegorical sense, more than man of Adam's race simply.

XXX. 1–10. "And thou shalt make an altar to burn incense upon: *of* shittim wood shalt thou make it.

2. "A cubit *shall be* the length thereof, and a cubit the breadth thereof; foursquare shall it be, and two cubits *shall be* the height thereof: the horns thereof *shall be* of the same.

3. "And thou shalt overlay it with pure gold, the top thereof, and the sides thereof round about, and the horns thereof; and thou shalt make unto it a crown of gold round about.

4. "And two golden rings shalt thou make to it under the crown of it, by the two corners thereof, upon the two sides of it shalt thou make *it;* and they shall be for places for the staves to bear it withal.

5. "And thou shalt make the staves *of* shittim wood, and overlay them with gold.

6. "And thou shalt put it before the vail that *is* by the ark of the testimony, before the mercy seat that *is* over the testimony, where I will meet with thee.

7. "And Aaron shall burn thereon sweet incense every morning: when he dresseth the lamps, he shall burn incense upon it.

8. "And when Aaron lighteth the lamps at even, he shall burn incense upon it, a perpetual incense before the Lord throughout your generations.

9. "Ye shall offer no strange incense thereon, nor burnt sacrifice, nor meat offering; neither shall ye pour drink offering thereon.

10. "And Aaron shall make an atonement upon the horns of it once in a year with the blood of the sin offering of atonement; once in the year shall he make atonement upon it throughout your generations: it *is* most holy unto the Lord."

The golden altar of incense (see Sketches P and Q) indicates the same magnitude as the brazen altar of burnt-offering; for by the four equal sides, and the four horns, the Four Ages of Man are indicated. When atonement is made upon the horns of the altar the blood of the sacrifice is sprinkled upon it seven times; which indicate or memorialize (see Diagram 38) the seven semidivisions of the times: to each of which the promise holds (see Lev. xvi. 29, 30) that their

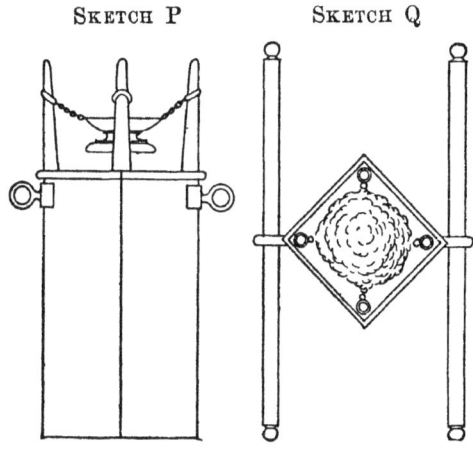

Golden Altar of Incense.

transgressions shall be forgiven, even as further indicated (see Lev. vi. 1–7) in the offering of the trespass-offerings. These promises eventually were redeemed by Jesus Christ as indicated (Heb. ix. 15), "And for this cause he is the mediator of the new testament, that by means of death, for the redemption of the transgressions *that were* under the first testament, they which are called might receive the promise of eternal inheritance;" hence it is evident enough that the blood of the trespass-offering points to the promise of forgiveness, while the time of the sprinkling of the blood is a memorial to the children of Israel of the past ages (see Diagram 38) that the promises given to them stand in full force and vigor, although they as races and instrumentalities have, apparently, passed away forever.

It also becomes evident that these forms are for signs and wonders; and if so, then they must be manifest to the great host which fell before man was brought forth for a sign and for a wonder; and, also, that they are manifest to the Advesary and his immediate army of adherents,—for the dwellers in the land of the valley of the shadow of death cannot realize the strength of these forms, although they are included in them; while man otherwise is blind to their full and proper significance. It is further made evident by the sacrifices that atonement by substitution is impossible,—the rulings of the First Covenant being inexorable, therefore no other way of redemption now can be brought forward than that arising from the death of Jesus Christ the Son of God; who, as man, paid the penalty of man's transgression,—not by substitution, but by the actual fulfilment in the flesh of man of all the laws, statutes, and judgments which stood against man.

The fulfilment of these laws required Christ's manifestation in the flesh of man; hence he made his advent in the world as the flesh of man. Pure substitution, however, does not require such a manifestation; neither does it require pain or tribulation of any kind on the part of the substitute; it simply requires the power of undoing Death's work. This realization, however, while relieving transgressive man for the time being would leave the normal condition worse than that which existed previous to the entering in of the Law or First Covenant; for while death reigns as an absolute possibility transgression in a manner is restrained.

The life and labors of Jesus Christ, however, embodied every vitality whereby the old order of things should be done away with beyond all doubt or question, never to return, and a new order instituted; from which it follows that the signs and wonders done in and by the House of Man are the indications to the great hosts which peopled the indefinite past that sin will be imputed as sin, and that the penalties attached to sin must be paid by all transgressors irrespective of host. Jesus Christ, therefore, is the foundation of the Second Covenant; a covenant through which individual righteousness, or righteousness by works as a life-giving source, is made old, obsolete, and, as Paul says, ready to vanish away.

The wisdom shown in and by the institution of the First Covenant, however, is unmistakable; for through it Evil is overthrown. If the First Covenant had not entered, sin could not have been imputed. If sin could not be imputed, the offence could not abound. If the offence abounded not, judgment could not be rendered against the transgressor; hence sin, being unimputed as sin, would exist continually as a hurtful aggressive element. But by the entering in of the Law or First Covenant, sin was imputed, and the offence did abound; and, as the ruling is fixed beyond all change, judgment certainly will be rendered against the transgressor. All hosts—" for *there is* no man that sinneth not"—must come under its judgments; even as man himself, in Christ, came under its judgments. But Christ, by an absolute death, paid the penalty of his (man's) transgression beyond all question or doubt; hence, through the institution of the First

Covenant, Evil will be everthrown and its kingdom made desolate forever; for Christ will never reinstate Evil or recall it from the fatal pit.

Now while this fearful ruling rests over all hosts, the gospel, embodying the principles of the Second Covenant, was preached unto Abraham that in him (see Gal. iii. 8) all families of the earth shall be blessed; which carries with it the assurance that a highway will be prepared for the escape of all God's creatures, irrespective of host; that (see Isa. lxv. 17–25) Jerusalem may be free from weeping, and that the wolf and the lamb may feed together. Through the golden altar of incense the possibility of the latter expression is indicated, besides which (see I. John v. 6) Christ came,— not by water only, but by water and blood, which is significant of indirect and direct regeneration (see also St. John ii. 1–10).

Pertainings of the altar of incense upon indirect regeneration are further given as follows:

Spaces a, a, Diagram 38, indicate the Four Ages of Man; b, b indicate the Four Ages by the land through which Abraham passed in his journey from Ur of the Chaldees to Canaan; c, c indicate the first seven semidivisions of the Four Ages by the seven times the blood of the sacrifice is sprinkled before the mercy-seat; d, d indicate the first seven semidivisions of the Four Ages by the first seven months of the year; the seventh month (see Lev. xvi. 29–34) being the one during which the yearly atonement is made (see, also, verse 10); e, e indicate pertaining of altar of incense to time; f, f indicate the earth as a great altar of sacrifice; g, g indicate time; h, h indicate pertaining of

Ex. xxx. 1–10, considered as allegory.

DIAGRAM 38.

THE ALTAR OF INCENSE.

Creation of a body for the Word of God in and as the very beginning of the creation of God
First day —Creation of light
Second day —Creation of the firmament
Third day —Creation of vegetation
Fourth day —Creation of sun, moon, and stars.
Fifth day —Creation of fishes and fowl
Sixth day —Creation of cattle, creeping thing, and beast of the earth
The Son begotten   Beginning of Time.
Pre-Euphratic Era
Creation of the Euphratic or First race (Adam's)

Dividing in the midst of the Euphratic age

Creation of the Hiddekelic or Second race.
Destruction of the Euphratic or First race.

Dividing in the midst of the Hiddekelic age.

Creation of the Gihonic or Third race.
Destruction of the Hiddekelic or Second race

Dividing in the midst of the Gihonic age

Creation of the Pisonic or Fourth race
Antediluvian Epoch
Tenth day of the seventh month   Deluge of Noah   Destruction of the Gihonic or Third race   An atonement made
Advent of the Messiah as the Son of man
The day of Jesse (see prophecy, Isa xi 1–10)
Messianic Epoch or Month
Crucifixion, absolute death, and resurrection of the Messiah as Jesus Christ
Judgmental Era
Thousand Years' Era
Era of Destruction.
End of Time.

staves; *i, i* indicate the years of the first three epochs of the Pisonic or Fourth age.

By verse 10 an atonement shall be made once a year upon the horns of the altar of incense. This atonement (see Lev. xvi. 29, 30) shall be made on the tenth day of the seventh month; hence a special relation exists between the altar of incense and the seventh month, whereby a special pertaining of this altar to the seventh month is indicated.

In the allegoric sense the seventh month, by the Decade System, pertains to the seventh semidivision of the Four Ages or the first half of the Pisonic age. The tenth day of the seventh month probably points to the Deluge of Noah, at which time a general atonement was made by the general sweeping away of the creature, even as a special atonement is made by the special slaughter of the burnt sacrifice.

From the time of the Deluge man of Adam's race (see Lev. xvi. 29–31) will enter into a rest as far as the subjugatory labors are concerned, but the indication is clear that at or from this time the Messiah as Subjugator must come forward and take up this portion of man's mission; hence it is stated (Lev. xvi. 32–34), "And the priest, whom he shall anoint, and whom he shall consecrate to minister in the priest's office in his father's stead, shall make the atonement, and shall put on the linen clothes, even the holy garments.

"And he shall make an atonement for the holy sanctuary, and he shall make an atonement for the tabernacle of the congregation, and for the altar: and he shall make an atonement for the priests, and for all the people of the congregation."

INDICATIONS OF THE BOOK OF EXODUS. 269

The priest shadowed by these verses doubtless is the Messiah; wherefore the golden altar of incense will point to his labors for the redemption of the creature world. In this light, therefore, the diagonal of the altar of incense, as allegory, will reach from the time of the Deluge down to the day of Jesse the son of Obed; for the first half of the Pisonic age is divided into three chief divisions, viz., from the creation of the Pisonic race to the Deluge, from the Deluge to the advent of the Messiah the Prince in the day of Abraham, and from the advent of the Messiah the Prince unto the dividing of the Pisonic age, at which time the Messiah made his great atonement for the creature world.

The length of the altar of incense is one cubit, and the breadth is one cubit, from which the diagonal is found to be one and four-tenths cubits; hence, by allowing one cubit to each chief division (see Diagram 38), the diagonal will, by proportion, cover the years from the Deluge of Noah to the day of Jesse. Why to the day of Jesse? Because by the great prophecy (see Isa. xi. 1–10) the Messiah, as a branch, shall spring out of the roots of Jesse, the girdle of whose loins shall be righteousness, and faithfulness shall be the girdle of his reins; he shall smite the earth with the rod of his mouth, and with the breath of his lips shall he slay the wicked. What more shall follow? Why, "The wolf also shall dwell with the lamb, and the leopard shall lie down with the kid; and the calf and the young lion and the fatling together; and a little child shall lead them.

" And the cow and the bear shall feed; their young

ones shall lie down together: and the lion shall eat straw like the ox.

"And the sucking child shall play on the hole of the asp, and the weaned child shall put his hand on the cockatrice' den.

"They shall not hurt nor destroy in all my holy mountain: for the earth shall be full of the knowledge of the Lord, as the waters cover the sea."

If the labors of the Messiah shall thus separate the good from the evil in the animal kingdom, and the good only be retained, what shall be done with it? or who will raise his hand to sweep it from existence? Who, in that day, could stand and brave Messiah's wrath, condemning both creative and redemptive work? The blood that stains the altar's golden horns will surely be restored,—for the blood is the life,—and not one drop unseen shall pass away; for Messiah, clothed with linen robes (see II. Sam. vi. 12-14; Acts vii. 44, 45),—not Aaron,—shall minister the priestly measures, in his Father's stead, that shall bring forth the promised fruit.

The four sides of the altar of incense are equal, hence the diagonals are equal, and normal to each other, by which a perfect square is indicated, and upon which, as a base, a perfect unit of labor is brought to notice. This unit of labor pertains to the Messiah through the priesthood of Aaron; hence, inasmuch as the flesh of the sacrifice is eaten by Aaron and his sons, after the natural life has passed away, that it may be consecrated and sanctified, and as the blood of the sacrifice is put upon the horns of the altar of incense in the general atonement—the horns of the altar (see Diagram 28) indicating the Four Ages

INDICATIONS OF THE BOOK OF EXODUS.

—so the future welfare of the sacrificial offering is indicated; while by the prophecy (see Isa. xi. 1–10) the fruit of the atonement, consecration, and sanctification of the creature world, is shadowed forth.

If the creature shall thus live after the natural life shall have passed away, then the indication becomes well marked that such creature can be made worthy of regeneration, and hence that, eventually, the spirit of such creature will be transferred from the earthy body with which it was clothed in the day it was created, into the body that was prepared in the beginning of the creation of God suitable for this purpose.

If the Almighty created a blemishable body for the creature that it might partake of natural life, then the indication is clear that, in his infinite wisdom, his plan for the establishment of a kingdom of righteousness, peopled with a great variety of living intelligences, fully comprehended the creation of an unblemishable body in which the creature irrespective of host might partake of eternal life.

XXX. 11–16. " And the Lord spake unto Moses, saying,

12. " When thou takest the sum of the children of Israel after their number, then shall they give every man a ransom for his soul unto the Lord, when thou numberest them; that there be no plague among them, when *thou* numberest them.

13. " This they shall give, every one that passeth among them that are numbered, half a shekel after the shekel of the sanctuary : (a shekel *is* twenty gerahs:) a half shekel *shall be* the offering of the Lord.

14. " Every one that passeth among them that are

numbered, from twenty years old and above, shall give an offering unto the Lord.

15. "The rich shall not give more, and the poor shall not give less, than half a shekel, when *they* give an offering unto the Lord, to make an atonement for your souls.

16. "And thou shalt take the atonement money of the children of Israel, and shalt appoint it for the service of the tabernacle of the congregation; that it may be a memorial unto the children of Israel before the Lord, to make an atonement for your souls."

Spaces a, a, Diagram 39, indicate the Four Ages of Man; b, b indicate pertainings of the children of Israel to the Four Ages (see Ezek. xlviii. 30-34); c, c indicate the numbers of the children of Israel that pertain to the Four Ages; d, d indicate ransom money pertaining to each of the Four Ages; e, e indicate the years of the Four Ages in a direct line from the creation of Adam's race unto the end of time; f, f indicate time (total); g, g, total number of the children of Israel that were numbered, and their pertainings to time; h, h indicate total ransom money, and its pertaining to time; i, i indicate the bounds of time as set according to the number of the children of Israel, or time from the creation of Adam's race unto the end thereof.

The record is made (Deut. xxxii. 8), "When the Most High divided to the nations their inheritance, when he separated the sons of Adam, he set the bounds of the people according to the number of the children of Israel." This record contains a clear indication that the bounds of man of Adam's race, in regard to time,

INDICATIONS OF THE BOOK OF EXODUS. 273

Ex. xxx. 11–16, *considered as allegory.*

DIAGRAM 39.

THE ATONEMENT MONEY AS A MEMORIAL.

Creation of a body for the Word of God in and as the very beginning of the creation of God
First day —Creation of light
Second day —Creation of the firmament.
Third day —Creation of vegetation
Fourth day —Creation of sun, moon, and stars
Fifth day —Creation of fishes and fowl
Sixth day —Creation of cattle, creeping thing, and beast of the earth

The Son begotten   Beginning of Time
Pre Euphratic Era
Creation of the Euphratic or First race (Adam's)

The earth in the Euphratic age

Creation of the Hiddekelic or Second race
Destruction of the Euphratic or First race

The earth in the Hiddekelic age

Creation of the Gihonic or Third race.
Destruction of the Hiddekelic or Second race.

The earth in the Gihonic age.

Creation of the Pisonic or Fourth race
Antediluvian Epoch
Destruction of the Gihonic or Third race   Deluge of Noah.
Epoch of replenishment (see Gen ix 1)
Advent of the Messiah as the Son of man in the day of Abraham
Messianic Epoch
The Pisonic age as divided into two equal parts   Crucifixion, absolute death, and resurrection of the Messiah as Jesus Christ
Judgmental Era
Thousand Years' Era
Era of Destruction.
End of Time.

are limited by some proportionate relation to the number of the children of Israel. The number of the children of Israel that were numbered (see xxxviii. 25, 26) was six hundred thousand and three thousand and five hundred and fifty; hence this number is proportionate to the years from the creation of man of Adam's race unto the end of time.

The separation of the sons of Adam finds place or fulfilment in the Four Ages of Man; wherefore should the number of the children of Israel pertaining to one of these ages be given, and should the years thereof be determined, then the ratio that exists between them would be the same as that existing between the total number of the children of Israel and the total years of the people.

By the chronology of the book of Daniel (see Dan. ix. 1, 2, 25–27), the years of the first half of the Pisonic or Fourth age are found to be three thousand nine hundred and thirty years; consequently the total years would amount to twice this, or seven thousand eight hundred and sixty.

The tribes of Israel that appertain to the Pisonic age (see Ezek. xlviii. 34) are Gad, Asher, and Naphtali; the total number of these three tribes as numbered (see Num. i. 25, 40–43) was one hundred and forty thousand five hundred and fifty; hence as 140,550 : 603,550 :: 7860 : 33,752, or to the years from the creation of Adam in the Euphratic age unto the end of time (see Diagram 39, spaces i, i).

The prophet Ezekiel also gives by name the tribes that appertain to each of the three remaining ages, while the number pertaining to each tribe is given (see

Num. i. 1–49), with the exception of Levi, which tribe Moses, by divine command, was forbidden to number among the children of Israel. From these records the approximate years from the creation of one race of men to the creation of the next are readily obtained by simple proportion (see results, Diagram 39, spaces e, e).

The bounds of the people of Adam's race being thus set according to the number of the children of Israel, so the aggregate number of bekahs, or half shekels, of atonement money (see Diagram 39) points to the same magnitude; hence the ten gerahs of the half shekel that is given by every man that was numbered—be he rich or poor—memorialize (see Diagram 18, spaces d, d) the ten chief divisions of time as pertaining to man of Adam's race, or time from the creation of the Euphratic race unto the end. From this position the indication follows that the twenty gerahs of the full shekel may point (see Diagram 18, spaces e, e) to the twenty chief divisions of the grand epoch from the beginning of the creation of God down to the end of time; and from the indication that burdens pertaining to the creative days are transmitted from generation to generation (see, also, Diagrams 24, 25) until they shall be banished forever in the latter day.

These indications are further confirmed by verse 16; for the atonement money shall be appointed for the service of the tabernacle of the congregation that it may be a memorial unto the children of Israel. The tabernacle of the congregation (see Diagram 27) pertains to the twenty chief divisions of the grand epoch from the beginning of the creation down to the end of time; hence the atonement money truly becomes a memorial to the children of Israel of creatures that existed far beyond the call of man of Adam's race. In this light, therefore, the consecration and sanctification of the flesh of the burnt sacrifice, after natural life shall have passed away, clearly points to a restoration of the creature—whether animal, plant, or mineral—that the new earth (see Isa. xlv. 17–25) be other than a bloomless waste whereon the sole survivor, man, shall find his final home and resting-place.

XXX. 17–21. "And the Lord spake unto Moses, saying,

18. "Thou shalt also make a laver *of* brass, and his foot *also of* brass, to wash *withal:* and thou shalt put it between the tabernacle of the congregation and the altar, and thou shalt put water therein.

19. "For Aaron and his sons shall wash their hands and their feet thereat:

20. "When they go into the tabernacle of the congregation, they shall wash with water, that they die not; or when they come near to the altar to minister, to burn offering made by fire unto the Lord:

21. "So they shall wash their hands and their feet, that they die not: and it shall be a statute forever to them, *even* to him and to his seed throughout their generations."

Spaces *a, a*, Diagram 40, indicate the Four Ages of Man; *b, b* indicate the Four Ages by the great image of Nebuchadnezzar's dream (see Dan. ii. 31–48); *c, c* indicate the Four Ages through the peculiar hallowing of Aaron as priest (see Sketch O, also Diagram 34); *d, d* indicate the tabernacle as pertaining by divisions (see Diagram 27) to the grand epoch from the begin-

INDICATIONS OF THE BOOK OF EXODUS. 277

Ex. xxx. 17–21, *considered as allegory.*

DIAGRAM 40.

THE LAVER OF BRASS.

Creation of a body for the Word of God in and as the very beginning of the creation of God.

First day —Creation of light   Creation of matter

Second day —Creation of the firmament.

Third day —Creation of vegetation

Fourth day —Creation of sun, moon, and stars.

Fifth day —Creation of fishes and fowl

Sixth day —Creation of cattle, creeping thing, and beast of the earth
The Son begotten   Beginning of Time   Position of Laver.
Pre-Euphratic Era divided in the midst
Creation of the Euphratic or First race (Adam's).

Dividing in the midst of the Euphratic age.

Creation of the Hiddekelic or Second race.

Destruction of the Euphratic or First race

Dividing in the midst of the Hiddekelic age.

Creation of the Gihonic or Third race

Destruction of the Hiddekelic or Second race.

Dividing in the midst of the Gihonic age

Creation of the Pisonic or Fourth race
Antediluvian Epoch
Deluge of Noah   Destruction of the Gihonic or Third race.
Epoch of replenishment (see Gen IX 1)
Advent of the Messiah the Prince as the Son of man
Messianic Epoch
Crucifixion, absolute death, and resurrection of the Messiah as Jesus Christ   Dividing of the Pisonic age
Judgmental Era
Thousand Years' Era.
Era of Destruction.
End of Time

ning of the creation of God down to the end of time;
e, e indicate the altar of burnt-offering in its pertaining
to the earth as an altar of sacrifice; *f, f* indicate the
pertaining of the tabernacle of the congregation as a
whole to the grand epoch from the beginning to the
end of time.

By the text the laver of brass shall be put between
the tabernacle of the congregation and the altar; wherefore (see Diagram 40) the position of the laver, in the
allegoric sense, is established in the beginning of the
Pre-Euphratic Era, or between that part of the grand
epoch shadowed by the altar and the remaining portion that pertains to the tabernacle of the congregation.
At or about this time the Word of God was begotten
as the Son of God that he might do the will of God.
What is the will of God? It is this (Ps. ii. 7, 8), "I
will declare the decree: the Lord hath said unto me,
Thou art my Son; this day have I begotten thee.

"Ask of me, and I shall give *thee* the heathen *for*
thine inheritance, and the uttermost parts of the earth
for thy possession."

Thus at the time the Son is begotten the earth is
already in existence, and the heathen—living intelligences—have been brought forth. Of these creatures
the Lord said to the Son in the day he was begotten,
"Ask of me and I shall give *thee* the heathen *for* thine
inheritance, and the uttermost parts of the earth *for*
thy possession."

As an historical stand-point the day in which the Son
was begotten (see Lev. xxvii.) is in the beginning of the
Pre-Euphratic Era; which corresponds with the beginning of time; hence the conditions shadowed by

the quotations from Ps. ii. become (see Diagram 40) tangibly manifest. If, therefore, the creatures that peopled the epoch from the beginning of the creation down to the day the Son was begotten shall be given to the Son, then some means must have been devised for their preservation and restoration, or the essence of the gift—that is, intellectual life as pertaining to individual embodiments—would already have passed out of existence forever. The clay remodelled cannot fill the called-for measures of the psalm, and thus confirm the wisdom of the gift; for one long grave would meet the retrospective glance, and raise a shudder rather than a pleasing consciousness of work well done. Did the Son seek only clay, and ask for it a king's protection and regard? No, forever no; for (see Ps. xxi. 4) " he asked life of thee, *and* thou gavest *it* him, *even* length of days for ever and ever." But the clay, what will he do with the clay, the earthly possessions of clay? He will break them (see Ps. ii. 9) with a rod of iron; he will dash them in pieces like a potter's vessel," and, hence, as they came from nothing, so unto nothing shall they return.

If the clay he thus destroyed, whence shall come the habitation of the souls that fostered life in homes of earthy mould? The indications are that the habitations of the restored creature will be of the body that was created for the Word of God in and as the very beginning of the creation of God suitable for this purpose; but, on the ground that the Son in the body created for him has the pre-eminence in all things, the indication follows that when the spirit of the creature leaves its earthy body it cannot at once be regenerated or born into the body that was created for the Son, inasmuch as the Word of God did not invest this body (see Diagram 40) until ages, indeterminate in extent, had passed away.

At any time, however, after the Word of God invested the body that had been created for the Word of God in and as the very beginning of the creation of God, the work of regeneration may be inaugurated, but the consecration and sanctification of the creature, through prescribed channels, may have been in force from the beginning.

If, in the priesthood of Aaron, the flesh of the creature shall be eaten that it may be consecrated and sanctified, then, through the general eating of creature flesh by prescribed channels, general creature life—whether animal or plant—may be consecrated and sanctified also.

If through the flesh the creature is consecrated and sanctified after the natural life shall have passed away, then the indication is well marked that restoration will, eventually, pertain to the creature so consecrated and sanctified ; and if restored, then regenerated also, or born into the body that was created in the beginning suitable for this purpose.

The position of the laver (see Diagram 40) points in a special manner to the eventual regeneration and restoration of the creature world that existed on the earth previous to the creation of man of Adam's race ; hence, inasmuch as water shall be put into the laver, and inasmuch (see I. John v. 6) as Jesus Christ—who is the begotten Son of God—came by water as well as by blood, so through the water in the laver, that has

INDICATIONS OF THE BOOK OF EXODUS. 281

position before the creation of man of Adam's race, the possible regeneration of the creature world that existed on the earth prior to the creation of man of Adam's race is brought to notice.

Indications have been set forth that regeneration cannot find accomplishment before the Word of God shall have invested the body created in the beginning of the creation suitable for this purpose, but that consecration and sanctification may pertain to the creature before this investment; hence physical peculiarity must descend from generation to generation that regeneration as a physical condition may be realized. If animal life as a genus is traceable through many stages of imperfection, then the existence of a law or laws governing transmission of blood becomes manifest; but if transmission of blood be not governed by a law or laws, then the records concerning it would be but little more than coincidence of chances. The records, however, in their strength, prove the law of transmission; hence physical peculiarity must descend, or the function of the law would produce like results independent of precedent, which cannot be.

If, therefore, physical peculiarity descend from generation to generation, in known or unknown forms, then, through such descent, regeneration may pertain to the creature world when, through the prescribed channels, the regenerative body shall have been eaten by such creature world, either directly or indirectly (see St. Matt. xv. 21–28; xxvi. 26).

From the positions thus set forth indications become manifest that the universal preying of animals upon each other may (see Rom. viii. 28) " work together for good to them that love God, to them who are called according to *his* purpose," the evidence being clear that man is not the only host called according to the purpose of God.

The possible regeneration of the creature world that existed before the creation of man of Adam's race having been indicated, the work is further taken up through the anointing of Aaron that he may minister unto the Lord in the priest's office. Inasmuch, therefore, as Aaron the priest (see Diagram 34, also Sketch O) shadows the Four Ages of Man, and inasmuch as Aaron as priest shall wash his hands and his feet in the laver that is established in the beginning of the Pre-Euphratic Era, so the pertainings of Aaron as shadow (see Diagram 40) will extend from the Pre-Euphratic Era unto the end of time.

In the light that Aaron as priest shadows the Four Ages of Man, then, by the shadow, the general priesthood of man is brought to notice, and hence, as a priesthood, they shall eat of those things wherewith the atonement was made (see xxix. 33) to consecrate and to sanctify them; by which the future welfare of the creature world as pertaining to the earth will eventually be considered.

By the Law of Iniquity the names, blood, characteristics, and iniquity of the creature world are transmitted to the Pisonic or Fourth age; hence in this age the things that were consecrated and sanctified will be considered; and if considered, then they will be made clean. Wherefore, inasmuch as the Pisonic or Fourth age is shadowed by the feet of the great image of Nebuchadnezzar's dream (see Diagram 34), it follows that, by the Law of Iniquity, the iniquity of the whole image, or of the whole Four Ages, is borne by the feet; hence (see St. John xiii. 3–11) when in the Fourth age the Messiah as Jesus Christ shall wash away the sins of the Fourth age, then the whole image will be clean. This is evident, for the sins òf the Four Ages, through the descent thereof from generation to generation, fell upon the Fourth, and from the Fourth they fell upon the Messiah as the Son of man, who, in his great atonement, washed away the sins of the world with his blood, in strict fulfilment of all laws and covenants.

The laver of brass, as already indicated, points in an especial manner to the preservation and restoration of God's creatures that existed before the creation of man of Adam's race (see Diagram 25), whereby the animate and inanimate, in beauty and variety, will ever find a place of kingly glory.

XXX. 22–33. "Moreover the Lord spake unto Moses, saying,

23. "Take thou also unto thee principal spices, of pure myrrh five hundred *shekels*, and of sweet cinnamon half so much, *even* two hundred and fifty *shekels*, and of sweet calamus two hundred and fifty *shekels*,

24. "And of cassia five hundred *shekels*, after the shekel of the sanctuary, and of oil olive a hin:

25. "And thou shalt make it an oil of holy ointment, an ointment compound after the art of the apothecary: it shall be a holy anointing oil.

26. "And thou shalt anoint the tabernacle of the congregation therewith, and the ark of the testimony,

27. "And the table and all his vessels, and the candlestick and his vessels, and the altar of incense,

28. "And the altar of burnt offering with all his vessels, and the laver and his foot.

29. "And thou shalt sanctify them, that they may be most holy: whatsoever toucheth them shall be holy.

30. "And thou shalt anoint Aaron and his sons, and consecrate them, that *they* may minister unto me in the priest's office.

31. "And thou shalt speak unto the children of Israel, saying, This shall be a holy anointing oil unto me throughout your generations.

32. "Upon man's flesh shall it not be poured, neither shall ye make *any other* like it, after the composition of it: it *is* holy, *and* it shall be holy unto you.

33. "Whosoever compoundeth *any* like it, or whosoever putteth *any* of it upon a stranger, shall even be cut off from his people."

Spaces a, a, Diagram 41, indicate the Four Ages of Man; b, b indicate pertainings of the four principal spices by name to the Four Ages; c, c indicate pertainings of the four principal spices to the Four Ages according to quantity; d, d indicate apportionment by quantity of the four principal spices to the chief divisions of time according to the Decade System (see Diagram 18); e, e indicate time; f, f indicate pertaining of hin of oil to time.

Thus the holy anointing oil as compounded points to the consecration and hallowing of time as a link of eternity that is set apart for the fulfilment of the will of God. Time, however, is not all that is thus consecrated and hallowed, but the instrumentalities pertaining to time or the Four Ages of Man (see Diagram 41) are consecrated and hallowed also.

INDICATIONS OF THE BOOK OF EXODUS. 285

Ex. xxx. 22–33, considered as allegory.

DIAGRAM 41.

THE HOLY ANOINTING OIL.

Creation of a body for the Word of God in and as the very beginning of the creation of God
First day —Creation of light   Creation of matter
Second day —Creation of the firmament
Third day —Creation of vegetation
Fourth day —Creation of sun, moon, and stars
Fifth day —Creation of fishes and fowl
Sixth day —Creation of cattle, creeping thing, and beast of the earth
The Son begotten   Beginning of Time
Pre-Euphratic Era divided in the midst
Creation of the Euphratic or First race (Adam's)

Dividing in the midst of the Euphratic age

Creation of the Hiddekelic or Second race
Destruction of the Euphratic or First race.

Dividing in the midst of the Hiddekelic age.

Creation of the Gihonic or Third race
Destruction of the Hiddekelic or Second race

Dividing in the midst of the Gihonic age

Creation of the Pisonic or Fourth race.
Antediluvian Epoch
Deluge of Noah   Destruction of the Gihonic or Third race.
Epoch of replenishment (see Gen ix 1)
Advent of the Messiah as the Son of man in the day of Abraham
Messianic Epoch
Crucifixion, absolute death, and resurrection of the Messiah as Jesus Christ   Dividing in the midst of the Pisonic age
Judgmental Era
Thousand Years' Era
Era of Destruction
End of Time

The consecration of time, and the instrumentalities therein, become clearly manifest from inspection of Diagram 41; for the four principal spices pertain to the Four Ages, and, hence, the weight of the four spices must pertain to the Four Ages also; wherefore, in accordance with the order given in the text, the myrrh—first in order—pertains to the Euphratic or First age. The Euphratic age is divided into four chief divisions (see Diagram 18, spaces e, e); hence the five hundred shekels of myrrh, by apportionment, would give just one hundred and twenty-five to each of these four divisions.

The sweet cinnamon—second in order—pertains to the Hiddekelic or Second age, which (see Diagram 18) is divided into two chief divisions; hence the two hundred and fifty shekels of cinnamon, by apportionment, would give just one hundred and twenty-five to each of these two divisions.

The sweet calamus—third in order—pertains to the Gihonic or Third age. The Gihonic age (see Diagram 18) is also divided into two chief divisions; hence the two hundred and fifty shekels of calamus, by apportionment, would give just one hundred and twenty-five to each of these two divisions.

The cassia—fourth in order—pertains to the Pisonic or Fourth age. This age (see Diagram 18, spaces d, d), in accordance with the Decade System, is divided into four chief divisions; hence the five hundred shekels of cassia, by apportionment, would give just one hundred and twenty-five to each of these four divisions also.

Thus by the apportionment of the principal spices each age has neither more nor less shekels than are required to indicate the chief divisions thereof, whereby the existence of the Four Ages of Man and of the chief divisions of time become further confirmed. Inasmuch, therefore, as the holy anointing oil that is compounded with the principal spices shall not be poured upon the flesh of man (see verse 32), so the special pertaining thereof is to the things that are consecrated and hallowed in and during the limits of time.

The indication now follows—inasmuch as the four principal spices pertain to the Four Ages and as the hin of oil is compounded with and permeates these spices—that the hin shadows time as a whole (see Diagrams 37, 41).

The holy anointing oil not only points to the consecration and hallowing of instrumentalities in the purpose of God during time, but it also points to the existence of a body that, in excellence, is far beyond the one pertaining to man of Adam's race. This body, therefore, must be the one created in the beginning for the Word of God; hence the indication follows that only through regeneration or by being born into this body can the creature be truly anointed with this holy oil, —the holy oil pertaining to the Four Ages,—for upon man's flesh it shall not be poured; hence again, as the tabernacle of the congregation (see Diagrams 26, 27), the ark of testimony (see Diagram 21), the table and his vessels (see Diagram 22), the altar of incense (see Diagram 38), the altar of burnt-offering with all his vessels (see Diagram 28), and the laver and his foot (see Diagram 40) shall be anointed with this holy oil, so the general regeneration, preservation, and restoration of the creature world is indicated.

The anointing of Aaron and of his sons in the priest's garments, that they may minister unto the Lord in the priest's office, also point to the possible regeneration of the creature world; more especially as (see xxix. 32, 33) they shall eat those things wherewith the atonement was made, to consecrate and to sanctify them.

XXX. 34-38. "And the Lord said unto Moses, Take unto thee sweet spices, stacte, and onycha, and galbanum; *these* sweet spices with pure frankincense: of each shall there be a like *weight*:

35. "And thou shalt make it a perfume, a confection after the art of the apothecary, tempered together, pure *and* holy:

36. "And thou shalt beat *some* of it very small, and put of it before the testimony in the tabernacle of the congregation, where I will meet with thee: it shall be unto you most holy.

37. "And *as for* the perfume which thou shalt make, ye shall not make to yourselves according to the composition thereof: it shall be unto thee holy for the Lord.

38. "Whosoever shall make like unto that, to smell thereto, shall even be cut off from his people."

Spaces *a, a*, Diagram 42, indicate the Four Ages of Man; *b, b* indicate the pertainings of the four principal spices of the holy anointing oil to the Four Ages (see Diagram 41); *c, c* indicate pertaining of the spices for the perfume or holy confection to the Four Ages; *d, d* indicate the Four Ages as four grand divisions by the like weight of spices pertaining to each; *e, e* indicate time; *f, f* indicate pertaining of the perfume, as a holy confection, to time.

By Diagram 41, labors and history pertaining to the

Ex. xxx. 34-38, considered as allegory.

DIAGRAM 42.

THE PERFUME AS A HOLY CONFECTION.

Creation of a body for the Word of God in and as the very beginning of the creation of God
First day —Creation of light   Creation of matter
Second day —Creation of the firmament
Third day —Creation of vegetation
Fourth day —Creation of sun, moon, and stars
Fifth day —Creation of fishes and fowl
Sixth day —Creation of cattle, creeping thing, and beast of the earth.
The Son begotten   Beginning of Time
Pre-Euphratic Era
Creation of the Euphratic or First race (Adam's)

First Grand Division of Time.

Creation of the Hiddekelic or Second race

Destruction of the Euphratic or First race

Second Grand Division of Time.

Creation of the Gihonic or Third race

Destruction of the Hiddekelic or Second race

Third Grand Division of Time.

Creation of the Pisonic or Fourth race.
Antediluvian Epoch
Deluge of Noah   Destruction of the Gihonic or Third race
Epoch of replenishment (see Gen ix. 1)
Advent of the Messiah as the Son of man.
Messianic Epoch
Advent of the Messiah born of the Virgin
Crucifixion, absolute death, and resurrection of the Messiah as Jesus Christ   Fourth Grand Division of Time
Judgmental Era
The thousand years' reign of the Messiah
Era of Destruction
End of Time   "It is finished"   The Word returns to the Father

creature world were brought into notice, but, by Diagram 42, the labors shadowed pertain more particularly to the Messiah in his great mission for the subjugation of Evil, and for the regeneration, preservation, and restoration of the creature world.

Therefore in the beginning of the creation of God a body was prepared for the Word of God that was pure and unblemishable; later the earthy body was created, into which the spirit of the living creature was born or generated. This earthy body is blemishable, notwithstanding which, the spirit of the living creature—for a wise purpose—was clothed with it, and thus partook of its possible blemishability.

In due time the Word of God came forward (see Diagram 42) and invested with life the pure unblemishable body that had been prepared for the Word of God, and thus the Word was begotten as the Son of God; from which time (see Ps. xl. 6, 7; Heb. x. 4–9) special mission must pertain to the Word as the Son of God. The indication now presents itself that to transfer the spirit of the living creature from the blemishable earthy body into the pure unblemishable body that was created for the Word of God in the beginning of the creation forms or constitutes, through the priesthood of Melchizedek, a portion of the wonderful mission of the Son of God.

If the first bringing forth of the living creature is the first generation of the living creature, then the transfer of the spirit of the living creature from the earthy body into the pure unblemishable body that was created for the Word in the beginning must be regeneration; and if regeneration, then regeneration in the full sense of the term, a regeneration that embodies and includes all that is promised by regeneration throughout the Scriptures.

The perfection of the labors of the Messiah is indicated (see Diagram 42) by the like weight of the spices that pertain to and shadow the Four Ages. In the beginning of the Euphratic age, or the First Age of Man, the Son was begotten that he might do the will of God; hence as his weight was when he thus came forward in the beginning of the Euphratic age, so a like weight is found for him in the three succeeding ages, whereby (see Diagram 42, spaces f, f) his labors in these ages are as a perfume for a " sweet-smelling savor" unto the Lord. Myrrh in the First age, frankincense in the Fourth,—perfume attesting all! Wise were the men who from their open treasure-box brought forth their gifts of gold, of frankincense, and myrrh, and spread before the new-born King these tokens of his mighty triumphs in the past. Wherefore, whatever more to them the future may unfold, work done must have its place, and every unsuspected recess must reveal its crumpled page of history; hence the perfume rising with the lapse of time will prove the weight alike that marks the perfect labors of the One that came to do the will of God.

XXXI. 12-18. "And the Lord spake unto Moses, saying,

13. "Speak thou also unto the children of Israel, saying, Verily my sabbaths ye shall keep: for it *is* a sign between me and you throughout your generations; that *ye* may know that I *am* the Lord that doth sanctify you.

292 INDICATIONS OF THE BOOK OF EXODUS.

14. "Ye shall keep the sabbath therefore; for it *is* holy unto you. Every one that defileth it shall surely be put to death: for whosoever doeth *any* work therein, that soul shall be cut off from among his people.

15. "Six days may work be done; but in the seventh *is* the sabbath of rest, holy to the Lord: whosoever doeth *any* work in the sabbath day, he shall surely be put to death.

16. "Wherefore the children of Israel shall keep the sabbath, to observe the sabbath throughout their generations, *for* a perpetual covenant.

17. "It *is* a sign between me and the children of Israel for ever: for *in* six days the Lord made heaven and earth, and on the seventh day he rested, and was refreshed.

18. "And he gave unto Moses, when he had made an end of communing with him upon mount Sinai, two tables of testimony, tables of stone, written with the finger of God."

Spaces *a, a,* Diagram 43, indicate the Four Ages of Man; *b, b* indicate appertainings of the children of Israel to the Four Ages (see Ezek. xlviii. 30–34); *c, c* indicate the first seven semidivisions of the Four Ages (see Gen. xv. 7–10); *d, d* indicate the age in which the Messiah as Jesus Christ died an absolute death, that in this death the creature world might have life; *e, e* indicate time; *f, f* indicate the grand epoch from the beginning of the creation of God down to the end of time as the seven days of Gen. i., ii.

By verse 13 the sabbath is a sign between the Lord and the children of Israel that the children of Israel may know that the Lord doth sanctify them. The

Ex. xxxi. 12–18, *considered as allegory.*

DIAGRAM 43.

THE SEVEN DAYS OF THE WEEK.

Creation of a body for the Word of God in and as the very beginning of the creation of God

First day —Creation of light. Creation of matter

Second day —Creation of the firmament

Third day —Creation of vegetation.

Fourth day —Creation of sun, moon, and stars.

Fifth day —Creation of fishes and fowl

Sixth day —Creation of cattle, creeping thing, and beast of the earth.
The Son begotten   Beginning of Time.
Pre-Euphratic Era
Creation of the Euphratic or First race (Adam's)

The earth in the Euphratic age.

Creation of the Hiddekelic or Second race

Destruction of the Euphratic or First race.

The earth in the Hiddekelic age

Creation of the Gihonic or Third race

Destruction of the Hiddekelic or Second race

The earth in the Gihonic age

Creation of the Pisonic or Fourth race, after which the Most High God, the Sublime Unity, rested from his labors
"Ye shall keep the sabbath therefore, for it *is* holy unto you Every one that defileth it shall surely be put to death" (verse 14)
"The Lord looked down from heaven upon the children of men, to see if there were any that did understand, *and* seek God
"They are all gone aside, they are *all* together become filthy *there is* none that doeth good, no, not one ' (Ps xiv 2, 3)
The universal death of the creature world in the death of Jesus Christ the Messiah at the dividing of the Pisonic age
Judgmental Era
Thousand Years' Era
Era of Destruction
End of Time   The fruits of sanctification realized.

children of Israel thus sanctified are not merely the progeny of Jacob the son of Rebekah, but they are the people of the Four Ages to which the twelve tribes of Israel appertain (see Diagram 43, spaces *b, b*). In harmony with this indication the seven days of the calendar week shadow the first seven semidivisions of the Four Ages; of which the seventh day is the day in which the Most High rested " from all his work which he had made" (see Diagram 43, spaces *c, c*).

The seven days of the calendar week not only shadow the first seven semidivisions of the Four Ages but (see verse 17) they shadow the seven creative days also. On the seventh day, however, the Most High rested from his labors; hence (see Diagram 43, spaces *f, f*) the seventh day or sabbath of the Lord is represented by the period of time covered by the Pisonic or Fourth age.

The two tables of testimony given Moses upon Mount Sinai (see verse 18) shadow (see Diagrams 17, 19) the entering in of the Law with the advent of man of Adam's race (see, also, xx. 1–18; Deut. ix. 10); but the proof of the general failure of man of Adam's race in his mission for the subjugation of Evil is made manifest by the Deluge of Noah; wherefore, because of this general failure, the One who came forth in the beginning of time, that he might do the will of God, will take up the subjugatory labors, and will realize the fruits that pertain to and follow with the sanctification of the creature world (see Diagram 43, spaces *d, d*).

The text indicates that the work involved in the creation of the heaven and the earth was completed in six days; and that on the seventh day the Lord rested

INDICATIONS OF THE BOOK OF EXODUS. 295

from his labors, and was refreshed; from which it becomes manifest that the government must rest upon one of his own choosing. This one is the only begotten Son, the man for whom a body was prepared suitable and fitting as a governor, a ruler, a subjugator, and a redeemer. If, therefore, the government of all things shall rest upon his shoulder, the indication is clear that some great plan has been fully conceived and perfected by the Infinite Majesty, and that, after the sixth day, he rests from his labors, while the details are being carried out and fulfilled by the only begotten Son, the chosen One, in whom dwells all the fulness of the Godhead bodily. This very resting of the Most High is a certain indication of the immutability of his designs as set forth in his purpose, whereby a new order of things will be established for the government and ruling of all hosts. It is equally evident that, when this new order of things shall have become established, the government must return unto the Father, that developments pertaining to the new order may be signified and brought into existence.

Now, although it is stated, Acts xv. 18, " known unto God are all his works from the beginning of the world," it does not follow that they are all signified or expressed, but, rather, that the revelations made are more particularly those appertaining to the Grand Epoch that extends from the beginning of the creation of God down to the end of time, during which the great purpose seeks and reaches fulfilment. The resting of the Lord God upon the seventh day, in which he was refreshed, further indicates the wonderful perfection of his plan and purpose, and that not one single point is possessed of doubtful import, whereby any disturbing element shall arise to mar its beauty, its glory, and the inestimable grandeur of its fruit.

XXXII. 1-6. "And when the people saw that Moses delayed to come down out of the mount, the people gathered themselves together unto Aaron, and said unto him, Up, make us gods, which shall go before us; for *as for* this Moses, the man that brought us up out of the land of Egypt, we wot not what is become of him.

2. "And Aaron said unto them, Break off the golden earrings, which *are* in the ears of your wives, of your sons, and of your daughters, and bring *them* unto me.

3. "And all the people brake off the golden earrings which *were* in their ears, and brought *them* unto Aaron.

4. "And he received *them* at their hand, and fashioned it with a graving tool, after he had made it a molten calf: and they said, These *be* thy gods, O Israel, which brought thee up out of the land of Egypt.

5. "And when Aaron saw *it*, he built an altar before it; and Aaron made proclamation, and said, To morrow *is* a feast to the Lord.

6. "And they rose up early on the morrow, and offered burnt offerings, and brought peace offerings; and the people sat down to eat and to drink, and rose up to play."

Spaces *a, a*, Diagram 44, indicate the Four Ages of Man; *b, b* indicate the Four Ages of Sinai, Elim, Horeb, and Canaan (see Diagrams 14, 15, 16); *c, c* indicate the Four Ages by the countries through which Abraham passed in his journey from Ur of the Chal-

INDICATIONS OF THE BOOK OF EXODUS. 297

Ex. xxxii, considered as allegory.

DIAGRAM 44

THE MOLTEN CALF.

Creation of a body for the Word of God in and as the very beginning of the creation of God
First day —Creation of light   Creation of matter.
Second day —Creation of the firmament
Third day —Creation of vegetation
Fourth day —Creation of sun, moon, and stars.
Fifth day —Creation of fishes and fowl
Sixth day —Creation of cattle, creeping thing, and beast of the earth
The Son begotten   Beginning of Time
Pre-Euphratic Era
Creation of the Euphratic or First race (Adam's).

The earth in the Euphratic age.

Creation of the Hiddekelic or Second race

Destruction of the Euphratic or First race

The earth in the Hiddekelic age

Creation of the Gihonic or Third race

Destruction of the Hiddekelic or Second race.

The earth in the Gihonic age

Creation of the Pisonic or Fourth race.
Antediluvian Epoch
Deluge of Noah   Destruction of the Gihonic or Third race
Epoch of replenishment (see Gen ix 1)
Advent of the Messiah as the Son of man
The exodus of the children of Israel
The earth in the Pisonic age   Crucifixion, absolute death, and resurrection of the Messiah as Jesus Christ
Judgmental Era
Thousand Years' Era
Era of Destruction.
End of Time

dees to Canaan (see Gen. xii., xiii.); *d*, *d* indicate the first three ages as the wilderness; *e*, *e* indicate apportionment of the forty days and forty nights, during which Moses fasted, to the Four Ages; *f*, *f* indicate time; *g*, *g* indicate pertaining of Aaron as priest to time.

The exodus of the children of Israel from the land of Egypt, and the crossing of the Red Sea, as simple history, shadows the exodus or bringing out from the Egypt of the past (see Diagrams 17, 44) of the great hosts that peopled the Egypt of the past. Wherefore, as by the simple history, the children of Israel came out from the land of Egypt and were safely passed through the Red Sea, so by this history, as allegory, the names, iniquity, blood, and characteristics of the people of the past ages were brought out from their dark land, and were safely passed through the Deluge of Noah in harmony with the laws governing such transmissions.

The wanderings of the children of Israel in the wilderness also shadow history pertaining to the first Three Ages of Man, by which (see Diagram 17) Mount Sinai, as shadow, finds place in the beginning of the Euphratic age at or about the time man of Adam's race was created.

By xxiv. 12–18, the Lord commanded Moses to come up into the mount, and be there; which command Moses obeyed, and he was in the mount forty days and forty nights. As the cloud covered Sinai six days, and as upon the seventh day the Lord called unto Moses, so the first seven semidivisions of the Four Ages are shadowed or memorialized; and as Moses was in the mount forty days and forty nights, so (see Diagram 44, spaces e, e) by the apportionment thereof, the same time is covered, whereby the allegorical position of Sinai becomes chronologically established at or about the time man of Adam's race was created.

Moses was commanded to come up into Sinai that he might receive " tables of stone, and a law, and commandments" which the Lord had written; by xxxi. 18, Moses was given the tables of stone written with the finger of God; by Deut. x. 3-5, the words written on the tables of stone were the Ten Commandments; hence by the allegoric stand-point of Sinai, the Ten Commandments were given forth as law at or about the time man of Adam's race was created. The law, however, is for the government of all hosts; wherefore inasmuch as (see xxxii. 15) the two tables of testimony were written on both sides, so, from Sinai as an historical stand-point, the writing can be seen (see Diagram 44) by the dwellers of the Pre-Euphratic Era as well as by those dwelling in the House of Man. The indications are that by the simple history, as shadow, these two stones pertain more especially to the ages of man under the veil or to the divisions of time during which, as shadow, the cloud abode upon Sinai; for, because of the veil, the people of these ages may be considered as magnitudes independent of those pertaining directly to the Fourth age, which are not under the veil.

By the simple history (see xxiv. 18) Moses was in the mount forty days and forty nights, during which time the people became impatient (see verses 1-6), and demanded of Aaron that he should make them gods, to go before them. In accordance with this demand Aaron made a molten calf from the golden earrings of the people. This calf the people worshipped as the gods that brought them up out of the land of Egypt.

Moses in Sinai places the allegorical stand-point in the Euphratic age; also by the golden earrings of the people (see Diagrams 34, 40), and by the molten calf or heifer (see, also, Gen. xv. 7-10), the Euphratic or First age is further indicated. In this light the text points to the fall of man of Adam's race in the First age, a lamentation for which is taken up as follows (Amos v. 1, 2, 16-24): "Hear ye this word which I take up against you, *even* a lamentation, O house of Israel.

"The virgin of Israel is fallen; she shall no more rise: she is forsaken upon her land; *there is* none to raise her up. . . .

"Therefore the Lord, the God of hosts, the Lord, saith thus; Wailing *shall be* in all streets; and they shall say in all the highways, Alas! alas! and they shall call the husbandman to mourning, and such as are skilful of lamentation to wailing.

"And in all vineyards *shall be* wailing: for I will pass through thee, saith the Lord.

"Woe unto you that desire the day of the Lord! to what end *is* it for you? the day of the Lord *is* darkness, and not light.

"As if a man did flee from a lion, and a bear met him; or went into the house, and leaned his hand on the wall, and a serpent bit him.

"*Shall* not the day of the Lord *be* darkness, and not light? even very dark, and no brightness in it?

"I hate, I despise your feast days, and I will not smell in your solemn assemblies.

INDICATIONS OF THE BOOK OF EXODUS. 301

"Though ye offer me burnt offerings and your meat offerings, I will not accept *them;* neither will I regard the peace offerings of your fat beasts.

"Take thou away from me the noise of thy songs; for I will not hear the melody of thy viols.

"But let judgment run down as waters, and righteousness as a mighty stream."

Thus the fall of the Euphratic race carries with it a blight that none can displace or render harmless; hence in all the vineyards (see Song of Sol. i. 5, 6) shall be wailing, and destruction (see Diagram 44) shall surely visit each great city in the day the Lord shall visit them.

XXXII. 7–14. "And the Lord said unto Moses, Go, get thee down; for thy people, which thou broughtest out of the land of Egypt, have corrupted *themselves:*

8. "They have turned aside quickly out of the way which I commanded them: they have made them a molten calf, and have worshipped it, and have sacrificed thereunto, and said, These *be* thy gods, O Israel, which have brought thee up out of the land of Egypt.

9. "And the Lord said unto Moses, I have seen this people, and, behold, it *is* a stiffnecked people:

10. "Now therefore let me alone, that my wrath may wax hot against them, and that I may consume them: and I will make of thee a great nation.

11. "And Moses besought the Lord his God, and said, Lord, why doth thy wrath wax hot against thy people, which thou hast brought forth out of the land of Egypt with great power, and with a mighty hand?

12. "Wherefore should the Egyptians speak, and say, For mischief did he bring them out, to slay them in

the mountains, and to consume them from the face of the earth? Turn from thy fierce wrath, and repent of this evil against thy people.

13. "Remember Abraham, Isaac, and Israel, thy servants, to whom thou swarest by thine own self, and saidst thou unto them, I will multiply your seed as the stars of heaven, and all this land that I have spoken of will I give unto your seed, and they shall inherit *it* forever.

14. "And the Lord repented of the evil which he thought to do unto his people."

Thus by the simple history of the text as allegory conditions pertaining to the beginning of the Euphratic age are further indicated. Inasmuch, however, as Moses has not made known to the people the law and commandments written upon the two tables of stone, the indication may follow that the Law had not entered in at the time for the government of the people; but, in all probability, commandments without attached penalty were issued and in force as guiding principles. This indication is strongly marked (Rom. v. 13), "For until the law sin was in the world; but sin is not imputed when there is no law." If sin existed before the law entered, then commandments must have been in force that sin, by the commandments, be made manifest as sin.

The threatened destruction of the people, and the possible elevation of Moses into a great nation (see verses 9, 10) carry the indications that the people shadowed by the text pertain to the Pre-Euphratic Era and to the beyond thereof, and that Moses is representative of man of Adam's race. Moses, however,

INDICATIONS OF THE BOOK OF EXODUS. 303

interceded and besought the Lord for this people, calling to the Lord's remembrance the promises to Abraham, to Isaac, and to Israel, that their seed should be multiplied as the stars of heaven, and that they should inherit forever the land spoken of by the Lord.

That the seed of Abraham, of Isaac, and of Israel are not merely the descendants of Abraham, Isaac, and Jacob is clearly indicated in Gal. iii. 7–9; for by the gospel as preached unto Abraham, "In thee shall all nations be blessed." If, therefore, the promise to Abraham be retroactive, then (see Diagram 44) the limit of the promise cannot be reached until the day a body was created for the Word of God, in and as the very first-born of all creatures, comes in full view.

The destruction, however, that shall come upon the people is shadowed (see Amos v. 1–3) by the fall and smiting of Israel, while the mercy of the Lord, through which Israel was preserved, is indicated by the escaping remnant of one hundred out of a thousand, and of ten out of a hundred (see, also, Isa. i. 9; vi. 13; Rom. ix. 26–30). From the position as thus set forth indications follow that others than man of Adam's race are shadowed by the text, and that they shall participate in the mercy of the Lord.

XXXII. 15–18. "And Moses turned, and went down from the mount, and the two tables of the testimony *were* in his hand; the tables *were* written on both their sides; on the one side and on the other *were* they written.

16. "And the tables *were* the work of God, and the writing *was* the writing of God, graven upon the tables.

17. "And when Joshua heard the noise of the people as they shouted, he said unto Moses, *There is* a noise of war in the camp.

18. "And he said, *It is* not the voice of *them that* shout for mastery, neither *is it* the voice of *them that* cry for being overcome; *but* the noise of *them that* sing do I hear."

By xxiv. 13, 14, Moses rose up, and his minister Joshua; and Moses went up into the mount of God, while Aaron and Hur, and the elders, and the people remained behind. The record does not say that Joshua, the minister of Moses, went up into the mount with Moses, but the indication is well implied that he did accompany him. This indication is borne out by the text (xxxii. 15-18) in that Joshua talked with Moses when Moses went down from the mount. Owing to the sacredness of the mount, indications arise that Joshua the minister of Moses—not Jehoshua or Oshea the son of Nun (see Num. xiii. 8, 16) of the tribe of Ephraim—is the Messiah as the Son of man. Hence, inasmuch as, by the simple history (see verse 16), the tables were the work of God, and as the writing was the writing of God, graven upon the tables (see, also, xxxi. 18), so the inference becomes manifest that the preparation and graving of the tables was the work of the Messiah as Joshua the minister of Moses.

If the Messiah made his advent as the Son of man in the day of Abraham (see St. John viii. 56-58), and if the Messiah (see I. Chron. xvii. 4, 6) went from tent to tent, and from one tabernacle to another (see, also, Num. xxiv. 1-9), then it is highly probable that the Old Testament records will reveal, to a greater or less extent, the tabernacles in which the Messiah walked in the fulfilment of his great mission as the Son of man.

Therefore, in the light that Joshua the minister of Moses is the Messiah, then his remark to Moses, " *There is* a noise of war in the camp" (see, also, verse 25), points to conditions that actually environ the camp, but which are under the veil, even to Moses; wherefore Moses replied, "*It is* not the voice of *them that* shout for mastery, neither *is it* the voice of *them that* cry for being overcome; *but* the voice of *them that* sing do I hear."

The war thus indicated probably points to the aggression of Evil upon the creature world even to the beyond of the Euphratic age; but, as shown by the words of Moses, this aggression may, to the deluded throng, find vent in songs of mirth mistaken for those of true joy.

XXXII. 19-24. "And it came to pass, as soon as he came nigh unto the camp, that he saw the calf, and the dancing: and Moses' anger waxed hot, and he cast the tables out of his hands, and brake them beneath the mount.

20. "And he took the calf which they had made, and burnt *it* in the fire, and ground *it* to powder, and strewed *it* upon the water, and made the children of Israel drink *of it*.

21. "And Moses said unto Aaron, What did this people unto thee, that thou hast brought so great a sin upon them?

22. "And Aaron said, Let not the anger of my lord wax hot: thou knowest the people, that they *are set* on mischief.

23. "For they said unto me, Make us gods, which

shall go before us: for *as for* this Moses, the man that brought us up out of the land of Egypt, we wot not what is become of him.

24. "And I said unto them, Whosoever hath any gold, let them break *it* off. So they gave *it* me: then I cast it into the fire, and there came out this calf."

Spaces *a, a*, Diagram 45, indicate the Four Ages of Man; *b, b* indicate the Four Ages by the countries shown Abraham by the Lord (see Gen. xii., xiii.); *c, c* indicate the Four Ages as Sinai, Elim, Horeb, and Canaan; *d, d* indicate apportionment of the forty days and forty nights during which Moses fasted; *e, e* indicate apportionment of the three thousand men slain on account of the molten calf; *f, f* indicate time; *g, g* indicate pertaining of Aaron as priest to time (see Diagrams 34, 40).

The exodus of the children of Israel from the land of Egypt under the leadership of Moses, as simple history, shadows the bringing forth of the names, iniquity, blood, and characteristics of those pertaining to the first three ages of man into the Pisonic or Fourth age; wherefore the crossing of the Red Sea by the children of Israel shadows the transmission of the names, iniquity, blood, and characteristics of those of the past ages through the Deluge of Noah.

The iniquity of those who peopled the first three ages of man is made manifest by the molten calf; hence, as by the allegory, the molten calf was made in the Euphratic or First age (see Diagram 44), and as it was destroyed in the Gihonic or Third,—the Gihonic age (see Diagrams 16, 17, 19, 44, 45) being shadowed by Horeb, and in Horeb (see Deut. ix. 8–16)

INDICATIONS OF THE BOOK OF EXODUS. 307

Ex. xxxii., considered as allegory.

DIAGRAM 45.

THE MOLTEN CALF.

Creation of a body for the Word of God in and as the very beginning of the creation of God
First day —Creation of light   Creation of matter.
Second day —Creation of the firmament
Third day —Creation of vegetation
Fourth day —Creation of sun, moon, and stars
Fifth day —Creation of fishes and fowl
Sixth day —Creation of cattle, creeping thing, and beast of the earth
The Son begotten   Beginning of Time
Pre-Euphratic Era
Creation of the Euphratic or First race (Adam's)

The molten calf in the Euphratic age (see xxxii. 1-4)

Creation of the Hiddekelic or Second race

Destruction of the Euphratic or First race.

The molten calf in the Hiddekelic age

Creation of the Gihonic or Third race

Destruction of the Hiddekelic or Second race

The molten calf in the Gihonic age (see Deut ix 8-16)

Creation of the Pisonic or Fourth race
Deluge of Noah, as shadowed by the Red Sea   Destruction of the Gihonic or Third race
Epoch of replenishment (see Gen ix 1)
Advent of the Messiah as the Son of man
The Red Sea as shadowing the Deluge of Noah
The Pisonic age   Crucifixion, absolute death, and resurrection of the Messiah as Jesus Christ
Judgmental Era
Thousand Years' Era
Era of Destruction.
End of Time

the worship of the calf culminated in its destruction,—so the iniquity or sin (see Deut. ix. 21) that pertained to the First age is found transmitted to the Third as represented by Horeb.

By the text, Moses took the calf and burnt it in the fire, and ground it to powder, and strewed it upon the water, and made the children of Israel drink of it; by Deut. ix. 21, Moses took the calf and burnt it with fire and stamped it, and ground it small as dust, and cast the dust thereof into the brook that descended out of the mount; hence from these records indications follow that the events surrounding the destruction of the molten calf occurred in the latter part of the Gihonic or Third age; hence, again, the threatened destruction of the people by the Lord (see Deut. ix. 25) was that pertaining to the Deluge of Noah. This indication is further pointed to (see Deut. ix. 17, 18, 25) by the apportionment of the forty days and forty nights (see Diagram 45) during which Moses fasted; for by the apportionment, as shadow, past time is indicated from the Deluge of Noah back to Mount Sinai as established in the Euphratic or First age (see similar apportionment, Diagram 44), whereby Moses could communicate with the Lord on Sinai.

Now, although the molten calf was burnt with fire, and ground to powder, yet total destruction was not fulfilled upon it; for after the dust of it had been cast upon the water the children of Israel were made to drink of it. From the positions already set forth the indications follow that, through this piece of simple history as shadow, the names, iniquity, blood, and characteristics of those who dwelt in the ages of man prior to the Deluge, fell upon the escaping remnant of that great day of the Lord.

Indications further follow that the three thousand men slain on account of the molten calf shadow, by apportionment (see Diagram 45) the first three ages of man; and that as these men were slain by the tribe of Levi, so by the priesthood of the tribe of Levi, as made manifest through the consecration of Aaron and his sons (see xxviii. 40, 41), the general priesthood of man is indicated.

If man is consecrated as a priesthood, and if the names, iniquity, blood, and characteristics of the fathers are transmitted to the children, then, through the consecration of the children (see verse 29), the blessing of the Lord will surely fall upon the children, whereby such blessing will pertain to the fathers also, or else "a little leaven" will not leaven the whole lump. The indications are, however, that this blessing fulfils to the children through their regeneration or by their being born into the body that was created for the Word in the beginning of the creation of God, and, hence, to the fathers also; for the regeneration of the fathers, as an actual physical fact, is reached through the children that bear their names, iniquity, blood, and characteristics (see Job xiv. 19–22.)

By the simple history the three thousand men slain by the Levites probably were of those who withstood Moses after his return from the mount, and who were unwilling to give up their idolatry.

XXXII. 30–35. "And it came to pass on the morrow, that Moses said unto the people, Ye have sinned a great sin: and now I will go up unto the Lord;

peradventure I shall make an atonement for your sin.

31. "And Moses returned unto the Lord, and said, Oh, this people have sinned a great sin, and have made them gods of gold.

32. "Yet now, if thou will forgive their sin—; and if not, blot me, I pray thee, out of thy book which thou hast written.

33. "And the Lord said unto Moses, Whosoever hath sinned against me, him will I blot out of my book.

34. "Therefore now go, lead the people unto *the place* of which I have spoken unto thee: behold, mine Angel shall go before thee: nevertheless, in the day when I visit, I will visit their sin upon them.

35. "And the Lord plagued the people, because they made the calf, which Aaron made."

In the allegoric sense the great and special sin recorded above was committed in the latter part of the Gihonic or Third age, and probably is connected with the abomination which maketh desolate (see Dan. viii. 8–14; St. Matt. xxiv. 15–18) that was set up in the latter part of the Gihonic age, or (see Rev. xiii. 18) in the six hundred threescore and sixth generation of man from the creation of the Euphratic or First race. The excessive idolatry that existed upon the earth at this time culminated in the Deluge of Noah; for (see Deut. ix. 21, 25) the Lord said he would destroy the children of Israel because of the molten calf.

Moses, however, sought to avert the calamity by an atonement, but the Lord said, "Whosoever hath sinned against me, him will I blot out of my book," which

INDICATIONS OF THE BOOK OF EXODUS. 311

reply carries with it the conviction that the Deceiver rather than the deceived (see Rev. xiii. 4–18) shall be blotted out of God's book. This indication is strengthened by the text where the Lord said, "Therefore now go, lead the people unto *the place* of which I have spoken unto thee: behold, mine Angel shall go before thee."

The place spoken of by the Lord is the land of Canaan; hence, inasmuch as by the simple history Moses brought the children of Israel out of the land of Egypt, and as they crossed the Red Sea, so by this history as allegory (see Diagrams 14, 15, 16, 17) the bringing forth of the people of the Egypt of the past, their passage through the Deluge of Noah, and their entry into the land of Canaan as the earth in the Pisonic age (see Diagram 45) is indicated and brought to notice.

The atonement Moses sought to make (see verse 32) was probably in relation to an absolute destruction of the later generations of children upon whom the iniquity of the fathers rested, whereby, through this destruction or blotting out, the fathers might go free. Such an atonement, however, would not be equitable; for (see Ezek. xviii. 18–20) "*As for* his father, because he cruelly oppressed, spoiled his brother by violence, and did *that* which *is* not good among his people, lo, even he shall die in his iniquity.

"Yet say ye, Why? doth not the son bear the iniquity of the father? When the son hath done that which is lawful and right, *and* hath kept all my statutes, and hath done them, he shall surely live.

"The soul that sinneth, it shall die. The son shall

not bear the iniquity of the father, neither shall the father bear the iniquity of the son; the righteousness of the righteous shall be upon him, and the wickedness of the wicked shall be upon him."

Thus the transmission of iniquity from father to son does not relieve the original transgressor from the penalty of transgression; wherefore the atonement offered by Moses was valueless, and, hence, as such, could not be accepted by the Lord.

The quotation from Ezekiel carries with it the clear indication that the iniquity pertaining to man, which falls upon the Messiah, as the Son of man, in no way vitiates the Messiah's claim to life, and in no way brings him into condemnation as the begotten Son of God, clothed with the body that was prepared for him in and as the very beginning of the creation of God; for because he fulfils all the laws and statutes of the Lord "he shall surely live."

XXXIII. 1–7. "And the Lord said unto Moses, Depart, *and* go up hence, thou and the people which thou hast brought up out of the land of Egypt, unto the land which I sware unto Abraham, to Isaac, and to Jacob, saying, Unto thy seed will I give it:

2. "And I will send an Angel before thee; and I will drive out the Canaanite, the Amorite, and the Hittite, and the Perizzite, the Hivite, and the Jebusite:

3. "Unto a land flowing with milk and honey: for I will not go up in the midst of thee; for thou *art* a stiffnecked people: lest I consume thee in the way.

4. "And when the people heard these evil tidings,

they mourned: and no man did put on him his ornaments.

5. "For the Lord had said unto Moses, Say unto the children of Israel, Ye *are* a stiffnecked people: I will come up into the midst of thee in a moment, and consume thee: therefore now put off thy ornaments from thee, that I may know what to do unto thee.

6. "And the children of Israel stripped themselves of their ornaments by the mount Horeb.

7. "And Moses took the tabernacle, and pitched it without the camp, afar off from the camp, and called it the Tabernacle of the congregation. And it came to pass, *that* every one which sought the Lord went out unto the tabernacle of the congregation, which *was* without the camp."

By xvii. the people murmured against Moses, and thirsted for water, neither was there any water for their cattle. In this strait Moses was commanded to smite the rock in Horeb,—Horeb (see Diagram 16) shadowing the Gihonic age, even to the overlap with the Hiddekelic,—the fulfilment of which gave an abundance of drink for both man and beast. The conditions thus set forth indicate history connected with the great Hiddekelic famine which swept away the Hiddekelic race, and the overlapping portion of the Gihonic; wherefore, as, by the simple history, the children of Israel at that time were before Horeb,—Horeb shadowing the Gihonic age,—so the immediate text also takes up history pertaining to the Gihonic age; for the children of Israel stripped themselves of their ornaments by the Mount Horeb; the allegorical stand-point of Mount Horeb being in the overlap of the Gihonic and Pisonic ages.

The threatened destruction of the Gihonic race is indicated by the words (verse 5), " I will come up into the midst of thee in a moment, and consume thee: therefore now put off thy ornaments from thee, that I may know what to do unto thee," yet these people must be brought into the promised land which the Lord sware unto Abraham as a father of nations, to Isaac, and to Jacob.

When, therefore, by the simple history, Moses brought the children of Israel out of the land of Egypt, the great races which existed previous to the flood were brought forth with the hosts of Israel,—that is, their names were raised up among their brethren, and their iniquity to a great extent was assumed and borne by the Seed, the Messiah. This bringing forth is indicated (verse 7) as follows: " And Moses took the tabernacle, and pitched it without the camp, afar off from the camp, and called it the Tabernacle of the congregation. And it came to pass, that every one which sought the Lord went out unto the tabernacle of the congregation, which was without the camp." If there were none other than the children of Israel simply to seek the Lord, no particular indication seems to be given why Moses should thus have pitched the tabernacle without the camp; but should the other hosts of man be considered, then the placing of the tabernacle without the camp becomes fraught with great significance, and it truly becomes the tabernacle of the congregation,—that is, it becomes the tabernacle of the whole House of Man; and perhaps, through the House of Man as a priesthood, the tabernacle of other hosts also.

XXXIII. 8-10. " And it came to pass, when Moses

went out unto the tabernacle, *that* all the people rose up, and stood every man *at* his tent door, and looked after Moses, until he was gone into the tabernacle.

9. " And it came to pass, as Moses entered into the tabernacle, the cloudy pillar descended, and stood *at* the door of the tabernacle, and *the Lord* talked with Moses.

10. " And all the people saw the cloudy pillar stand *at* the tabernacle door : and all the people rose up and worshipped, every man *in* his tent door."

These verses further indicate the presence of others than the children of Israel: for they, as a body, are now in their tents, every man in his tent door, while (see verse 7) the tabernacle had been removed and pitched without the camp ; probably in obedience to the command (xxxii. 34), " Therefore now go, lead the people unto *the place* of which I have spoken unto thee : behold, mine Angel shall go before thee."

The indication now comes forth that the Lord dwelt in the tabernacle, and that people other than the children of Israel, the progeny of Jacob, simply sought him there: which people, doubtless, are those whose names were raised up by the Seed during the years of his manifestation in the flesh of man from the day of Abraham to the exodus. In this light the Messiah as the Son of man (see verse 7) must have gone into the tabernacle of the congregation.

XXXIII. 11. " And the Lord spake unto Moses face to face, as a man speaketh to his friend. And he turned again into the camp ; but his servant Joshua, the son of Nun, a young man, departed not out of the tabernacle."

From this verse it is clear that the Lord spake face to face with Moses, even as a man speaks unto his friend; therefore the Lord must have been manifest to Moses as a tangible presence. If the Lord visibly manifested himself to Moses as a man, it should not be deemed incredible that Melchizedek, priest of the most high God, who is clothed with divine attributes, was God manifest as man when he met Abraham and blessed him and called him possessor of heaven and earth. The Lord which spoke with Moses was, with little doubt, either Melchizedek or the Seed, the Messiah: but as, in this portion of his labors as man, the Seed was unrecognized of men, the indication is strongly given that the Lord which spake to Moses face to face was Melchizedek, priest of the most high God, the Faithful Witness, the Angel which went before the hosts of Israel; one whose labors throughout the Four Ages of Man are unmistakably manifest by the Scriptures of the prophets.

But who is Joshua, the son of Nun, the young man that departed not out of the tabernacle, as called for by the text? This mysterious personage seems, in some way, to be identified with the Seed, the Messiah; while the reading of the text calls for the presence of the Seed at the door of the tabernacle of the congregation that he may seek the Lord with the great and precious roll of names he bears with him. By verses 8-10 all the children of Israel abode in their tents; and, therefore, the indication comes forth that this Joshua, by his presence in the tabernacle, not only seeks the Lord, but that he is there by some inherent right, and that he represents one of the two bands (see Gen. xxxii. 10)

INDICATIONS OF THE BOOK OF EXODUS. 317

into which Jacob was divided. Joshua, the son of Nun, of the tribe of Ephraim, cannot be the Messiah; but Joshua, the minister of Moses, who entered within the tabernacle, may have been the Messiah as Joshua the Son of the Eternal; for the word "Joshua" means the Lord, the Saviour, while the word "Nun" means eternal: from which the above deduction becomes manifest. The indication also follows that the Lord which spake face to face with Moses, as a man speaketh to his friend, may have been this Joshua as the seed of Abraham that was called in Caleb the son of Jephunneh, Caleb the son of Jephunneh, in all probability, being identical with Nahshen, prince of the house of Judah. The general interpretation remains undisturbed whether Moses spake face to face with the Lord as Melchizedek or with the Lord as the Messiah; for, in all probability, both were present at the time. Indications are clear that Joshua, the minister of Moses, has unquestionable access to the most sacred places.

The people of the preceding ages and their history have, to some extent, been indicated in xxxii., xxxiii. 1–6; while by the tabernacle of the congregation and its appertainings their presence and existence are further represented, but not made visibly manifest; therefore, although Moses (see xxxii. 34) is commanded to lead the people unto the place which the Lord had spoken of, he evidently does not yet know who these people are; for (see iii. 13) he did not even know the name of their God. This indication the context confirms as follows:

XXXIII. 12, 13. "And Moses said unto the Lord, See, thou sayest unto me, Bring up this people: and thou hast not let me know whom thou wilt send with me. Yet thou hast said, I know thee by name, and thou hast also found grace in my sight.

13. "Now therefore, I pray thee, if I have found grace in thy sight, shew me now thy way, that I may know thee, that I may find grace in thy sight: and consider that this nation *is* thy people."

Thus Moses confesses his ignorance of the people whom he is commanded to bring up. The children of Israel simply he knows well enough; for they are now abiding in their tents: hence the people is a host of which he is in ignorance, and of which he has been in ignorance from the first, even though the Lord (see iii. 4) did know him by name, and called him to bring the children of Israel out of Egypt. Now, however, Moses prays for light that he may know that this people is the Lord's people; in reply to which the Lord says (verse 14), "My presence shall go *with thee*, and I will give thee rest;" which indicates the actual physical presence of the Messiah, who bears with him the names of those lying in the dark valley waiting for their deliverance from captivity. The reply also indicates the successful termination of the Messiah's labors; for Moses is assured of rest also.

It is not clear that Moses even yet comprehends who is to go with him; for he says (verses 15, 16), "If thy presence go not *with me,* carry us not up hence.

"For wherein shall it be known here that I and thy people have found grace in thy sight? *is it* not in that thou goest with us? So shall we be separated, I and thy people, from all the people that *are* upon the face of the earth;" from which it becomes manifest that the

Lord's people are more in number than the progeny of Jacob the son of Rebekah; for before this man Jacob went down into Egypt (see Gen. xxxii. 9, 10), he had become two bands; one of which—the Messiah —was under the veil, and which, under the veil, multiplied exceedingly, and came out of Egypt an exceeding great host.

This host is the one of which Moses is in comparative ignorance, and they are those which peopled the two great ages immediately preceding the Deluge of Noah; ages which, figuratively (see Diagrams 44, 45) are indicated as the land of Egypt. That the land of Egypt is typical or representative of the Gihonic and Hiddekelic ages is clear enough from many figures, but it is especially noticeable from Ezek. xxix. 8-12: "Therefore thus saith the Lord God; Behold, I will bring a sword upon thee, and cut off man and beast out of thee.

" And the land of Egypt shall be desolate and waste; and they shall know that I *am* the Lord: because he hath said, The river *is* mine, and I have made *it*.

" Behold, therefore I *am* against thee, and against thy rivers, and I will make the land of Egypt utterly waste *and* desolate, from the tower of Syene even unto the border of Ethiopia.

" No foot of man shall pass through it, nor foot of beast shall pass through it, neither shall it be inhabited forty years.

" And I will make the land of Egypt desolate in the midst of the countries *that are* desolate, and her cities among the cities *that are* laid waste shall be desolate forty years: and I will scatter the Egyptians among the nations, and will disperse them through the countries."

320   INDICATIONS OF THE BOOK OF EXODUS.

The Tower of Syene (see Sketch R) indicates in all probability the same magnitude as the Tower of Babel; the Tower of Babel was built (see Gen. xi. 1-9) during the overlap of the Euphratic and Hid-

SKETCH R.

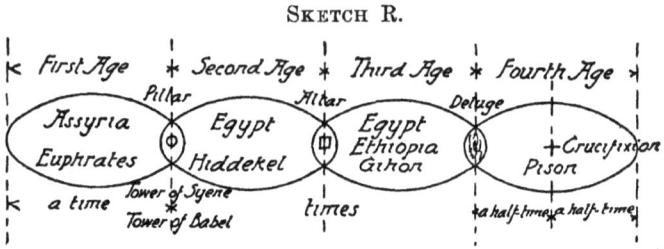

dekelic races; while the river Gihon (see Gen. ii. 13) compasses the whole land of Ethiopia; hence the land of Egypt from the Tower of Syene, or of Babel, unto the extreme border of Ethiopia, as shadow (see Sketch R), would include both the Hiddekelic and the Gihonic ages. Moreover the text of Ezekiel is against the rivers of Egypt, which by the figure of the river of Eden (see Gen. ii. 10-14) are the rivers Hiddekel and Gihon. Again, the land of Egypt shall be made desolate in the midst of the countries that are desolate; by which Egypt as a whole is in the midst of the Four Ages; one of which, the Euphratic or First (see Sketch R) is on the one side of Egypt, while the Pisonic or Fourth age is on the other side of it. Still, again, by the Decade System of Chronology, Egypt shall be desolate forty years; for (see Dan. ix. 2) the seventy years of the desolation of Jerusalem pertain to the seven semidivisions of the Four Ages from the first creation

---

* The Messiah's

INDICATIONS OF THE BOOK OF EXODUS. 321

of man of Adam's race until the Saviour Jesus Christ entered into his kingdom, which, in all probability, was immediately after his resurrection; whereby ten years pertain to each semidivision of the Hiddekelic and Gihonic ages.

The prophet Isaiah, in taking up the burden of Egypt, also indicates the limits of the figurative land of Egypt as follows (Isa. xix. 18-20), " In that day shall five cities in the land of Egypt speak the language of Canaan, and swear to the Lord of hosts; one shall be called, The city of destruction.

" In that day shall there be an altar to the Lord in the midst of the land of Egypt, and a pillar at the border thereof to the Lord.

" And it shall be for a sign and for a witness unto the Lord of hosts in the land of Egypt: for they shall cry unto the Lord because of the oppressors, and he shall send them a saviour, and a great one, and he shall deliver them."

The pillar (see Gen. xi. 1-9; also Sketch R) is established in the border of Egypt or the overlap of the Euphratic and Hiddekelic ages; and the altar must necessarily be placed in the midst of Egypt or in the overlap of the Hiddekelic and Gihonic ages; hence, as the pillar and altar are for signs and witnesses because of the oppressor, their positions are confirmed by the overwhelming of these great nations when their days had run out. The positions of the altar and pillar, therefore, as allegory, indicate the unity of the Hiddekelic and Gihonic ages under the name of Egypt.

If these great nations existed, then the plan of re-
v

322 INDICATIONS OF THE BOOK OF EXODUS.

Ex. xxxiii. 12, 13, considered as allegory.

DIAGRAM 46.

THE PEOPLE MOSES BROUGHT OUT OF EGYPT.

Creation of a body for the Word of God in and as the very beginning of the creation of God
First day —Creation of light   Creation of matter
Second day —Creation of the firmament.
Third day —Creation of vegetation
Fourth day —Creation of sun, moon, and stars
Fifth day —Creation of fishes and fowl
Sixth day —Creation of cattle, creeping thing, and beast of the earth

The Son begotten   Beginning of Time
Pre-Euphratic Era
Creation of the Euphratic or First race (Adam's)

Dividing in the midst of the Euphratic age

Creation of the Hiddekelic or Second race

Destruction of the Euphratic or First race

Dividing in the midst of the Hiddekelic age

Creation of the Gihonic or Third race

Destruction of the Hiddekelic or Second race

Dividing in the midst of the Gihonic age

Creation of the Pisonic or Fourth race
Antediluvian Epoch
Deluge of Noah   Destruction of the Gihonic race.
Epoch of replenishment
Advent of the Messiah as the Son of man
Messianic Epoch
Crucifixion absolute death, and resurrection of the Messiah as Jesus Christ   Dividing of the Pisonic age
Judgmental Era
Thousand Years' Era
Era of Destruction
End of Time

INDICATIONS OF THE BOOK OF EXODUS. 323

demption calls for their return from the land of their captivity; and this return is indicated by the text of Exodus when Moses prays the Lord for light that he may consider them the Lord's people. The conditions, shadowed by the text of Exodus, Isaiah, and Ezekiel, are recapitulated and further indicated by Diagram 46.

Spaces *a, a,* Diagram 46, indicate the Four Ages of Man; *b, b* indicate the Four Ages as the four rivers of Eden (see Gen. ii. 10–14); *c, c* indicate the Four Ages as four countries (see Gen. ii. 10–14); *d, d* indicate the Four Ages by the countries through which Abraham passed in his journey from Ur of the Chaldees to Canaan, Canaan representing the earth in the Pisonic or Fourth age as the promised land; *e, e* indicate the first seven semidivisions of the Four Ages, and the apportionment of the seventy years' desolation of Jerusalem (see Dan. ix. 2), or to the time from the creation of the Euphratic race (Adam's) down to the crucifixion of the Messiah at the dividing of the Pisonic or Fourth age; *f, f* indicate time; *g, g* indicate pertaining of Moses as leader of the hosts of Israel.

Inspection of Diagram 46 will show that the rivers of Egypt are the Hiddekel and Gihon; therefore that which is cried against them by the prophet Ezekiel is cried against the land of Egypt thus shadowed. It will be seen, further, that the spaces from the Tower of Syene to the border of Ethiopia include the rivers Hiddekel and Gihon; hence the waste and desolation prophesied against this land by the prophet, in which both man and beast shall be cut off from it, found fulfilment in the Deluge of Noah, which took place (see Diagram 46, spaces *b, b*) in the border of Ethiopia, or, otherwise, in the border of Egypt.

The prophet Daniel (see Dan. ix. 2) "understood by books the number of years, whereof the word of the Lord came to Jeremiah the prophet, that he would accomplish seventy years in the desolation of Jerusalem." These seventy years, by apportionment (see Diagram 46, spaces *e, e*) shadow, by the Decade System of Chronology, the first seven semidivisions of the Four Ages; wherefore, by the apportionment already made, the forty years' waste and desolation, prophesied against Egypt by the prophet Ezekiel, shadow the four semidivisions of the Hiddekelic and Gihonic ages.

Further, inasmuch as Egypt shall be desolate in the midst of countries that are desolate, so (see Diagram 46, spaces *d, d*) this condition is clearly manifest in that Ur of the Chaldees, which represents the Euphratic or First age, is on the one side, and Canaan, which represents the Pisonic or Fourth age, is on the other. Moreover the cities that shall be laid waste (see Diagram 46, spaces *e, e*) are represented by the first seven semidivisions of the Four Ages; hence, as by apportionment of the seventy years' desolation of Jerusalem (see Dan. ix. 2), ten years pertain to each semidivision, so the forty years' desolation of cities among cities points to the four semidivisions of Egypt as the Hiddekelic and Gihonic ages.

According to the quotation from Isaiah, as already given, five cities in the land of Egypt shall speak the language of Canaan. Four of these cities (see Diagram

46, spaces *d, d*) are readily perceived as the four semi-divisions of the Hiddekelic and Gihonic ages (see, also, Ezek. xxix. 12), while the fifth city is the one pertaining to the Euphratic age that overlaps the Hiddekelic. These five cities, therefore, shall speak the language of Canaan; hence the allegorical stand-point is brought down into the overlap of the Gihonic and Pisonic ages, the latter being shadowed by Canaan. From this stand-point the allegoric positions of the altar and pillar are confirmed; for in this day (see verse 19) the altar and pillar have existence; wherefore the pillar must be in the remote border of Egypt or in the overlap of the Euphratic and Hiddekelic ages, while the altar is in the overlap of the Hiddekelic and Gihonic ages.

From these indications the city that shall be called the city of destruction clearly is the one in which the language of Canaan shall be spoken, or, otherwise, it is the one in which the great Deluge of Noah finds place; and at which time the names, iniquity, blood, and characteristics pertaining to those of Egypt and Assyria (see Isa. xix. 23–25; also Diagram 46, spaces *d, d*) were transmitted to Canaan as the age in which the Redeemer made his advent, and in which God blessed the work of his hands. Indications are now quite clear that Moses seeks for information regarding these hosts, that he may consider them the Lord's people.

XXXIII. 17–23. "And the Lord said unto Moses, I will do this thing also that thou hast spoken: for thou hast found grace in my sight, and I know thee by name.

18. "And he said, I beseech thee, shew me thy glory.

19. "And he said, I will make all my goodness pass before thee, and I will proclaim the name of the Lord before thee; and will be gracious to whom I will be gracious, and will shew mercy on whom I will shew mercy.

20. "And he said, Thou canst not see my face: for there shall no man see me, and live.

21. "And the Lord said, Behold, *there is* a place by me, and thou shalt stand upon a rock:

22. "And it shall come to pass, while my glory passeth by, that I will put thee in a cleft of the rock, and will cover thee with my hand while I pass by:

23. "And I will take away mine hand, and thou shalt see my back parts; but my face shall not be seen."

By the fulfilment of this promise Moses will be put in possession of the great, leading, vital points involved in the plans for the overthrow of evil and for the redemption of the creature world, from the creation of force and matter upon the first day, until the entering into the sublime rest of the Creator upon the last day; for by the vision God was in the beginning, and God was in the end of it. Inasmuch, therefore, as God was in the beginning, it follows that his face could not be seen; for God is the greatest of all infinities; hence a less magnitude could not behold and comprehend him. In the end, however, by the plan he as a Person of the Trinity became manifest to man as man, and, consequently, as such he could be visible to man through this finite manifestation without bringing detriment to the beholder.

XXXIV. 1-4. "And the Lord said unto Moses, Hew thee two tables of stone like unto the first: and I will write upon *these* tables the words that were in the first tables, which thou brakest.

2. "And be ready in the morning, and come up in the morning unto mount Sinai, and present thyself there to me in the top of the mount.

3. "And no man shall come up with thee, neither let any man be seen throughout all the mount; neither let the flocks nor herds feed before that mount.

4. "And he hewed two tables of stone like unto the first; and Moses rose up early in the morning, and went up unto mount Sinai, as the Lord had commanded him, and took in his hand the two tables of stone."

The first two tables of stone, which Moses broke beneath the mount, pertained, as shadow, to the people from the creation of the Euphratic race down to the destruction of the Gihonic race. Inasmuch, therefore, as these stones—which, as shadow, had been prepared in or towards the beginning of the Euphratic age— were broken at the end of the Gihonic age, so the general failure of man of Adam's race during the first three ages is indicated; hence, in this light, the second set of tables will pertain to the Pisonic or Fourth age; the age in which the Messiah as man will take up the subjugatory and redemptive labors.

The preparation of this second set of tables, however, does not vitiate the rulings of the first set in the past ages,—both sets being given forth from Sinai, while Sinai shadows the Euphratic age,—hence the condemnation that rested upon the people in the past still clings to them.

XXXIV. 5–9. "And the Lord descended in the cloud, and stood with him there, and proclaimed the name of the Lord.

6. "And the Lord passed by before him, and proclaimed, The Lord, The Lord God, merciful and gracious, longsuffering, and abundant in goodness and truth,

7. "Keeping mercy for thousands, forgiving iniquity and trangression and sin, and that will by no means clear *the guilty;* visiting the iniquity of the fathers upon the children, and upon the children's children, unto the third and to the fourth *generation.*

8. "And Moses made haste, and bowed his head toward the earth, and worshipped.

9. "And he said, If now I have found grace in thy sight, O Lord, let my Lord, I pray thee, go among us; for it *is* a stiffnecked people; and pardon our iniquity and our sin, and take us for thine inheritance."

In this proclamation the Law governing the descent of iniquity is set forth as follows: " Visiting the iniquity of the fathers upon the children, and upon the children's children, unto the third and to the fourth *generation.*" It is evident that this Law must have been active from the first transgression of man, inasmuch as it is active at the time the proclamation is made, and it was active also when the Ten Commandments were communicated to Moses from Sinai.

By the Law of Iniquity, iniquity is transmitted from father to son as a debt, the penalty of which must be paid; for one great object in the establishment of the First Covenant was (see Rom. v. 20) that the offence might abound. If, however, the offence did not abound, sin could not be imputed, and, in consequence, judgment could not be rendered. If the First Covenant entered that the offence might abound, it is clearly manifest that the penalty attached to the offence is irrevocable, otherwise the forgiveness of sin might clear the guilty, whereby the abounding of the offence would become a nullity. But the text indicates that forgiveness will by no means clear the guilty. Why? Because forgiveness simply transfers the debt, while the transgressive power still remains intact;' hence forgiveness of the debt, simply, will not prevent accumulation; neither will forgiveness, simply, pay the debt.

By the Edenic Law forgiveness cannot clear the guilty, and, therefore, the iniquity, transgression, and sin are transmitted from father to son by the Law of Iniquity to the end that every jot and tittle of the vast debt may be paid by the one that assumes it, and thus forgives it.

Why should not forgiveness be the ruling principle? Because it provides no way for the abolition of the aggressive Evil Power; but by the abounding of the offence; but by the abounding of judgment based upon the Edenic Law, the Evil Kingdom will, finally, be abolished; while forgiveness will wax old and vanish with the First Covenant.

If, therefore, forgiveness does not clear the guilty, then the descent of iniquity from father to son is a matter of paramount importance,—not that the father is made clear thereby,—for through it the whole burden falls upon the man for whom a body was prepared suitable for this purpose. This Man (see

Gal. iii. 16) was Christ the seed of Abraham; this Man (see Gen. xxi. 12) was called in Isaac; and this Man (see Gen. xxviii. 4) was with Jacob; hence the establishment of the Law governing the descent of iniquity clearly indicates why it was necessary that the Redeemer should thus take upon himself the flesh of sinful man. It was that he could assume the iniquity and pay the penalty of man's transgression according to the rulings of the Law. These fulfilments would leave the great Judge (see Psalm li. 4) justified when he spoke, and clear when he judged the great hosts of evil; for the fall of man having been foreseen at the time of his predestination according to the purpose of God, his redemption was provided for in the plan as indicated above. This plan, therefore, will leave God's great attributes free, clear, and without blemish in the judgment of all hosts.

The Law or the First Covenant is now resolved into three comprehensive embodiments. First embodiment: Thou shalt not eat of the tree of the knowledge of good and evil, which is a prohibition against all manner of evil indulgences and shortcomings. Second embodiment: In the day thou eatest thereof thou shalt surely die; this indicates the irrevocable penalty attached to transgression. Third embodiment: Visiting the iniquity of the fathers upon the children, and upon the children's children, unto the third and to the fourth generation; which indicates the transmission of the debt and the accompanying penalty of transgression.

These three features or embodiments comprehend the whole law as contained in the First Covenant, through the fulfilment of which evil is overthrown, and the era of absolute righteousness ushered in; wherefore, as Paul says (Gal. iii. 24), "The law was our schoolmaster *to bring us* unto Christ." It is evident enough that man of Adam's race is not the only host which is brought to Christ through the agency of the law, but that the highway has been prepared for those which fell before man was brought forth as an instrumentality in the work; for (Rom. v. 13) "until the law sin was in the world;" but, as Paul further says, "Sin is not imputed when there is no law;" therefore the fallen host which existed before the advent of man was under the dominion of the evil kingdom, although sin was not imputed to them.

The continuance of this state could never bring them any nearer to righteousness or free them from evil influences; but the institution of the law was a means whereby they might be delivered from their bondage to the Adversary, for through the law sin was adjudged sin, the offence abounded, judgment was rendered, the penalty of transgression was paid by the One who possessed the power of returning from the dead. Hence, through the involved labors, a highway was opened to the creature world, whereby the justification of thought and action was made by the faith of the Word of God, and not by the faith gendered through free agency under the law.

It is evident that, sin being dead, the faith of the Word of God can bring forth only righteous works. This particular faith, however, is obtainable only through regeneration; wherefore works in the kingdom of righteousness become proof of the faith of the regenerative body, which is Christ's; hence, because of existing transgression, the entering in of the law or First Covenant with the advent of man of Adam's race embodies a clear indication that a highway which is not of the First Covenant has been prepared for those who fell, or who were under bondage to the Adversary previous to the advent of man, and, therefore, the Law, through its irrevocability forced regeneration, thus becoming a school-master or means for bringing them also unto Christ.

The Law of Iniquity states substantially that the iniquity of the fathers shall be visited upon the children, and upon the children's children, unto the third and to the fourth generation, whereby the Four Ages of Man are indicated (see Diagram 47) through which iniquity shall descend. It will be found, that with the general depopulation of the earth at the end of each age a remnant was made to escape, the great mission of which involved the transmission of iniquity and blood from generation to generation. This remnant, generally, is indicated where the history appertaining to these depopulations is taken up in the Scriptures of the prophets (see, also, Diagrams 25, 46, 47), from which the indication becomes manifest that Jesus Christ the Messiah as the Son of man is the escaping remnant of and for the creature world.

Spaces a, a, Diagram 47, indicate the Four Ages of Man; b, b indicate the Four Ages as Sinai, Elim, Horeb, and Canaan; c, c indicate the Four Ages as four generations; d, d indicate the Four Ages by the fathers and children through whom the iniquity of the fathers and children falls upon the Messiah as the Son

INDICATIONS OF THE BOOK OF EXODUS. 333

Ex. xxxiv. 5-10, considered as allegory.

DIAGRAM 47.

THE LAW OF INIQUITY.

Creation of a body for the Word of God in and as the very beginning of the creation of God

1st day — Creation of light   Creation of matter
2nd day — Creation of the firmament
3rd day — Creation of vegetation
4th day — Creation of sun, moon, and stars
5th day — Creation of fishes and fowl
6th day — Creation of cattle, creeping thing, and beast of the earth
The Son begotten   Beginning of Time
Michael and his angels } Pre Euphratic Era
Satan and his angels
Creation of the Euphratic or First race (Adam's)   The Law enters in at this time

The earth in the Euphratic age

Creation of the Hiddekelic or Second race
Destruction of the Euphratic or First race

The earth in the Hiddekelic age

Creation of the Gihonic or Third race
Destruction of the Hiddekelic or Second race.

The earth in the Gihonic age.

Creation of the Pisonic or Fourth race
Antediluvian Epoch
Deluge of Noah   Destruction of the Gihonic race
Epoch of replenishment (see Gen ix 1)
Advent of the Messiah as the Son of man, upon whom finally the iniquity of the fathers rested (see Isa liii 6)
Advent of the Messiah as Jesus the Son of the Virgin
Crucifixion, absolute death, and resurrection of the Messiah as Jesus Christ in the body prepared for him in and as the very beginning of the creation of God, and into which body the creature world (see Diagram 25) is regenerated or born, that the creature world may die in Christ, and participate in the eternal life of Christ, alter his resurrection   The Judgmental Era.
Thousand Years Era.
Era of Destruction
End of Time

of man; *e, e* indicate time; *f, f* indicate pertaining of the First Covenant to time.

XXXIV. 10, 11. "And he said, Behold, I make a covenant: before all thy people I will do marvels, such as have not been done in all the earth, nor in any nation: and all the people among which thou *art* shall see the work of the Lord: for it *is* a terrible thing that I will do with thee.

11. "Observe thou that which I command thee this day: behold, I drive out before thee the Amorite, and the Canaanite, and the Hittite, and the Perizzite, and the Hivite, and the Jebusite."

These verses point to the trials and tribulations of the Messiah as the Son of man, which form a portion of the burden of the Pisonic or Fourth age.

Where the history of the Third age was taken up (see xxxii.) the tables of stone were broken under the mount; which indicated the ruling of the First Covenant in that age, while by the renewal of them (see verse 1) the same ruling in the Fourth age is indicated; hence the above verses relate to the history of the Fourth age, the stand-point of which as shadowed by the renewal of the two tables of stone, evidently, is about or immediately after the fall of the Adam of the Fourth or Pisonic race. The terrible thing which the Lord will do with the Messiah Seed of Abraham seems to relate more particularly to the four hundred years' affliction which Abraham was assured should befall his seed; for the Lord is about to drive out from before him the Amorite, and the Canaanite, and the Hittite, and the Perizzite, and the Hivite, and the Jebusite, which, by previous figures, means the Adversary and his host; a task that was too difficult for man otherwise to fulfil. In the labors for the subjugation of the earth and of every living thing that moves upon it, the Messiah will meet with excessive tribulation; for it is said (Gen. iii. 15), " I will put enmity between thee and the woman, and between thy seed and her seed; it shall bruise thy head, and thou shalt bruise his heel." But that no compromise shall exist between the two is clearly indicated (Ex. xxxiv. 12, 13), " Take heed to thyself, lest thou make a covenant with the inhabitants of the land whither thou goest, lest it be for a snare in the midst of thee:

" But ye shall destroy their altars, break their images, and cut down their groves." These commands are indicated more strongly still (Deut. xii. 2, 3), " Ye shall utterly destroy all the places, wherein the nations which ye shall possess served their gods, upon the high mountains, and upon the hills, and under every green tree:

" And ye shall overthrow their altars, and break their pillars, and burn their groves with fire; and ye shall hew down the graven images of their gods, and destroy the names of them out of that place;" from which the overthrow of Evil will be complete and thorough: for the Seed of Abraham, who is among the host of Israel, will fulfil this command to the very letter when he drives the Adversary and his host from the face of the earth and replenishes it with those of his own choosing.

The simple history of the children of Israel shows that they failed to fulfil the commands of the Lord, and, therefore, the commands themselves are evidence of the presence of the Subjugator and Replenisher in the work for the overthrow of Evil; for if the Lord knew that his commands would not be carried out by man of Adam's race, and there were none other to fulfil them, why should he have issued them? The commands were issued to the children of Israel as signs and wonders; and, though the children of Israel fail, even as man at the first failed to have dominion over and to subjugate the earth, they will be fulfilled in all their strength by the Subjugator and Replenisher Jesus Christ the only begotten Son of God.

XXXIV. 27, 28. "And the Lord said unto Moses, write thou these words: for after the tenor of these words I have made a covenant with thee and with Israel.

28. "And he was there with the Lord forty days and forty nights; he did neither eat bread, nor drink water. And He wrote upon the tables the words of the covenant, the ten commandments."

In these verses the record is given that Moses fasted forty days and forty nights; and neither ate bread nor drank water. This record possesses great value as an indication of the identity of the two prophets which (see Deut. xviii. 15-18) shall be raised up like unto Moses. It will be found (see I. Kings xix. 1-8) that the prophet Elijah fasted forty days and forty nights; and that (see St. Matt. iv. 1, 2) Jesus also fasted forty days and forty nights; hence in the matter of fasting these two were like unto Moses. The indication is very probable that Moses fulfilled two fasts of forty days and forty nights,—that is, one fast for each set of tables of stone.

XXXIV. 29-35. "And it came to pass, when Moses came down from mount Sinai with the two tables of testimony in Moses' hand, when he came down from the mount, that Moses wist not that the skin of his face shone while he talked with him.

30. "And when Aaron and all the children of Israel saw Moses, behold, the skin of his face shone; and they were afraid to come nigh him.

31. "And Moses called unto them; and Aaron and all the rulers of the congregation returned unto him: and Moses talked with them.

32. "And afterward all the children of Israel came nigh: and he gave them in commandment all that the Lord had spoken with him in mount Sinai.

33. "And *till* Moses had done speaking with them, he put a vail on his face.

34. "But when Moses went in before the Lord to speak with him, he took the vail off, until he came out. And he came out, and spake unto the children of Israel *that* which he was commanded.

35. "And the children of Israel saw the face of Moses, that the skin of Moses' face shone: and Moses put the vail upon his face again, until he went in to speak with him."

By this record the skin of Moses' face shone, and when he came out from the presence of the Lord he put a veil over his face. So, also, by I. Kings xix. 9-13, the prophet Elijah stood before the Lord on Mount Horeb; and, after hearing the still small voice, Elijah wrapped his face in his mantle, and went out, and stood in the entering in of the cave; which, from the similar conditions, indicates that the skin of Elijah's face shone like unto that of Moses on Mount Sinai. The first fast of Moses may, possibly, be identified with the forty days' fast of Elijah, as allegory.

By St. Matt. xvii. 1–3, Jesus was transfigured upon a high mountain, and his face shone as the sun, and there appeared unto him both Moses and Elias; hence the indication is comparatively clear that, in the shining face, both Elijah and Jesus as the Prophets are like unto Moses. The second fast of Moses may, possibly, be identified with the forty days' fast of the Messiah as Jesus Christ.

The words which Moses spoke to the children of Israel were the words of the First Covenant or the Law; but it is manifest that, although the Law, as simple history pertaining to the Fourth age, is defined by Moses at this time upon Sinai, they were given forth for the government of all hosts when man was first brought forth as an instrumentality in the great purpose established by Jehovah, the eternal King and Ruler.

The First Covenant (see II. Cor. iii. 7) embodies the ministration of death; and if the ministration of death was so glorious that the children of Israel could not steadfastly behold the face of Moses because of its glory, what was the object of its institution? As previously indicated, it was instituted that evil might be overthrown; for far in the indefinite past Evil existed as a baleful active kingdom: it threw down and trampled under foot mighty hosts, and brought into captivity innumerable creatures which were fitted for an eternity of happiness. During the unfolding of this link in the eternal chain of events, sin was not laid at the door of the high transgressors, but suddenly, though quietly, the still small voice spoke the glorious words through which a ministration entered whereby sin was laid against its engendering household. The institution of the First Covenant was, therefore, a great step towards the overthrow of Evil: for by it the offence would abound should transgression follow under its rulings; hence the wisdom of its establishment is unquestionable. The wisdom is unquestionable, because by the covenant the offence not only abounds, but judgment will be rendered. When judgment shall have been rendered, then the penalty must be paid; for the letter of the covenant provides no way or possibility of escape; wherefore, it really and truly, as Paul indicates, is the ministration of death. Why should there be a ministration of death? It is that Evil may be destroyed forever, that it may be destroyed never more to rise; hence it becomes exceedingly glorious on this account. The overthrow of Evil is one of the great paramount objects disclosed by the sacred writings. Man is an instrumentality in this work; he was predestinated as such, and he was called as such; but the grandest and most marvellous portion of his mission lies in his calling as a nation of priests, and a peculiar treasure unto the Lord above all people (see xix. 3-6).

It is shown by the fall of man in the garden of Eden that the kingdom of Evil has, with man, fallen under the penalty of the First Covenant, and that, through the covenant, death reigns over all the Evil host. This penalty, being irrevocable, must be paid, the wisdom and strength of the covenant depending upon its irrevocability; from which the certainty is absolute that the transgressions of man—even though he be an instrumentality in the purpose of God—also must come under the strictest ruling of the Law, lest Evil go free, and a flaw be disclosed in the plan for Evil's overthrow. Man's redemption, however, is amply provided for in the regeneration and in the death of Christ the Lord; which leaves the great Adversarial host altogether outside this pale; for (see I. John iii. 8) Christ came to destroy the works of the devil, not to establish them. The promise is given (Isa. xlix. 6), "It is a light thing that thou shouldest be my servant to raise up the tribes of Jacob, and to restore the preserved of Israel: I will also give thee for a light to the Gentiles, that thou mayest be my salvation unto the end of the earth;" by which it is clear that a highway will be opened through Christ for the restoration of all hosts which may seek to enter therein. At the same time, however, the ruling of the First Covenant or ministration of death will assuredly rest over those which turn aside from this highway; hence Evil will, with the expiration of the limits of time, be destroyed forever as an energy or power.

The transfiguration of Moses on Mount Sinai relates to the ministration of death,—that is, it relates to the going forth of the First Covenant for the government of all hosts. The transfiguration of Elijah on Mount Horeb (see I. Kings xix. 9-14) indicates the hosts which have fallen under the penalties of the First Covenant. The transfiguration of Jesus (see St. Luke ix. 28-36) indicates the payment of the penalty resting over those who have broken the First Covenant; for on the mount were these three, Moses, Elias, and Jesus, and they appeared in glory and spoke of Jesus' decease.

It is perfectly manifest that no one but Jesus can pay the penalty of transgression, and return again from the dead; for death, of himself, never looses the bonds of his prisoners. Moreover, if the transgressor die an absolute death by the decree of the Almighty, it is evident that he cannot return from thence through any other power than Christ, or such other power would be greater than the Almighty; hence, conversely, the Almighty can return from the grave against any power or any combination of powers which may strive against him. Through the death of Christ, therefore, the highway of justification may be, and is, prepared "even unto the end of the earth," whereby the ministration of death becomes an exceeding great glory; for by it the "precious is separated from the vile," and Evil is overthrown forever, while the fruit arising therefrom (see II. Cor. iii. 9–14) is a glory which by far excelleth, and, consequently, righteousness will dwell in the habitation of every creature that rejoices in its new-born life.

XXXVIII. 1–31. "And he made the altar of burnt offering *of* shittim wood: five cubits *was* the length thereof, and five cubits the breadth thereof; *it was* foursquare; and three cubits the height thereof.

2. "And he made the horns thereof on the four corners of it; the horns thereof were of the same: and he overlaid it with brass.

3. "And he made all the vessels of the altar, the pots,

and the shovels, and the basins, *and* the fleshhooks, and the firepans: all the vessels thereof made he *of* brass.

4. "And he made for the altar a brazen grate of network, under the compass thereof, beneath unto the midst of it.

5. "And he cast four rings for the four ends of the grate of brass, *to be* places for the staves.

6. "And he made the staves *of* shittim wood, and overlaid them with brass.

7. "And he put the staves into the rings on the sides of the altar, to bear it withal; he made the altar hollow with boards.

8. "And he made the laver *of* brass, and the foot of it *of* brass, of the lookingglasses of *the women* assembling, which assembled *at* the door of the tabernacle of the congregation.

9. "And he made the court: on the south side southward the hangings of the court *were of* fine twined linen, a hundred cubits:

10. "Their pillars *were* twenty, and their brazen sockets twenty; the hooks of the pillars and their fillets *were of* silver.

11. "And for the north side *the hangings were* a hundred cubits, their pillars *were* twenty, and their sockets of brass twenty; the hooks of the pillars and their fillets *of* silver.

12. "And for the west side *were* hangings of fifty cubits, their pillars ten, and their sockets ten; the hooks of the pillars and their fillets *of* silver.

13. "And for the east side eastward fifty cubits.

14. "The hangings of the one side *of the gate were*

fifteen cubits; their pillars three, and their sockets three.

15. "And for the other side of the court gate, on this hand and that hand, *were* hangings of fifteen cubits; their pillars three, and their sockets three.

16. "All the hangings of the court round about *were* of fine twined linen.

17. "And the sockets for the pillars *were of* brass; the hooks of the pillars and their fillets *of* silver; and the overlaying of their chapiters *of* silver; and all the pillars of the court *were* filleted with silver.

18. "And the hanging for the gate of the court *was* needlework, *of* blue, and purple, and scarlet, and fine twined linen: and twenty cubits *was* the length, and the height in the breadth *was* five cubits, answerable to the hangings of the court.

19. "And their pillars *were* four, and their sockets *of* brass four; their hooks *of* silver, and the overlaying of their chapiters and their fillets *of* silver.

20. "And all the pins of the tabernacle, and of the court round about, *were of* brass.

21. "This is the sum of the tabernacle, *even of* the tabernacle of testimony, as it was counted, according to the commandment of Moses, *for* the service of the Levites, by the hand of Ithamar, son to Aaron the priest.

22. "And Bezaleel the son of Uri, the son of Hur, of the tribe of Judah, made all that the Lord commanded Moses.

23. "And with him *was* Aholiab, son of Ahisamach, of the tribe of Dan, an engraver, and a cunning workman, and an embroiderer in blue, and in purple, and in scarlet, and fine linen.

24. "All the gold that was occupied for the work in all the work of the holy *place*, even the gold of the offering, was twenty and nine talents, and seven hundred and thirty shekels, after the shekel of the sanctuary.

25. "And the silver of them that were numbered of the congregation *was* a hundred talents, and a thousand seven hundred and threescore and fifteen shekels, after the shekel of the sanctuary :

26. "A bekah for every man, *that is,* half a shekel, after the shekel of the sanctuary, for every one that went to be numbered, from twenty years old and upward, for six hundred thousand and three thousand and five hundred and fifty *men.*

27. "And of the hundred talents of silver were cast the sockets of the sanctuary, and the sockets of the vail; a hundred sockets of the hundred talents, a talent for a socket.

28. "And of the thousand seven hundred seventy and five *shekels* he made hooks for the pillars, and overlaid their chapiters, and filleted them.

29. "And the brass of the offering *was* seventy talents, and two thousand and four hundred shekels.

30. "And therewith he made the sockets to the door of the tabernacle of the congregation, and the brazen altar, and the brazen grate for it, and all the vessels of the altar,

31. "And the sockets of the court round about, and the sockets of the court gate, and all the pins of the tabernacle, and all the pins of the court round about."

Spaces *a, a,* Diagram 48, indicate the Four Ages of Man; *b, b* indicate the Four Ages by the countries through which Abraham passed in his journey from

INDICATIONS OF THE BOOK OF EXODUS. 345

Ex. xxxviii. 1-31, *considered as allegory.*

DIAGRAM 48.

THE GOLD, SILVER, AND BRASS, AS CHRONOLOGY
(TABERNACLE OF THE CONGREGATION).

1st day	Creation of a body for the Word of God in and as the very beginning of the creation of God First day —Creation of light Creation of matter.
2nd day	Second day —Creation of the firmament
3rd day	Third day —Creation of vegetation
4th day	Fourth day —Creation of sun, moon, and stars
5th day	Fifth day —Creation of fishes and fowl
6th day	Sixth day —Creation of cattle, creeping thing, and beast of the earth The Son Begotten Beginning of Time War in heaven ⎫ Pre-Euphratic Era divided in Satan cast out into the earth ⎬ the midst Creation of the Euphratic or First race (Adam's)

The earth in the Euphratic age

Creation of the Hiddekelic or Second race.
Destruction of the Euphratic or First race.

The earth in the Hiddekelic age.

Creation of the Gihonic or Third race
Destruction of the Hiddekelic or Second race.

The earth in the Gihonic age.

Creation of the Pisonic or Fourth race.
Antediluvian Epoch
Deluge of Noah   Destruction of the Gihonic or Third race
Epoch of replenishment (see Gen ix. 1)
Advent of the Messiah as the Son of man in the day of Abraham.
Messianic Epoch
The earth in the Pisonic age   Crucifixion, absolute death, and resurrection of the Messiah as Jesus Christ.
Judgmental Era
Thousand Years' Era.
Era of Destruction
Approximate end of Time.

Ur of the Chaldees to Canaan (see Gen. xii., xiii.); *c, c* indicate pertaining of the image of Nebuchadnezzar's dream (see Dan. ii. 36-45) to the Four Ages; *d, d* indicate pertaining of the talents of gold and talents of brass to time from the creation of the Euphratic race down to the Deluge of Noah, or to the end of the Gihonic age (see, also, Diagrams 34, 40); *e, e* indicate the years, as through the male (see Lev. xxvii.), from the creation of the Euphratic race down to the Deluge of Noah; *f, f* (see page of Landmarks) indicate the years, as through the male, from the creation of the Euphratic race down to the end of the Euphratic age plus the overlapping portion of the Hiddekelic age; *g, g* (see page of Landmarks) indicate the years, as through the male, from the creation of the Hiddekelic race down to the Deluge of Noah or to the end of the Gihonic age plus the overlapping portion of the Pisonic age; *h, h* indicate the years, as through the male, from the creation of the Euphratic race to the end of the Euphratic age plus the overlapping portion of the Hiddekelic age, as shadowed by the talents and shekels of gold; *i, i* indicate the years, as through the male, from the creation of the Hiddekelic race to the end of the Gihonic age plus the overlapping portion of the Pisonic age, as shadowed by the talents and shekels of brass; *j, j* indicate the bounds of time as set according to the number of the children of Israel (see Deut. xxxii. 8); *k, k* indicate the number of the children of Israel that were numbered (see Num. i. 46); *l, l* indicate pertaining of the ransom money of the children of Israel, in silver bekahs (see Diagram 39), to time.

By Deut. xxxii. 8, the bounds of the people are set

INDICATIONS OF THE BOOK OF EXODUS. 347

according to the number of the children of Israel; by Num. i. 46 the number of the children of Israel that were numbered was six hundred thousand and three thousand and five hundred and fifty. By xxx. 11–16, xxxviii. 26, the ransom or atonement money of the children of Israel was six hundred thousand and three thousand and five hundred and fifty bekahs or half shekels; wherefore the ransom money also becomes an exponent of time (see Diagram 48, spaces j, j, k, k, l, l). The ransom money (see xxxviii. 25) was paid in silver; hence in this allegorical pertaining, the silver shadows time as set according to the number of the children of Israel,—that is, the years of time commencing with the creation of the Euphratic race. These years number thirty-three thousand seven hundred and fifty-two.

By the image of Nebuchadnezzar's dream the Euphratic or First age is shadowed by the head of gold, in harmony with which the talents of gold "for the work in all the work of the holy *place*" pertain to the Euphratic age also. The amount of gold thus occupied was twenty-nine talents, and seven hundred and thirty shekels, after the shekel of the sanctuary, or one hundred and seventy-five thousand four hundred and sixty bekahs. Wherefore, inasmuch as the silver bekahs become an exponent of time as set according to the number of the children of Israel, so also, by proportion, the golden bekahs will express a valuation of time pertaining to the Euphratic age, in that the gold pertains to the Euphratic age, while the bekahs shadow years thereof. Hence, by proportion, as 603,550 : 175,460 :: 33,752 : 9812, or to the years, as through the male (see Lev. xxvii.), from the creation of the Euphratic race unto the end of the Euphratic age plus the overlapping portion of the Hiddekelic age (see Diagram 48, spaces *e, e, h, h*). The establishment of the years of the Euphratic age, and of the overlapping portion of the Hiddekelic, as thus determined correspond very closely with those already given (see Diagram 48, spaces *f, f*, also page of Landmarks), by which the general approximation becomes well assured.

By the image of Nebuchadnezzar's dream the brass shadows the Gihonic or Third age. The Third age (see Diagrams 15, 16, 17, 19) is shadowed by Egypt, while Egypt, as a term, pertains to both the Hiddekelic and Gihonic ages; hence the brass may also shadow these two ages, even as the silver arm of the image (see Diagram 34) overlaps them both. Therefore, with this construction—which is fully supported by numerous allegories otherwise—the brass used in the service of the Tabernacle of the congregation, and its appointments, pertains to the Hiddekelic and Gihonic ages and to the overlapping portion of the Pisonic.

The quantity of brass thus utilized was seventy talents, and two thousand and four hundred shekels, or four hundred and twenty-four thousand eight hundred bekahs. As before, the silver shekels, as bekahs, constitute an exponent of time from the creation of the Euphratic race as set according to the number of the children of Israel; hence, by proportion, the bekahs of brass will express a valuation of years—as through the male—from the creation of the Hiddekelic race down to the Deluge of Noah, or to the end of the Gihonic age plus the overlapping portion of the Pisonic age; wherefore, by proportion, as 603,550 : 424,800 : :

INDICATIONS OF THE BOOK OF EXODUS. 349

33,752 : 23,755, or to the total years—as through the male—from the creation of the Hiddekelic race to the Deluge of Noah, or to the end of the Gihonic age plus the overlapping portion of the Pisonic age (see Diagram 48, spaces i, i).

The total years of the Hiddekelic age, as otherwise set, are ten thousand nine hundred and nineteen; the total years of the Gihonic age, as otherwise set, are eleven thousand two hundred and twenty-four; while the years from the creation of the Pisonic race to the Deluge of Noah, or the overlapping portion of the Pisonic age, are one thousand six hundred and fifty-six. The sum of these years (see Diagram 48, spaces g, g) amounts to twenty-three thousand seven hundred and ninety-nine; which is a very close approximation to the years as given above. Hence, the text is confirmative of the general chronology of the Scriptures, and of the chief divisions of time (see, also, Diagrams 21-31 inclusive).

The text further indicates that the Golden age is the age in which the Word of God was begotten as the Son of God that he might do the will of God in the body that was created for him in the beginning of the creation suitable for this purpose; which will, in part, comprehends the regeneration and restoration of the creature world that for ages lay captive in the treasure-house of Lucifer, the prince of Tyrus (see Ezek. xxviii. 1-19; Isa. xiv. 3-17, xxiii. 17, 18).

XL. 12-15. "And thou shalt bring Aaron and his sons unto the door of the tabernacle of the congregation, and wash them with water.

13. "And thou shalt put upon Aaron the holy garments, and anoint him, and sanctify him; that he may minister unto me in the priest's office.

14. "And thou shalt bring his sons, and clothe them with coats:

15. "And thou shalt anoint them, as thou didst anoint their father, that they may minister unto me in the priest's office: for their anointing shall surely be an everlasting priesthood throughout their generation."

Thus indications are given that the priesthood of Aaron is not merely a temporary exhibition of priestly power covering the epoch from the exodus of the children of Israel unto the absolute death of the Messiah as Jesus Christ, but that it is a priesthood the far-reaching value of which is covered by a veil. By the lifting of the veil, however, the involved magnitudes of the Aaronic order of priesthood become disclosed in their marvellous bearings upon the future welfare of the creature world; hence the simple history of the anointing and sanctifying of Aaron and his sons is, in allegorical sense, prolific with meaning of such glorious worth that every new-born ray of light that falls thereon will lighten newer bars of God's great page wherein the songs of "Moses" and the "Lamb" are found.

THE END.

www.ingramcontent.com/pod-product-compliance
Lightning Source LLC
Chambersburg PA
CBHW071227230426
43668CB00011B/1332